BUILDING COMMUNITY VIA SPORT: A BETTER TOGETHER SOCIETY

BUILDING COMMUNITY VIA SPORT

A Better Together Society

Stacy Warner

 SPORT & COMMUNITY DEVELOPMENT LAB

Copyright © 2025 by East Carolina University. All rights reserved.

ISBN 978-1-4696-9211-1 (paperback)
ISBN 978-1-4696-9212-8 (EPUB ebook)
ISBN 978-1-4696-9213-5 (UPDF ebook)

For product safety concerns under the European Union's General Product Safety Regulation (EU GPSR), please contact gpsr@mare-nostrum.co.uk or write to the University of North Carolina Press and Mare Nostrum Group B.V., Mauritskade 21D, 1091 GC Amsterdam, The Netherlands.

Cover illustration: Stephanie W. Dicken

Published by the ECU Sport & Community Development Lab
Distributed by the University of North Carolina Press

Dedication

This book is dedicated to the memory of Dr. Nelson "Coop" Cooper, Dr. Jimmie Grimsley, and Mrs. Eva Price, whose remarkable legacies and profound impact through teaching and community building continue to inspire many.

CONTENTS

xi   Preface

ONE
1   Ghost Runner

TWO
13   Perspective on Sport: Sport is Not a Dirty Word

THREE
28   So What? Why Sport Managers Need to Understand How to Build Community

FOUR
47   Common Interest: A Shared Mission, Goal, or Purpose

FIVE
62   Administrative Consideration: People-Focused

SIX
78   Creating Leadership Opportunities: Empowering Others

SEVEN
93   Social Spaces: A Place Where Everyone Knows Your Name

EIGHT
109   Equity in Administrative Decisions: The Importance of Clarity and Transparency

NINE
124   Now What? Measuring a Sense of Community in Sport

TEN
139   What's Next? A Call to Action and Community of Practice

147   Acknowledgments

151   References

171   Notes

BUILDING COMMUNITY VIA SPORT: A BETTER TOGETHER SOCIETY

PREFACE

To the reader:

This is not a traditional academic text; rather it is a culmination of stories and research that can guide sport leaders in creating and building community. The text is based on the Sport and Sense of Community Theory,[1] which puts forward the five factors needed for community to develop through sport. That theory is based on well over 130 interviews, exhaustive literature reviews, and many research inquiries. Over the past decade I have felt the gap between academic theory and practice widening. Yet, I continued to recognize outstanding examples of the factors from my career and the everyday. While my storytelling approach, seasoned with research, may be non-traditional for an educational read or err on the side of too academic for a leisure read, my intent is to engage current and future sport managers and demonstrate the applicability of research. We need to have well-researched theory to guide us and to help us understand the power of sport and why it can have an impact. Ultimately, with quality research and theory, our sport systems can and should be used to improve and better our society. It is a lofty goal, but one that is worthwhile. As a result, learning objectives and chapter summaries are included for the student and educator. At the end of each chapter, discussion questions are provided to consider and reflect on how your experiences may be similar or different than the examples included. These reflective questions are included for you to consider how you might play a role in achieving that lofty goal of making society better with sport.

In chapter 1, *Ghost Runner*, I recount nostalgic memories of playing pickup wiffleball in a small central Pennsylvania town. The chapter highlights the sense of community and belonging fostered through sport, even in informal settings. I then reflect on how these early childhood experiences shaped my lifelong fascination with the power of sport to bring people together. The narrative also touches on the impact of Title IX on sport participation for girls, the role of parental influence, and the broader societal implications of sport in creating a sense of community and belonging. My goal is to establish the foundation of the important role sport plays in individuals' lives, setting the stage on how sport is woven into our lives and impacts families, communities, education, politics, and economics. For the learner, chapter 1 objectives include:

- Understand the role of informal and formal sport in fostering community and belonging.
- Reflect on the impact of early sport experiences on personal development.
- Consider the influence of Title IX on sport participation for girls.
- Discuss the broader societal implications of sport in creating community.

In chapter 2, *Perspective on Sport: Sport is Not a Dirty Word*, I share my journey as a doctoral student and subsequent career as an Assistant Professor of Sport Management at East Carolina University (ECU). The chapter highlights my experiences in Greenville, NC, a city deeply rooted in sport culture. It discuss the challenges of integrating sport management within a kinesiology department and emphasizes the importance of interdisciplinary collaboration. I argue that sport should not solely be viewed negatively and underscore its potential to improve health and foster community. The chapter also critiques the U.S. sport system's failures in promoting health and suggests that sport can play a significant role in public health if managed effectively. This chapter provides additional context on how embedded sport is in some communities, as well as the challenge for sport management educators to advance the study of sport in an academic setting. I position sport as part of the solution to improving society and emphasize that sport is not inherently good or bad, but rather how we manage it that matters. For the learner, chapter 2 objectives include:

- Explore the integration of sport within a city and community.
- Consider where sport management belongs in an academic setting.
- Evaluate the potential of sport to improve public health and foster community.
- Critique the U.S. sport system's effectiveness in promoting health.

For chapter 3, *So What? Why Sport Managers Need to Understand How to Build Community*, I underscore the importance of community building through sport. In the *So What?* chapter, I discuss the practical application of academic research in sport management, highlighting the need for sport managers to better bridge the gap between theory and practice. I argue that building community through sport is essential for psychological safety, health outcomes, and social cohesion. Throughout the chapter I stress the timeliness of this issue, especially in the context of the COVID-19 pandemic, and the role of sport in various life stages, such as parenting, grieving, and aging. My goal is for the reader to think beyond the right now and see how sport managers can positively impact many lives in the future. Sport is not just a trivial activity, but rather a tool that can change and improve lives. For the learner, chapter 3 objectives include:

- Analyze the practical application of academic research in sport management.
- Discuss the importance of building community through sport for psychological safety and social cohesion.
- Reflect on the role of sport in various life stages and its relevance during and since the COVID-19 pandemic.

In chapters 4 through 7, I illustrate, describe, and define the five factors that contribute to building a sense of community through sport. Chapter 4, *Common Interest: A Shared Mission, Goal or Purpose*, delves into my experience at the 2009 Special Olympic World Games in Boise, Idaho, highlighting the powerful sense of community fostered through a Common Interest in sport. Within the chapter I describe the success of the scarf project, where volunteers knitted over 60,000 scarves for athletes, creating a tangible symbol of support and unity. I also explore how Common Interest, such as sport officiating and the rapidly growing sport of pickleball, can build communities and improve psychological well-being. Through providing illustrative examples of Common Interest, I intend to demonstrate that a shared interest in sport can bring together diverse groups, fostering a sense of belonging and addressing broader societal issues like mental health. For the learner, chapter 4 objectives include:

- Examine the importance of a shared interest in creating a sense of community.
- Analyze the impact of volunteer projects, like the scarf project, that can foster community building through highlighting a Common Interest.
- Discuss how sport can be a Common Interest and aid in improving psychological well-being through the creation and fostering of a community.

In chapter 5, *Administrative Consideration: People Focused*, I emphasize the importance of Administrative Consideration, or a people-focused approach, in fostering a sense of community within sport settings. The chapter highlights various examples, including the Fleet Feet franchise in Greenville, NC, YMCA director Keno Beezer, University of North Carolina at Chapel Hill (UNC) athletics administrator Larry Gallo, and CrossFit coaches, all of whom demonstrate genuine care, concern, and intentionality in their roles. These leaders create environments where individuals feel valued and supported, which is essential for building strong, healthy communities. The chapter also discusses the broader implications of Administrative Consideration at the organizational level, such as corporate social responsibility initiatives in sport. With these relatable examples, I demonstrate how and why Administrative Consideration is key to community building. For the learner, chapter 5 objectives include:

- Understand the importance of a people-focused approach in sport administration.
- Identify examples of effective leadership in sport settings.
- Discuss the broader implications of Administrative Consideration on community building.

In chapter 6, *Creating Leadership Opportunities: Empowering Others*, I explore the significance of creating Leadership Opportunities within sport and community organizations. I highlight the success of groups like F3 ENC (Fitness, Fellowship, and Faith of Eastern North Carolina) and FiA ENC (Females in Action of Eastern North Carolina), which provide peer-led workouts and leadership roles to their members, fostering a strong sense of community and personal growth. In chapter 6, I also discuss the importance of shared leadership, where everyone has the chance to lead, and how this approach enhances engagement and retention. Personal stories, such as that of Dr. Nelson "Coop" Cooper and Shannon Williams, illustrate the transformative impact of these opportunities. My goal for the chapter is to underscore that environments offering leadership roles and fostering trust and collaboration thrive, benefiting both individuals and the broader community. Simply, Leadership Opportunities are key to community building, and organizations need to become better at integrating others if they desire to build healthy community. For the learner, chapter 6 objectives include:

- Explore the significance of creating Leadership Opportunities within sport organizations.
- Analyze the impact of shared leadership on engagement and retention.
- Reflect on personal stories illustrating the transformative impact of leadership roles.

In chapter 7, *Social Spaces: A Place Where Everyone Knows Your Name*, I explore the critical role of Social Spaces in fostering community and belonging within sport settings. I highlight various examples, such as the iconic Cheers bar, tailgating traditions, and the unique social spaces created by sports fans and athletes. In the Social Spaces chapter, I emphasize that both physical and virtual spaces are essential for building and maintaining social bonds, providing a venue for interaction, support, and shared experiences. These spaces, whether stadiums, pubs, or online forums, enable individuals to connect on a deeper level, enhancing their psychological well-being and sense of community. For the learner, chapter 7 objectives include:

- Understand the role of Social Spaces in fostering community within sport settings.
- Identify various examples of physical and virtual Social Spaces.
- Discuss the importance of Social Spaces for psychological well-being and community building.

In chapter 8, *Equity in Administrative Decisions: The Importance of Clarity and Transparency*, I emphasize the importance of evenhandedness in administrative decisions within sport settings. I highlight how fair and transparent policies and procedures are crucial for fostering a sense of community. The chapter discusses various examples, including Sue Donohoe's efforts to improve transparency in the NCAA Women's Basketball Tournament selection process, Sedona Prince's viral TikTok video that led to significant changes in gender equity, and the NFL's Rooney Rule aimed at increasing diversity in coaching and executive positions. These examples illustrate that equitable decisions not only enhance individual satisfaction and engagement but also strengthen the overall cohesion and success of the community. My goal is to provide illustrative examples of Equity in Administrative Decisions and the role it plays in community building, distinguish between equity and equality, and focus on inclusive and transparent practices. For the learner, chapter 8 objectives include:

- Examine the importance of Equity in Administrative Decisions within sport.
- Analyze examples of efforts to improve transparency and diversity in sport administration.
- Discuss the impact of equitable decisions on community cohesion and success.

Within chapter 9, *Now What? Measuring a Sense of Community in Sport*, I discuss the importance of measuring a sense of community within sport settings to improve and optimize its positive contributions. I highlight the development and refinement of the Sense of Community in Sport (SCS) scale, which identifies key factors such as Administrative Consideration, Common Interest, Equity in Administrative Decisions, Leadership Opportunities, and Social Spaces. By providing a robust tool for empirical assessment, the SCS scale helps researchers and practitioners enhance the sense of community among sport participants, ultimately impacting their psychological well-being and social support networks. The chapter underscores the necessity of measurement in understanding and fostering community dynamics in various sport contexts. For the learner, chapter 9 objectives include:

- Understand the importance of measuring a sense of community in sport settings.
- Explore the development and application of the Sense of Community in Sport (SCS) scale.
- Discuss the key factors identified by the SCS scale and their impact on community dynamics.

Finally, in chapter 10, *What's Next? A Call to Action and Community of Practice*, I delve into the leadership and dual roles of Dr. Jerry McGee and Dr. Leroy T. Walker. Dr. McGee's ability to excel as both a university president and a college football official is highlighted. The chapter emphasizes the importance of integrating education with athletic achievement, a unique aspect of the U.S. higher education system. Dr. Walker's contributions are also discussed, focusing on his leadership qualities and the impact he had on both individuals and communities. My goal is to provide a historical perspective on two important thought leaders in sport and education in North Carolina and also articulate a call to action. The concept of a "community of practice" is introduced, illustrating how shared knowledge and support can foster collective growth. The chapter's central theme is encapsulated in the slogan "Excellence Without Excuse: A Shared Responsibility," encouraging readers to strive for excellence in all aspects of life. The chapter concludes with a call to action, urging the promotion of sport as a means to build stronger, more inclusive communities. For the learner, chapter 10 objectives include:

- Explore the dual roles of Dr. Jerry McGee and Dr. Leroy T. Walker in education and sport.
- Understand the concept of a "community of practice" and its impact on collective growth.
- Discuss the importance of integrating education with athletic achievement and striving for excellence.

CHAPTER 1

Ghost Runner

"Only he who can see the invisible can do the impossible."
—Frank L. Gaines

"There are two types of invisible structures that need to be considered in every whole system design: the 'emotional landscape' and the 'social landscape.'"
—Heather Jo Flores

"Ghost runner on second!" I yelled as I made my way back to a cardboard object being held down by a rock and signifying home plate. It was my turn to bat again, as my teammate pedaled his bike towards the voice in the distance telling him dinner was ready. The sun was starting to go down, but with our young eyes we still hoped to be able track the brilliant white wiffle ball off the yellow plastic bat and finish our pickup game. Of course, there were no lights pointed toward the grass field that was anchored by a bar and church in my small hometown in central Pennsylvania. It was also the time of day when the large maple tree that sat on the first base line provided some unwanted shade and blocked the light needed to continue to play. That field was a perfect pickup wiffle ball diamond which transformed into a touch Nerf football field when the fall temperatures arrived. Our parents loved that our playing field did not have lights, as they knew we would return home before dark, tired and hungry.

With that ghost runner on second base my opponents made the call, "Let's finish this game tomorrow." With a wave of disappointment quickly followed by an eagerness to meet again the next day to finish the game, I agreed and found my bike to pedal home. Like probably ninety-five percent of the games I have played in my career, I do not recall if my team won or lost that game, which I am sure we finished the next day. But I do recall the unmistakable bond that formed between all of us who played on the makeshift field. We had the simple shared interest of wanting to play a game, never hesitated to

Barely able to hold a regulation sized baseball bat, many youth are socialized into a sporting community around the age of five. Socialization into the sporting community starts early, often sparked by enthusiastic parents and siblings. Studies show that this early involvement plays a crucial role in fostering lifelong love for the game.

welcome anyone that wanted to join, and always found a way to keep the game going. That bond and feeling of wanting to play alongside other teammates is hard to describe. It is much like that invisible ghost runner. We all know it is there, standing right on second base, and we all agree upon its superficial existence. In fact, if I was able to hit the ball past the infield with that "ghost runner on second," everyone would accept that a run would have been earned and should be added to my team's score. Decades later I would never lose my fascination with how sport can bring people together and how that hard-to-define, invisible, yet real, feeling and bond is created in sport settings. As it is and has been for so many, sport was an important part of my childhood and gave me a place to belong.

The good news is I do not have to define that connection and bond, because we all know and agree it exists. We all have that innate desire to belong and, at some point in our lives, have felt part of something special.[1] For many individuals, a sport or a sport setting has allowed them to experience a sense of

Title IX has played a large role in the increased number of sport opportunities available for girls. Little League baseball was one of the few sport options for young girls from small towns.

community or belonging at some point. For others, sport and sport settings have created a time and experience where they felt they were not part of community and did not belong. Community psychology scholars have compared this sense of community to physical hunger.[2] You know when you are hungry, and you know how satisfied you feel when that need is fulfilled. Feeling a sense of community is similar to hunger, in that belonging is also an essential human need, and individuals know when that need is fulfilled and when it is not.

As pickup wiffle ball, with whoever was available to play, evolved into playing in an organized league, sport continued to provide a place that gave me a strong sense of community. My dad coached my older brother in Little League baseball, and they never hesitated to bring me to practice. I proudly served as their team's bat girl until I was old enough to play. During those early days my dad and brother always made sure I got a few swings and the chance to field a few balls while my mother helped with the Little League concession stand. My mom would always dream up tasks to make sure I was out of their way as they practiced. Penny candy or a single Swedish Fish, Sour Patch Kid, or

Tootsie Roll were quite popular then, and I would count them out in groups of twenty-five and put them in a small plastic bag. They would later be sold for a quarter, likely to a parent with child in tow, who also needed to keep him or her occupied while their sibling competed. The counting task was enough to keep me busy, but I still wanted to be on the field with the team.

When I finally turned nine, I began playing Little League baseball, and soon after, a Junior Olympic softball team emerged in an adjacent town. There were enough girls playing Little League in my hometown that our mothers decided to form a softball team. I am sure it stemmed from some concession stand conversation, but there were one or two girls on each Little League team in my hometown that likely would being play softball if that option existed. Their initiative to start a softball team had a bigger impact than I realized. Years later I would work on a research project, "More than just letting them play: Parental influence on women's lifetime sport involvement,"[3] and I recognized how foundational parental leadership was for many daughters. Our research studied seventeen NCAA Division I female head coaches and revealed that "Parental influence impacted their enduring involvement in sport by normalizing the sport experience, particularly in terms of gender, and by allowing them a voice in their own participation decisions" (p. 538).

Sport had not been an option for most of our moms, but our mothers and fathers normalized it for the twelve girls who played in my hometown's Little League. Title IX, the breakthrough legislation that was geared toward prohibiting discrimination based on sex in federally funded educational programs or activities, did not exist when our mothers were growing up. Because sport operates within the educational system in United States, this educational legislation had a tremendous impact on sport participation for girls. Ironically enough, I was born days after the landmark legislation deadline for high schools and colleges to be fully compliant with Title IX.[4] My life and my peers' lives were very different than our mothers' lives. We had opportunities in sport, and we had parents that socialized, normalized, and role modeled that sport was a gender-appropriate activity for girls—exactly what research would support years later.[5] My father took me to Little League baseball practices, and my mom would coach our town's first girls' softball team.

My mom knew very little about the sport of softball and was ambidextrous, so it was quite amusing as she would catch, then take her glove off and throw with the same hand that had the glove on seconds before. She, like the other Little League moms with daughters, did whatever she could to provide an opportunity for me and my peers. They knew that Little League baseball had provided a necessary foundation, and above all, she and the other mothers wanted us to have an opportunity to play together. As they created a sport opportunity for us, a community formed among our parents, as well. As youth sport has grown it is not uncommon for the parents of athletes to benefit from the community and the bond formed with other parents.[6] The power of sport does extend beyond athletes on the field.[7]

Sport and the community it provided continued to be a draw for me and my teammates, and many of us went on to play for a very successful high school softball team. Although I was an average player with an above-average level of persistence (those who know me well have referred to this as stubbornness), those playing days with talented athletes paid off and I was eventually offered a college scholarship at a NCAA Division II school in Pennsylvania. The United States' sport system is somewhat unique in that school-sponsored sport is expected in our education system. Sport existed in private boarding schools and colleges in the 1800s and were primarily student-led. In the early nineteenth century, the Public Schools Athletic League in New York City emerged, and sport started to be recognized for its valuable contribution to a student's public education.[8] Within a few years the Intercollegiate Athletic Association of the United States (IAAUS), which would eventually become the National Collegiate Athletic Association (NCAA) in 1910, was initiated by President Theodore Roosevelt with the aim of preserving college football because of its character building.[9] Due to budget concerns during the Great Depression, though, school-sponsored sport stopped, only to re-emerge after World War II.

School sport is embedded in the culture of the American education system, arguably because sport is a tool "to answer a need created by our pluralistic society and to help fulfill the peculiar mission of American higher education by providing a vehicle for a sense of community, [and] promoting student commitment to the institution"[10](p.158). This held true for me, as the opportunity to continue to play softball was a draw to further my education. Initially I wasn't even sure if I wanted to go to college. As a first-generation college student who grew up in a small town, the only college-educated individuals I had contact with were teachers. And I was sure I did not want to be a teacher. In light of my parents' adamant belief that I *had* to go to college and that I could not make a career out of my passion for sport, the opportunity to play college softball was the encouragement that I needed.

When I arrived on campus, I quickly found that sense of community and belonging among the other college athletes. As a first-generation college student and now a college professor, as much as I hate to admit it, I can say with certainty that sport served as a motivating factor to continue my education in college. At that age, I was not motivated by the pursuit of knowledge, personal growth, or the potential for career advancement that higher education could provide. Now that I am well into my career, I recognize that fine-tuning my motor skills to hit a moving object or field a ball and then throw a perfect strike to a teammate did very little to advance society. It did, however, teach me teamwork, persistence, and the importance of effort and fortitude. I definitely struck out more times than I got a hit in my college career, no matter how many extra pitches I saw in a batting cage and swings I took. Importantly, though, I never let go of that fascination with how sport could bring people together and improve our lives and why it was so embedded in U.S. educational system and our society.

Because sport had opened doors that allowed me to obtain a college degree, I began exploring master's degrees in Sport Management and found a program focused solely on college athletics at The University of North Carolina at Chapel Hill. During my second year of that master's program, I had the opportunity to complete an internship at the NCAA headquarters in the Division I Basketball Championship in Indianapolis. The timing of that internship could not have been more momentous. I was selected as the Men's and Women's Division I Basketball Championships intern, which was one of the more coveted internships. I have never been a big basketball fan, and that likely set me apart. I had the opportunity to spend a year learning from and being mentored by some of the best in the business, as that group based out of the NCAA headquarters office in Indianapolis was charged with overseeing the then-sixty-four teams that made the tournament to play for a national championship. With me they did not have to worry about having a fan on the staff, or someone that would be more enthralled with a game than any tasks that I was asked to do. It was 2001, and I started my internship in June. I would again have a front-row seat to the phenomenon of how sport could play a powerful role in our society and bring people together.

I vividly recall standing in a colleague's office at the NCAA headquarters in Indianapolis on the morning of September 11, 2001. We were watching a small TV that sat on top of a filing cabinet. I had only been on the job for a little more than two months, but I had gotten to know the staff and their routines quite well. I arrived a bit early that Tuesday morning as I had dropped off a friend from UNC at the Indianapolis airport. She had come into town

Members of the class of 2001-2002 NCAA Post-Graduate Internship cohort walk in front of the NCAA headquarters in Indianapolis. The cohort formed a memorable bond as they navigated the aftermath of the 9-11 tragedy and adapted to the new normal in terms of security and travel.

for a visit and was on her way back to Raleigh-Durham via the Washington, D.C. airport. The other staff and I stood there in disbelief and confusion as we watched the news report of a plane reportedly hitting the Twin Towers in New York. It initially looked like a small commuter plane that somehow got off track. We then watched, live and in real time, as the second plane hit the Twin Towers and the confusion in the news reports immediately followed.

That friend I dropped off at the airport was making a connection in Washington, DC. At the time she was working in NCAA compliance at UNC, and she knew the 1-800 number at the NCAA by heart. This was a time when cell phones were just emerging in everyone's pocket and pay phones were still everywhere. Her flight would be one of the last flights to safely land on U.S. soil that morning. When she was finally allowed to deboard and get into the airport terminal, that 1-800 number was one of the only numbers she could get to connect. Her words were of utter confusion; all I recall is her asking, "What is going on? The airport is empty. And they are not telling me where or when my next connecting flight is." It was like time stood still and the world seemed to stop for a few days as we learned it was an intentional terrorist attack. All planes were grounded in the U.S. for three days, as news was slow to report what had happened.

From a sport standpoint, all the major sporting organizations took an unprecedented pause in play. This was the first notable pause in play across sport organizations since the NBA and NHL rescheduled playoff games, and eventually MLB would postpone games, in the wake of the April 4, 1968, assassination of Martin Luther King Jr.[11] Following the 9/11 terrorist attacks, the NFL led the way by cancelling its Sunday games, and MLB, NASCAR, and Division I college football followed suit. "Although months away from the major basketball tournament and March Madness, administrators had to make changes. Savvy college basketball fans may recall NCAA administrators implemented the "pod system" for the first time during the 2002 tournament, with the goal of reducing travel and increasing regional play for teams. This was a direct response to the 9/11 attacks."[12] More importantly, though, when play resumed, I watched as sport played a vital role in bringing a nation together. Sport served as a healing agent and provided a sense of much-needed normalcy for many.

Few individuals can watch the video of then-President George W. Bush throwing the first pitch of Game 3 of the 2001 World Series in Yankee Stadium[13] without recognizing the power of sport to bring people together and build, or in this case rebuild, community and sense of togetherness. It was a time when nationalism was at an all-time high, and sport team affiliations were more divisive than political affiliations. The tattered American flag that was recovered after being buried by debris at the World Trade Center on September 11 later flew during the 2001 World Series. That iconic flag also flew over Salt Lake City as the U.S. hosted the 2002 Olympic Winter Games and was presented during the national anthem at both the 2002 Super Bowl XXXVI at the Louisiana Superdome and NCAA national basketball championship game at the Georgia Dome. I could have been anywhere that year that 9/11 happened, but the fact that I was privileged to observe top sport industry leaders respond to the tragic event shaped my career. I understood that the unifying strength that sport could provide for a society was uniquely woven into our culture.

I would go on to work in the sport industry for five years, with the thought of pursuing a Ph.D. in the back of my mind. After consulting with an academic, I was motivated to leave a job that I really enjoyed, as this person assured me that I would not regret quitting my job and becoming a full-time student again. But the first semester as a doctoral student at The University of Texas at Austin, I immediately regretted quitting a job I loved for the challenge of getting a Ph.D. The "you won't regret it" words from that colleague echoed in my mind. As I searched for a dissertation topic, I was overwhelmed by the different paths and quickly felt out of my element. During my seemingly never-ending search for a dissertation topic to research, one Sunday I heard a sermon on the importance of community. Community was always something that I knew sport provided and it fascinated me, but I didn't know if it could be a topic of study. The gist of that sermon was that we are built and designed to live in community. I am not much of a note taker, and I have more notebooks with only a few pages of incoherent thoughts than you would believe. But I scribed down something that day that has guided my research since I've heard it, although I did not realize its significance until over a decade later when I discovered it in one of the many abandoned notebooks: *"Our job is to create the soil and environment where good work can thrive."*

I could not get away from the idea and importance of community, and I began researching sport and community. I immersed myself in the previous written research and literature, and I kept coming back to college athletic department mission statements I had read. The common purpose and justification for intercollegiate athletics in almost every athletic department mission statement I could find mentioned that hard-to-define *sense of community*. "Duke

University is committed to excellence in athletics as part of a larger commitment to excellence in education... Athletics also plays an important role in *creating a sense of community* in the University."[14] "The intercollegiate athletic program aligns its objectives with the academic and developmental objectives of the College, integrates athletes with other students, and fosters a *sense of community* on the campus."[15] The same held true for the mission statements outlined by intramurals and club sports:

> "Campus Recreation & Wellness contributes to the holistic well-being of students, faculty, and staff by providing access to recreational and educational experiences, *fostering a sense of community and belonging*, and empowering individuals to cultivate positive wellness values and behaviors that last throughout and beyond their time at Elon."[16]

The idea that sport would foster a sense of community was embedded throughout sport organization mission statements, but no one seemed to acknowledge or understand what role a sport manager could play in fostering community.

At least with our imaginary ghost runner on second, we knew and agreed upon how it came about—there were not enough players, so we created an invisible runner! But there was no agreement on how this invisible sense of community developed around sport. So, my research set out to find out how a sense of community in sport was created. After numerous interviews and focus groups with over 130 athletes, I began to narrow down the key factors that lead to a sense of community. Eventually the results of that work were a published *Sport and Sense of Community Theory*,[17] and almost a decade later I still see each of the five factors playing a significant role in building community for individuals. In fact, they are applicable beyond sport settings, but my focus will be on sport because of how foundational it is in our society.

I am writing this book and sharing stories for a range of audiences—from the sport fanatic that never misses a chance to watch their team play, to the begrudging midlife adult that wants to improve their health through physical fitness but chose band or theater over athletics years ago and sees no value in sport. But foremost in my mind is the college student that may want to work in sport one day, or be a future health or social work professional, or the current professional well into their career that may or may not yet have noticed the powerful impact sport can have on a community and individuals. Ultimately, my hope is that more people will see the common ground that sport can provide to build a better society and better understand the five unique environmental factors that foster belonging (Common Interest, Administrative Consideration, Social Spaces, Equity in Administrative Decisions, and Leadership Opportunities). No matter where you are on the "sport fanatic" to "sees no value in sport" spectrum, this book hopefully will challenge you to see not what sport is, but what it could be if we better understand its potential impact on communities and on society as whole.

Conclusion

From childhood pickup games to collegiate athletics and professional roles in sport management, sport can foster a profound sense of community and belonging. This chapter underscores the invisible, yet powerful bonds formed through shared experiences in sport. Like a "ghost runner" in a backyard wiffle ball game—an unseen but universally acknowledged presence, there is something special about sport that drives connection and builds community. The broader societal impact of sport, particularly in times of crisis such as the aftermath of 9/11 when sport served as a unifying and healing force, are also noteworthy. Through reflection on your own sport experiences, I hope it is evident that it is important to explore how sport can be a platform for positive social change and specifically, community building through sport. This foundation and reflection will pave the way for a deeper understanding of the five environmental factors that foster a sense of community in sport, which will be explored in the subsequent chapters.

Discussion and Reflection Questions

1. How did the author's personal experiences in sport influence her educational and career choices? How did community and mentorship contribute to the author's professional development and shape her career path?
2. What is the significance of the "ghost runner" metaphor in the context of the chapter? How does it relate to the broader theme of connection through sport?

3. Discuss the impact of Title IX on sport participation for girls and women. How might sport opportunities differ today without this legislation?
4. Sport often fosters a sense of belonging and community and has a way of bringing people together. Reflecting on your own experiences, how have sport or similar experiences contributed to your sense of community and belonging? Do you see a parallel with the author's experiences?
5. Reflect on the role of sport in society during times of crisis, such as the 9/11 attacks, Boston Marathon bombing, or Hurricane Helene. How can sport help communities heal and find normalcy? Can you think of a similar example where sport have played a significant role in societal healing or bringing a group of people together?

CHAPTER 2

Perspective on Sport: Sport is Not a Dirty Word

"Sport has the power to change the world. It has the power to inspire. It has the power to unite people in a way that little else does."
—Nelson Mandela

"Sport is a universal language that can build more bridges between people better than anything else I can think of."
—Olympian Sebastian Coe

After three-and-a-half years as a doctoral student at The University of Texas at Austin, I graduated with my Ph.D. in Sport Management and a newfound perspective on sport. I was fortunate enough to land a tenure-track position as an Assistant Professor at East Carolina University (ECU) in Greenville, NC. I was open to going anywhere offering a job which would allow me to continue my research and get me into the classroom to share what I had learned along the way with future sport managers. ECU was an ideal spot for my first academic position. Greenville was close to my family, and I had an uncle and two cousins that were not only ECU alums but also avid ECU Pirate fans. They also had looked past their niece and cousin from the north initially coming to North Carolina and choosing to work for a rival school, UNC-Chapel Hill, a short ninety miles up the road.

ECU would end up being an ideal fit for me for two reasons. First, it was ideal because of the city, and second because I felt there was a grittiness about the institution and an openness to my research that I had not experienced at other institutions. Greenville, the home of ECU, is a small sport-loving community. It is the eleventh-largest city in North Carolina with a population around 94,000[1] and the home to many different youth sport programs, including numerous privately funded sport leagues and two impressive youth baseball leagues run by the city. The team representing Greenville North State Little League even made a Little League World Series run in 2017, which was the second time a Greenville team advanced to the prestigious Little League

Greenville, named "Sports Town USA" by Sports Illustrated, is a place where sport bring the community together –just like in this moment. The 2022 ECU Sport Management alums join their practicum supervisors at the Little League Softball World Series, showcasing the teamwork and dedication that make this city so special.
Photo credit: Buzz 252 & Bill Hudson.

World Series event. The other was in 1998 by Greenville Tar Heel.[2] ECU competes in sixteen NCAA Division I sports and is supported by one of the most loyal fan bases in college sport.[3] Moreover, Greenville was selected as the Little League Softball World Series host in 2020 due to the energetic sport atmosphere and support from the local community.[4] In 2024, the local Pitt County softball all-star team would represent North Carolina and become the 2024 Little League Softball World Series champs. The City of Greenville has been named "SportsTown USA" for North Carolina by Sports Illustrated and the National Recreation and Parks Association[5] and was designated "the sportiest city" in the U.S. based on how much people spend on sporting equipment.[6]

In 2024, during the Little League Softball World Series hosted at Elm Street Park in Greenville, a hurricane dumped a ton of rain on eastern North Carolina and caused multiple delays. I was miles away in Kansas City at the inaugural PickleCon event, but even from the Midwest I observed why ECU and Greenville were ideal fits for me. I was speaking on panels at the event and collecting some data for a research study. During breaks I would find my way to local restaurants that had televisions tuned in to ESPN. Being a former college softball player and growing up near Williamsport, PA, the home of the Little League Baseball World Series, I have an appreciation for Little League and enjoy tuning in each August for the Little League broadcasts.

During Little League Softball World Series in 2024, though, I was concerned about the amount of rain my hometown of Greenville was getting while trying to host the eight U.S. regional winners and four international regional tournament winners. As I watched I quickly noticed the games were not being played at Elm Street Park, but rather on ECU's campus. Although the first few games were played at Elm Street, the rain and numerous delays forced organizers to make a tough decision and move to ECU's softball field a few blocks away. I could not imagine the breakdown and re-setup that had to quickly occur, but because of drainage and location, the ECU field was playable. I do not know all the behind-the-scenes effort that had to occur for such a move to be pulled off, but as I observed the tournament, I really felt a strong sense of gratitude to work at ECU in sport management. The effort to move something like the Little League Softball World Series to ECU's campus, although only a few blocks away, had to take a tremendous amount of planning and foresight, but more importantly it demonstrated how the university and city are good neighbors to one another.

For a researcher that studies sport and community building and teaches sport management, I do not know if I could find a better example of the power of sport to bring people together or of how sport managers always need to be community- and people-focused. It was clear that the City of Greenville and ECU have built a mutually beneficial relationship. Every time the ECU logo popped up on ESPN behind home plate or in the outfield, I felt a sense of why ECU and Greenville were an ideal place to study and advance the importance of sport and community. I appreciated the grit and get-it-done culture that was on display as I watched the games from several states away, not only because I knew there were ECU sport management and recreation sciences alums that I have taught and worked alongside who had made that happen, but also because I am not sure there is another city, event organizing team, or university that would work so well together to serve the community and pull off a pivot of changing field location during a tournament.

Along with the city being a fit, the institution, so closely tied to the community of Greenville, was also ideal for me. ECU is fourth-largest college among the sixteen universities that comprise the UNC System.[7] Originally founded

North Carolina softball players celebrate after a strikeout at Max R. Joyner Family Stadium on ECU's campus during the 2024 Little League Softball World Series. Photo courtesy of ECU News Services.

as a teachers' college, today ECU is the only public university in the state with a dental school, medical school, and college of engineering.[8] ECU's motto is "Servire" or service. I noticed the university's commitment to service right away, as ECU was actively involved in the community. At other universities that I have had experienced as student or employee, there was a clear separation between the university and the city in which it resides. ECU is different. Along with a strong town-and-gown relationship, ECU was also different because it was classified as FirstGen Forward institution, and in 2021 about 35 percent of its freshman class qualified as first-generation students,[9] meaning their parent or guardian did not earn a bachelor's or higher degree. Not surprisingly, in 2024 the institution was one of only forty colleges and universities in the U.S. to receive a Carnegie Community Engagement Classification from the American Council on Education (ACE) and the Carnegie Foundation for the Advancement of Teaching. This designation acknowledges the work the university does in communities across the globe. So, there was a grittiness and openness to my sport and community building research with both the city and institution. However, I had a bit more trouble finding my fit in the kinesiology department.

Sport and the Academic Fit

As one kinesiology department colleague and full professor told me early in my career at ECU, "I don't understand what you do, but I'm glad you are good at it." For an assistant professor on the tenure track whose work would be judged by a committee of higher-ranking professors (associate and full professors) roughly five to six years into the job, I took it as a compliment. After all, I did not really understand what he did in his biomechanic lab either, but I, too, was glad he was good at it and that he never hesitated to give me shoe-buying advice. As I sat in my office surrounded by the kinesiology faculty colleagues who taught exercise physiology, biomechanics, health fitness and bioenergetics, I often questioned how my work in the social and community-building aspects of sport fit within the department. While my colleagues went to their labs to do sophisticated scientific testing on human movement, I was meeting someone in a coffee shop with a recorder and a much shorter research participant waiver.

I knew as a sport management professor that I found fulfillment and purpose in my teaching and research; much like my fellow kinesiology colleagues, I was driven to study and provide insight on how we can improve the human experience. I just happened to research how the human experience is improved through the social aspects of sport and sporting environments, while most others in my department were focused on cellular and physiological aspects of exercise and physical activity. Despite the large gap between our individual disciplines and approaches to research, I still recognized the common ground. After all, we were all striving to educate and discover how to better serve people through human movement. It is also well-accepted that multidisciplinary approaches tend to produce the best solutions and outcomes. Yet I always felt there was a "sport" stigma—perhaps the "dumb jock" stereotype—to overcome. I was all too aware of the separation between the disciplines focused more on the hard sciences and areas like mine, which centered on the social sciences and managerial implications.

Ironically, the American College of *Sport* Medicine (ACSM) annually hosts an Exercise is Medicine On-Campus (EIM-OC) initiative that promotes physical activity and exercise across college campuses. East Carolina

University's (ECU) Kinesiology department, which did house exercise physiology, biomechanics, physical education, exercise psychology, and sport management, annually boasts that ECU is recognized with EIM-OC gold or silver status. (Sport management moved to the Department of Recreation Sciences in 2024.) Although sport is one avenue for physical activity, "sport" was not mentioned throughout *The American College of Sport Medicine's* guideline for this initiative. Too frequently, the individual disciplines within kinesiology, including myself in sport management, operate in silos. That is, although we have the same common goal of improving the human experience, we do not communicate or consider how our unique thinking and knowledge could inform each other's approach. Each discipline boasts excellent researchers studying and providing insight on promoting wellness and enhancing life quality with the desire for their work to be translated and put into practice. Yet synergistic approaches are not always being capitalized on, especially for those interested in and studying sport.

The gaps within the kinesiology academic disciplines across the nation could be bridged with a greater focus on our common aim to improve the human condition and a more holistic approach. I am advocating that we *should* bridge this gap; my goal is to provide a perspective on how doing so may serve more individuals and broader society. One of the most obvious paths is to consider how sport can improve health. Since the emergence of sport in ancient times, sport and health have been intertwined. In an effort to prepare one's mind and body for war, exercises and competition were combined to create sport and mass entertainment.[10] As contemporary society has evolved, the need to justify and legitimatize sport has continued to be dependent upon sports' positive association with healthy bodies.[11] Yet our sport systems are failing when it comes to viewing sport as a health promotion tool. It is vital for all those involved in sport, exercise, or physical activity to critically consider why. If our common goal is truly to improve the human experience and we find ourselves in a position to promote or be an advocate for sport, we must no longer shy away from discussion of sport and health.

Why Not Include "Sport?"

In several kinesiology faculty meetings, I found myself uttering to my colleagues, "Sport is not a dirty word." In my zeal to advocate for students interested in pursuing a career in the sport industry, I tried to campaign for "sport" modules or course units to be added to new and existing courses. I distinctly recall when a "Physical Activity and Aging" course curriculum change was on the faculty agenda. The course was being revised, and the name of the course was being changed to Physical Activity Across the Lifespan. This created an opportunity for our sport management students. So much of sport management courses are focused on youth sport, college sport, or elite and professional sport, and a large segment of the population could benefit from future professionals thinking about sport across the lifespan. Yet recreational sport for adults, senior games, and master's sport participation are commonly overlooked. A Physical Activity Across the Lifespan course, in my mind, could expand students' view of sport and expose them to sport outside their current realm of thinking.

One assignment in the Physical Activity Across the Lifespan course required students to volunteer at the Greenville-Pitt County Senior Games. It was clear from the reported student outcomes that simply volunteering at these senior games revealed important insights and, most importantly, the experience better prepared students to serve an aging population.[12] Students were mostly surprised by the competitiveness of the seniors and the socialization that occurred at these events. Sport and its ability to bring people together does not change; our society just seemingly focuses on the youth. So, I went all-in with stats and figures on how creating a unit on sport and adding "sport" to the course title would help demonstrate and acknowledge that the most prominent and visible forms of physical activity in our U.S. society center on sport.

I threw out every practical argument that I could muster—from the fact that almost every major news media outlet dedicates twenty percent of coverage to sport to the fact that more college students and most alums can name their university's head football coach than their chancellor or university's president. The arguments seemed to fall on deaf ears. Kinesiology faculty meetings were always on Friday afternoons, and no one wants to have an extended conversation after a long work week, so that may have been a factor. Nonetheless, it provided a catalyst for more water cooler and hallway conversations, as well as the motivation for me to try to encourage others to consider, or better yet, proclaim, that "sport is not a dirty word."

Ironically, I am not a sport evangelist. A sport evangelist ascribes to the "great sport myth" and deems that sport is fundamentally pure and good. As I often remind students, sport is not an automatic car wash. You cannot just put someone in sport and assume they will come out on the other side of a sport experience all clean and shiny. Sport researchers also have not shied away from this reality, acknowledging that over-conforming to the sport norms and culture can lead to negative outcomes and antisocial behaviors.[13] And as sport scholars and teachers, we acknowledge that the outcomes of sport participation for youth are highly influenced by significant others and social connections.[14] Simply put, sport does not exist in a vacuum, and it's imperative that we critically examine it and challenge others to consider how it might be improved upon. This can be a difficult task, especially for those who have picked up this book.

If you are reading this, the odds are good that you have interest in sport or likely have had a positive experience with sport, unless it was an assigned book for a required general education class. If you have had a positive experience with sport, I would encourage you to consider that your positive experience makes you different from the countless others who did not have the ability, resources, time, or self-confidence to even try out for a sport. You are likely different from those that may have had a negative experience in sport and dropped out early in life. Whatever your experience with sport has been, my hope is more people will see the common ground and believe that the goal to improve the human condition *can* be accomplished through sport. Regardless of your field of study or profession, sport can have a positive impact. But we must first acknowledge our systemic failures and patterns that have led many to be resistant to sport.

Failure of sport - deficient delivery

The ability to use sport to promote health has met resistance because of how sport is— and has been—managed and delivered. Frankly, our U.S. sport systems are failing to properly serve our participants, and they continue to move away from their origins of exercising one's mind and body. The U.S. sport development system is also very disjointed and the pathways for sport participation are not clear or connected. That is, if someone wants to enter U.S. sport the path for them to participate and continue to advance into elite sport is not clear. Sport opportunities are made available through the education system or through a nonprofit or for-profit organizations.[15]

Except for an anti-trust exemption granted to professional baseball in 1922, Title IX, and the Amateur Sport Act of 1978[16], which established the United States Olympic Committee (USOC; now the USOPC, United States

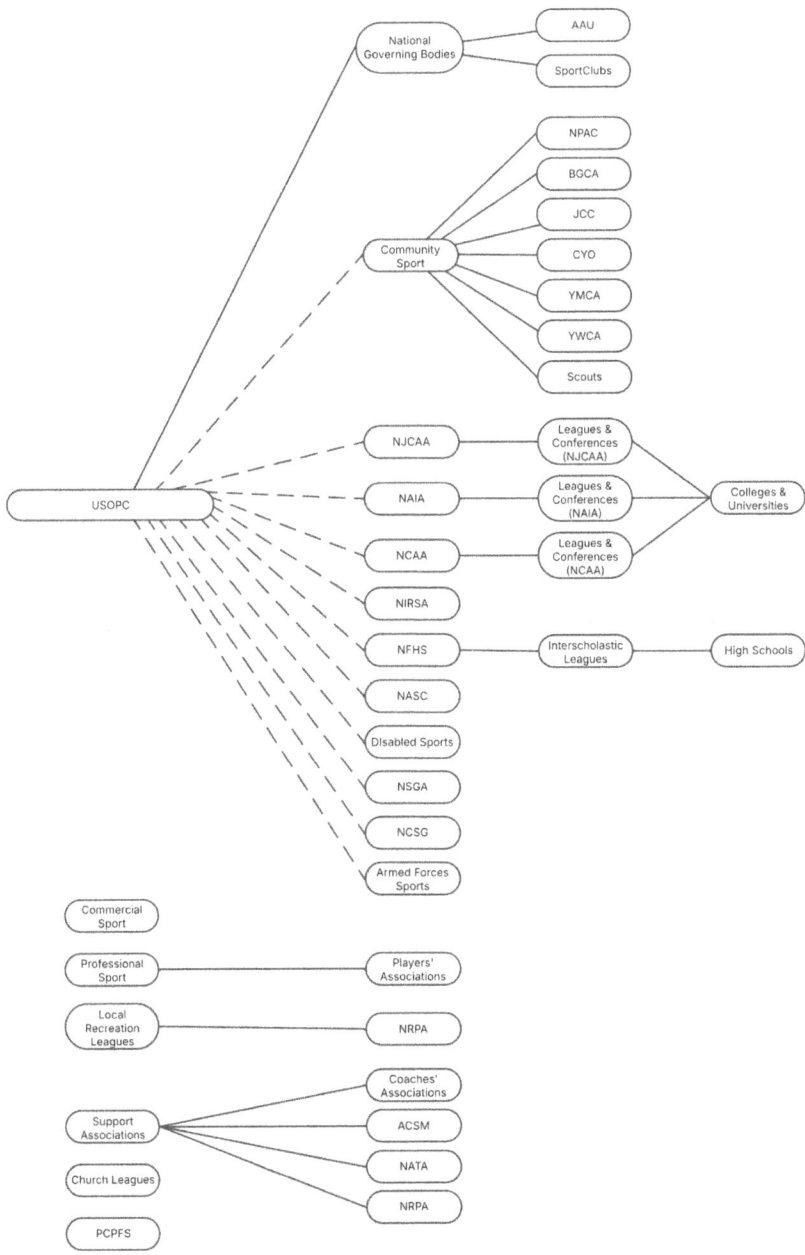

Unlike other countries, the U.S. sport system lacks a clear pathway for sport development and participation. The various non-profit sport organizations within the U.S. are not well-coordinated, making continued sport participation more difficult. Image concept is credited to Emily Sparvero and Laurence Chalip. Recreated by Austin Turner.

Olympic & Paralympic Committee) and provided for national governing bodies (NGBs) for each Olympic sport, there is no governmental legislation, position, or funding geared directly toward advancing our elite sport systems for public good. Most are surprised to learn the USOPC is a nonprofit organization that does not receive government funding.[17] The organization is financially dependent upon private donations and sponsorships, which drastically differs from other countries and their approach to national sport and national sport policies. For example, the European Sport Charter (i.e., sport for all model), was endorsed by the European Parliamentary Assembly in 1972 and passed in 1975 by the European ministers for sport.[18]

While many worldwide acknowledge sport's capacity to increase physical activity and exercise, scholars have been timid to proclaim sport as a means for improving health, especially in the U.S. In fact, Berg and colleagues[19] highlighted "the almost complete absence of the word sport" (p. 20) from U.S. public health discourse, nationwide health promotions, and physical activity guidelines. It is obvious that a sport-is-healthy versus sport-is-unhealthy paradox exists.[20] Although sport scholars are starting to make strides to addressing this,[21] greater progress can be made if we better recognize the potential contribution sport can make in the health realm.

If we are to position sport as a means to promote health, we must first critically consider sport and recognize a few of its chief failures. First, U.S. data has indicated that while the popularity of competitive/elite sport grew exponentially between 1985 and 2012, the obesity rates more than doubled.[22] While obesity rates are not entirely attributable to the growth of competitive/elite sport, this fact does indicate that offering more sport opportunities does not equal the achievement of important health benefits. Scholars continue to point out that sport participants are not meeting the recommended level of physical activity.[23] This is often due to an overemphasis on structure, drills, winning, and strategy.[24] That is, our sport systems are set up in a manner that stresses and places an overemphasis on winning.

The second failure of our sport system is that the overemphasis on competition can increase the likelihood of injuries and unnecessary stress. Extensive research continues to conclude that increased training loads for adolescent athletes contribute to injuries and illness. While the physical repercussions have been noted by researchers for some time, recently scholarly attention has turned to better understanding athlete mental health and the stress placed on athletes.[25] The third major failure of our sport system is that many adults view "sport participation" in terms of sedentary fanship. Fanship not only decreases time spent playing sport,[26] but it is also thought to encourage unhealthy eating and excessive alcohol consumption.[27] Inoue, Berg, and Chelladurai's (2015) work has called for researchers and sport managers to better address the health issues of sport spectators.[28] Specifically, their efforts identify the positive and negative health effects of spectator sport and acknowledge that more needs to be done in this area to address important social issues.

By acknowledging the three major failures of our sport system, one can understand why sport has been left out of the health conversation. And we can also understand why some may consider sport a dirty word when the focus is on improving health and the human condition. That is, our sport systems are at times failing to deliver positive health outcomes. However, we also must look at the successes within our sport systems. As Laurence Chalip pointed out almost two decades ago in his *Towards a Distinctive Sport Management Discipline* article, [29] sport has the advantage of offering hedonic rewards and social structures, which have direct implications on health. My own work has focused on sport and community building and the importance of those social structures, but it was not until I was invited to work on a paper entitled, *What about Sport? A Public Health Perspective on Leisure-Time Physical Activity*, that I recognized the proverbial mountain that needed to be climbed to push the conversation forward.

What about sport? A public health perspective on leisure-time physical activity

In this research, funded by the Texas Governor's Advisory Council on Physical Fitness (GACPF), forty-two interviews were conducted with community leaders, program organizers, and residents representing a large urban area, small urban area, and rural area. The goal was to better understand how to increase participation in community sport and other leisure-time physical activity programs to combat obesity. The results demonstrated that the commonly marketed emphasis in such programs, 'It's good for you,' did not appear in the data, nor did the factor of improved physical appearance. That is, individuals are not motivated as much by health and physical appearance outcomes as marketers and administrators tend to think.

Instead, the results from the interviews demonstrated and further reinforced Chalip's earlier work, that hedonic rewards and opportunities for social

A family celebrates after completing a 5K at The Color Run. This untimed, fun-run event emphasizes the joy and social benefits of participating in sport with others. By organizing and promoting activities that highlight enjoyment and fun, we can positively impact both individuals and the community. Photo courtesy of Lynn Mona.

interaction are two overlooked, yet primary benefits sought by participants. "Hedonic rewards comprised the personal satisfaction and pleasure the participants described as a benefit that they seek in sport and other leisure-time physical activities. That is, the participants readily cited how much better they felt after engaging in sport and leisure-time physical activity and the enjoyment involved" (p. 25). For example, one Texas resident identified as Aaron stated, "I'm terrible, but I'd love to play soccer, or ultimate Frisbee, or flag football... I might start doing more of that and workout less traditionally as I get older, just because it's fun." The "it's fun" was somewhat expected. But what stood out to me was that "The opportunity for social interaction and the sense of community that developed was the other most frequently cited reason the residents wanted to participate in sport and other leisure-time physical activities" (p. 26). One participant in the research explained:

> "First of all, people tend to be more engaged with physical activity and more consistent with it if it's a group activity; they have other people they're doing it with, friends, teammates. There's an element of camaraderie and fun when you do it that way. People tend to stay motivated when it's not just them going to exercise in the morning by themselves. People have a better retention, from my experience, when they're involved either with a team or at least a group of people they're training and exercising with, or they have a goal they're training toward." (p. 26)

This work only further reinforced the fact that creating a sense of community and a place to belong through sport is fundamental. The "how" to create community, though, was still elusive to many. The following chapters will provide examples on the "how" to create community through sport. Specifically, I will outline the necessary Common Interest, Administrative Consideration, Social Spaces, Equity in Administrative Decisions, and Leadership Opportunities — the key elements that comprise the Sport and Sense of Community Theory. If we want to ensure that sport is not considered a dirty word, we must consider these environmental factors that can create a healthy community for individuals to belong. In doing so, we can help create the soil and environment where a "better-together" society can thrive.

Conclusion

It is important to identify the transformative power of sport and its potential to improve the human experience. Despite the challenges and systemic

The Sport and Sense of Community Theory (Warner, 2016) provides a practical guide for sport managers to improving the athlete, fan, employee, or other stakeholders experience. The theory addresses the environmental factors needed to build or enhance the sense of belong experienced by individuals within various sport settings. Importantly, the theory can and should be applied to enrich, develop, strengthen and build better community through sport. Image created by Kathryn Adkins.

failures within the U.S. sport system, sport should not be dismissed as a mere trivial activity. Instead, it should be recognized for its capacity to foster community, promote health, and enhance social interactions. It is also important to highlight the significance of interdisciplinary collaboration and the need to bridge gaps between different academic disciplines to fully leverage the benefits of sport. It is also important to underscore the shortcomings of the current sport delivery systems, such as the overemphasis on competition and unclear sport pathways while still enhancing the physical, social, and hedonic rewards. By acknowledging these issues and focusing on creating inclusive, community-oriented sport environments, we can ensure that sport is positioned as an opportunity to reinforce improved health and well-being. This sets the stage for a call for a more holistic approach to sport management that integrates health promotion and community building while reinforcing that sport should not be viewed as "a dirty word" but rather as a powerful tool that can improve society and individuals' lives for the better.

Discussion and Reflection Questions

1. What challenges did the author face when integrating sport management within a kinesiology department, and how did she address these challenges?
2. Why is interdisciplinary collaboration so important, especially in the context of sport? How can different academic disciplines work together to improve the human experience through sport?
3. Discuss the reasons why sport is often excluded from public health discourse. What are the potential benefits of including sport in health promotion strategies?
4. What are the key failures of the U.S. sport system identified by the author? How do these failures impact participants' health and well-being? What steps can be taken to address these failures and improve the delivery of sport programs?
5. Reflect on how your own experiences with sport align with or differ from the issues discussed in the chapter. How have your personal experiences shaped your view of sport's role in health and community?

CHAPTER 3

So What? Why Sport Managers Need to Understand How to Build Community

"There is nothing so practical as a good theory."
—Kurt Lewin

"He who loves practice without theory is like the sailor who boards a ship without a rudder and compass and never knows where he may cast."
—Leonardo da Vinci

"So what?" That is the question my dear friend promised she would start asking me after presenting research one day at a stuffy academic conference. This friend, who is now a teaching professor at a major institution, and I had a handshake agreement when we were both doctoral students trying to find our way through our respective Ph.D. programs. We were both pursuing advanced degrees so that we could eventually teach. Both of us were at highly respected "R1" institutions, which means they are classified as research intensive universities where the faculty places a strong emphasis on research. Both of us were, and still are, practitioners at heart. We both at the time had worked in the sport industry for five to six years after earning our master's degrees in sport-related fields. Eventually, we both discovered our passion for teaching and desire to help the next generation find success in the sport industry. For us, though, there was a large gap, perhaps even a disconnect, between academic programs, especially those with a research focus, and the sport industry. And we both wanted to make sure we never ventured too far from our practical days working in that industry.

That "So what?" agreement with my dear friend and colleague came about after a conversation regarding the minutiae that is sometimes associated with academic research. When you are a practitioner, you want the brief version of research and its practical applications. Fortunately, in sport management research this is typically expected to be included in a peer-reviewed research article, but it is often packaged with a lengthy explanation of the theoretical support, justification for the methodological process, and sometimes even the epistemological framework. The epistemological frameworks in quantitative and qualitative studies explain the approaches researchers use to understand and generate new knowledge. Quantitative researchers typically tend to follow a positivism or post-positivism approach, while qualitative researchers take a constructivism or interpretivism approach. I am sure it was after an epistemological conversation in class, with my head aching, when I called this "So what?" agreement friend. I likely said, "Who gets this, who cares, and why does it matter?"

Now that I am a fully tenured professor, I can admit that conversation happened, and I still cringe when thinking or even typing the word "epistemological." At the time I would have rhetorically answered myself, "It matters because the people judging my work care. I have to get my research published, so I can have job security and do what I care about one day." Today, I will tell you it matters because there is a lot of cursory, shoddy research and unscrupulous or impatient individuals who want to make false claims about new knowledge. The more rigorous the research is, the more credible it will be, and consequently, the more impact sport can have on our society. So, you must know a bit about the epistemological approach (still cringing) to produce quality meaningful research. Today, I will also tell you, I am still committed to my "so what?" agreement with my friend and colleague and hope I will be answering the "so what?" question, as to why building community through sport matters, throughout this text.

Given the importance of translating research into relatable practical examples for sport managers, I propose that there are three key reasons why community building through sport deserves our attention. So what? Why does building community in sport matter? First, it matters because in our genetic make-up we have a desire to belong, and this impacts health outcomes. Second, it matters because it is timely to better understand how sport can play a role in community building. Third, finding a sense of community through sport matters and is important for every individual, and it is especially impactful at specific times when major life events occur. That is, being in community is particularly impactful at various major life occurrences that all individuals likely can relate to at some point in their lifetime (i.e., parenting, aging, and grieving).

The Human Condition, Social Beings, and Health Outcomes

All humans are inherently social beings, and being part of community is embedded in our genetic makeup. Therefore, it is important for leaders to learn how to build community through sport to help fulfill this fundamental human need. If you look back in history, over time civilizations have developed through community. Or if you think about a pack of wolves or sheep, the animals at the center of the community are the safest. The same is true for a group of people, the individuals at the center of community, those surrounded by the community members, are the safest. The same is true for each living being, and our society has evolved around this concept. So, belonging to community has to do with both our safety and physiological needs and is embedded in our overall well-being and survival. In Maslow's hierarchy of needs, belonging is an essential component. According to Maslow's theory, right after the physiological needs (i.e., food and shelter) and safety needs are met, individuals have the need for belonging.[1] That is, humans have an inherent need to feel a sense of belonging and acceptance within social groups. The U.S. Surgeon General report summarizes this need:

> "Social connection is a fundamental human need, as essential to survival as food, water, and shelter. Throughout history, our ability to rely on one another has been crucial to survival. Now, even in modern times, we human beings are biologically wired for social connection. Our brains have adapted to expect proximity to others. Our distant ancestors relied on others to help them meet their basic needs. Living in isolation, or outside the group, means having to fulfill the many difficult demands of survival on one's own. This requires far more effort and reduces one's chances of survival. Despite current advancements that now allow us to live without engaging with others (e.g., food delivery, automation, remote entertainment), our biological need to connect remains."

The size and context of the social group does not matter; individuals just have an inherent need to belong to something. If a sense of community and belonging does not exist, individuals will struggle with mental health concerns and feelings of loneliness, which has been identified by the U.S. Surgeon General[2] as an epidemic. Loneliness is now considered an epidemic, because it is a widespread undesirable phenomenon that has become a significant U.S. public health issue.

Fifteen Cigarettes a Day: Health Concerns and the Loneliness Epidemic

The best answer to the "So what? Why should we care about building community via sport?" was answered in the 2023 U.S. Surgeon General's report on loneliness. The report, *Our Epidemic of Loneliness and Isolation: The U.S. Surgeon General's Advisory on the Healing Effects of Social Connection and Community*, highlights the severe impact of loneliness and social isolation on public health. The report notes that even before the COVID-19 pandemic, about half of U.S. adults reported experiencing considerable levels of loneliness. What the report shockingly touted was that the detrimental health impacts of this reported loneliness and social isolation were equated to smoking fifteen cigarettes a day. Because of the pivotal 1964 Surgeon General's report, "Smoking and Health," which officially linked smoking to serious health issues and inspired several modern-day health and anti-smoking campaigns along with legislative actions aimed at reducing smoking rates, it is now well accepted that smoking is bad for one's health. This widespread knowledge makes this an especially meaningful analogy.

Loneliness is equal to smoking fifteen cigarettes a day because like cigarettes, loneliness and social isolation significantly increase the risk of various health issues, including heart disease, stroke, dementia, depression, and anxiety. From an economic standpoint, the report suggests that a lack of social connection contributes to billions of dollars in healthcare costs due to its association with various physical and mental health conditions. The report is a call to action from the U.S. Surgeon General for a national strategy to enhance social connection, as well as a call to individuals, communities, workplaces, health systems, and governments to address this public health crisis and improve social connections. The report states:

> "Extensive scientific findings from a variety of disciplines, including epidemiology, neuroscience, medicine, psychology, and sociology, converge on the same conclusion: social connection is a significant predictor of longevity and better physical, cognitive, and mental health, while social isolation and loneliness are significant predictors of premature death and poor health. In fact, the benefits of social connection extend beyond health-related outcomes. They influence an individual's educational attainment, workplace satisfaction, economic prosperity, and overall feelings of well-being and life fulfillment."

Clearly, there are well-documented and negative impacts to individuals not being in community, and sport organizations have an opportunity to address this very timely issue.

The Right Time to Build Community is Now

My second response to the "So what? Why should we care about building community via sport?" question is because individuals are lacking community and need to be in community for society to thrive. As scholars have continued to note the benefits of sport, the sense of community that develops around sport continues to be cited as a primary benefit.[3] The importance of this benefit was specifically highlighted when sport organizations were faced with cancelling seasons and postponing events due to the Coronavirus pandemic that hit the world in the spring of 2020. The tagline "We're all in this together" echoed throughout commercials, trended on Twitter, and was reiterated by professional athletes across the globe. It was evident that the innate need for community was at the forefront of many minds. Shortly after the COVID-19 pandemic, a colleague and I wrote:

> "We will concede it is still the feeling of safety that must be provided by sport systems, but more so than ever we argue that it is the togetherness that will be fundamental to the recovery of the sport industry. Our goal is to highlight the role and importance of sport fostering community, from the youth and adult participatory levels to professional and amateur spectator sport. To aid in the successful recovery of our sport systems, we must first acknowledge what fans and athletes have been missing because of the COVID-19 pandemic. We hope that sport managers will recognize that the most successful sport systems are those that create a healthy community and attachment for participants. As scholars across various disciplines have continued to note the benefits of experiencing togetherness or a sense of community, sport scholars have demonstrated that the sense of community derived from sport continues to be a primary benefit and justification for sport."[4]

Two texts that have especially underscored this are *Bowling Alone: The Collapse and Revival of American Community* by Robert Putnam and *Fractured: Why Our Societies Are Coming Apart and How We Put Them Back Together Again* by Jon Yates. Strikingly, *Bowling Alone* was published in 2000 while *Fractured* was written just over two decades later in 2021. Both texts emphasize the timely importance of sport and the need for sport to positively contribute to this communal impact. But the fact that little progress has been made in twenty years indicates a change is needed now.

Bowling Alone by Robert Putnam

In his book, Putnam explored the decline of social capital, or decrease in informal social connectedness, among individuals in the United States during the late 20th century. He defined social capital as "connections among individuals—social networks and the norms of reciprocity and trustworthiness that arise from them."[5] Putnam's main argument was that Americans have become increasingly disconnected from family, friends, neighbors, and democratic structures, and that this has led to a decline in civic engagement and community life in general. The book was entitled *Bowling Alone* because Putnam noted that while more Americans were bowling than ever before, they were doing so alone rather than in leagues. That is, even though more individuals were participating in the sport of bowling, fewer individuals are participating with others in bowling leagues and consequently, not reaping the social benefits of being in community. Putnam's work emphasized the importance of rebuilding social capital and communities to improve individual well-being and societal health. Further he suggested various ways to address the decline in community connectedness, offering the idea that participation in group activities, including sport leagues, could help foster social connections and build communities.

Fractured by Jon Yates

In his book, *Fractured: Why Our Societies Are Coming Apart and How We Put Them Back Together Again*,[6] Jon Yates, similarly to Putnam, argued that our societies are becoming increasingly divided due to a lack of social cohesion. Yates argued that people tend to surround themselves with others who are similar to themselves, a phenomenon he refers to as "people like me syndrome." This idea is supported by the common idiom "birds of a feather flock together" and extensive sociological research on homophily, which is the principle that contact between similar people occurs at a higher rate than among dissimilar people.[7] For example, a 2019 Public Religion Research Institute polling study reported: "A substantial minority of Americans, however, report less frequent interactions with people who are different than they are. About one in five

Americans say they seldom or never interact with someone who does not share their race or ethnicity (twenty-one percent) or religion (twenty-two percent), nearly one quarter (twenty-three percent) say they seldom or never interact with someone who does not share their political party, and nearly one third (thirty-one percent) say they seldom or never interact with someone who does not share their sexual orientation."[8]

A concern with homophily networks, according to researchers, is the fact that strong communities are diverse,[9] more economically and socially vibrant,[10] demonstrate more prosocial behaviors,[11] and tend to be more successful at problem solving[12] and perform better on group tasks.[13] Homophily networks, or those with only like-minded and similar individuals, can create echo chambers where individuals are only exposed to similar viewpoints.[14] This can reduce critical thinking and the opportunity to apply innovative problem solving to issues that a community may face. Yates' book emphasized the importance of creating a "common life," where people from diverse backgrounds engage in shared activities and institutions. Yates further noted that building community through fostering more diverse connections can help bridge societal divides and lead to stronger communities. He, like Warner and Martin,[15] saw the COVID-19 pandemic as an opportunity to create a more united society by fostering such connections. Importantly, Yates also referenced sport as a means to address and help bridge societal divides and foster unity. One notable example Yates used is the English football team, and he discussed how sport can create shared experiences and build connections among people from different backgrounds, contributing to social cohesion.

The Story of the '96 Euro

"I can remember it easily: jumping up and down, beer spilling out of my glass, celebrating with strangers. If I close my eyes, I can see the pub unfolding as we walk in. We came early to get a good spot. We chatted, nestling the beer I thought we wouldn't get served, watching the highlights of the previous match over our shoulders. I can feel the nervousness in my stomach before kick-off. Would we score? Could we stop them scoring? Would I get served another beer? I was sixteen: old enough to sneak into a pub and young enough to believe England could win the European Championship. It was all we talked about that summer. When we weren't revising for our exams, we dreamt of England winning the trophy," Yates recalled in the prologue of *Fractured*.[16]

Yates' prologue continued with contrasting the English and Dutch teams, who both found themselves in Group A of the 1996 UEFA European Football Championship. The Euro '96 was being hosted by England, and English and Dutch teams would play an exhilarating match at the world-renowned Wembley Stadium.[17] Less than a week prior to the 1996 Euro Championship, the England team was faced with controversy. On a return trip from Hong Kong, the team's celebratory rowdy antics carried over onto the plane on the flight back to London. When the English footballers landed at the Heathrow airport, their plane was greeted by police officers who were called by Cathay Pacific airline officials to inspect the damage to the interior of the plane. When Cathay Pacific airline officials learned they could not pursue criminal damages because of overseas justification issues, the airline quickly filed a complaint with the Football Association in England. Before the Football Association in England could address the issue, the story was leaked to the media, and the English team faced intense media scrutiny and public criticism for their off-field antics.

Remarkably, not a single English player would take responsibility for the damages or name a teammate as being a guilty party. Instead, the entire English squad took responsibility and agreed to pay for the damages caused during their boisterous behaviors in the Cathay Pacific plane cabin. The payment for the unruly celebratory damages would come from the match fees that they would earn from their first two games. David Davies, the executive director of the Football Association in England at the time, attempted to fend off any negative publicity and bad press for a single player by saying it was the team that took "collective responsibility."[18] The agreement within the squad for taking collective responsibility resulted in an increase in camaraderie and solidarity among the team. Many, including Yates, considered this strengthened bond a major contributing factor to their on-field success a few short days later as they vied for the 1996 Euro Championship.

In contrast, the Dutch team, despite being incredibly talented, was fractured along racial lines, with a group of Black players feeling marginalized and undervalued. The Dutch national football team in the mid-1990s faced internal divisions, particularly between the predominantly White players and a talented group of Black, Surinamese players, including Michael Reiziger, Edgar Davids, Patrick Kluivert, and Clarence Seedorf. Reiziger was quoted in the press discussing how the four players formed a separate group because of how easily they could talk and joke with each other due to their shared culture. This group, dubbed "the Cabal" by the press, felt marginalized and undervalued by both the manager and their White Dutch teammates, who, it was accidentally revealed, were being paid up to six times more than them. According to Yates and others, this division ultimately led to their downfall.[19] The fact that Yates uses this Euro '96 story in his prologue to *Fractured*, as well as Putnam's use of sport to entitle his book, *Bowling Alone*, further illustrate the important and sustained timeliness of the broader discussion on societal cohesion and how well-managed shared sport experiences can bring people together.

Life Stages and Sense of Community

My third and final response to, "So what? Why should we care about building community via sport?" is that it can impact everyone at a variety of different life stages. Although U.S. sport tends to focus primarily on youth sport participants, sport and sport-related programming can and should serve more people. This can be accomplished by thinking through people's innate need to belong, especially during specific life stages when community and group-level support are especially needed and beneficial. Sport and community are important parts of the social fabric of life, and the following will touch upon three life stages: new life and parenthood, the grieving, and the aging.

Runner by Marriage, Community Builder and Designated Team Mom by Choice

It was a particularly cold Saturday, and we were wrapped in layers of moisture-wicking, yet breathable clothing as we ventured out on a long run from a local coffee shop. We always started as a group of twenty or so on those long training runs, but inevitably within the first mile that group of twenty evolved to a smaller group of three to five people who naturally ran at the same pace. Katie 2, Dee, and I would end up in a group. If you are wondering why Katie 2 was not just Katie, it's because she shared her first name (and eventually her last name too) with a runner who would become her sister-in-law, Katie 1. I initially met Dee and Katie 2 through FiA when we decided to train for a half-marathon. Despite being winded by running with Katie 2, Dee, and I would use those Saturdays to catch up with one another. Dee was an especially gifted storyteller on those runs, and the time would fly by.

"I do not like running, but I always look forward to Saturdays with you all." Katie 2 perfectly described what we were all likely feeling one cold long run

Katie 2 (far right) poses with her husband and in-laws before a Thanksgiving Turkey Trot —a tradition that was about more than just the miles. The runs weren't just exercise; they were about moments of connection, conversation, and quiet support. Katie 2 married into a family of Boston qualifier runners and when she became a first-time mom she found community support for herself and others through the sport.

day. There was something about the time together and the conversation on those runs that made a meaningful impact on our days and the week ahead. It was a community built by running, and support at the group level that each of us did not recognize how much we needed. Katie 2, who never saw herself as runner, would eventually go on to run several half marathons and marry into a family of runners. Her husband and in-laws are the kind of family that run a turkey trot on Thanksgiving instead of lounging on the couch watching a televised parade. So, this was a different kind of family culture, and Katie 2 adapted. When Katie 2 became a first-time mom and settled into all the joys and sleeplessness of motherhood, it was that community and support that she would recognize she was missing and craving. She was also on the advisory board at Awaken Coffee, a local coffee shop that employs individuals with intellectual disabilities. Their website states, "With 80 percent of people with disabilities unemployed nationwide, Awaken Coffee creates a path for people with intellectual and developmental disabilities to become more valued, accepted and included in our community."

Along with her hidden passion for running, Katie 2 has a heart to serve individuals with disabilities. Combining these two things and considering her desire to be in community with others, Katie 2 made an Instagram post inviting other new parents to join her at Awaken Coffee for a run or walk one Friday morning. Katie 2 was admittedly nervous about putting herself and the idea out there. She was concerned no one would show that Friday morning, although I tried to assure her that how she was feeling–wanting to be around and in community with other parents–was exactly how others were likely feeling. Sure enough, the first Friday fifteen parents with strollers showed up. I did not think of it at the time to further reassure her, but the saying from Field of Dreams is true. "If you build it, they will come." And the strollers and parents kept showing up, and still show up, on Fridays at 7:30 a.m. at Awaken Coffee (or another designated spot).

Interestingly enough, a recent report explains why parents and all those strollers showed up at Awaken Coffee that Friday morning. According to a 2023 American Psychological Association survey, forty-eight percent of parents say, "most days their stress is completely overwhelming," compared with twenty-six percent of other adults who reported the same. Meanwhile only twenty percent of adults report that "most days they are so stressed they can't function," compared to forty-one percent of parents.[20] Clearly, the additional stressors of parenthood are impactful, and we also know social isolation and lack of social support can lead to even greater parental stress.[21]

Bringing the community together, one stroller at a time. What started with an Instagram invite from Katie 2 turned into a weekly tradition of connection and support. Join them every Friday at 7:30 a.m. at Awaken Coffee or follow @babyandweclub on Instagram.

According to the 2023 *Under Pressure: The U.S. Surgeon General's Advisory on the Mental Health & Well-Being of Parents* report, parents and guardians were more likely to be lonely than non-parents.[22] A 2021 Cigna survey found that approximately sixty-five percent of parents and guardians, and seventy-seven percent of single parents, experienced loneliness, compared to fifty-five percent of non-parents. Furthermore, forty-two percent of parents who experienced loneliness *always* felt left out compared to twenty-four percent of non-parents who experienced loneliness.[23] Parents experiencing loneliness are four times as likely as non-lonely parents to feel excluded (twenty-three percent versus six percent). These statistics are even more staggering for parents of children with disabilities. Thus, it was even more significant for the community, as a whole, that Katie 2 chose Awaken Coffee, a place operated by amazingly welcoming people, especially those with differing abilities, as the starting point for the Friday morning runs or walks. Of parents of children with disabilities, fifty-eight percent said they felt left out, sixty percent said they lacked companionship, and forty percent said they felt drained.

In a *New York Times* guest editorial, U.S. Surgeon General Vivek H. Murthy said: "The stress and mental health challenges faced by parents — just like loneliness, workplace well-being and the impact of social media on youth mental health — aren't always visible, but they can take a steep toll. It's time to recognize they constitute a serious public health concern for our country. Parents who feel pushed to the brink deserve more than platitudes. They need tangible support."[24] So, while Katie 2 never intentionally set out to become a runner, she did become a community builder and designated team mom for the Friday morning Awaken Coffee runners and walkers. She also demonstrated the importance of community at this life stage. While this group was more about the desire to socialize with other parents in community, there is no doubt that the little ones in the strollers are also benefiting.

The Grieving and the Importance of a Supportive Community

Years before Katie 2 organized her group at Awaken Coffee, Eva, a physical education colleague, recognized the same need for parents and wanted to be part of the solution as well. Eva designed and implemented the home school physical education program operated by the-then Exercise and Sport Science department at ECU. Like Katie 2, Eva merged her passions. Her passions were for physical education and preparing future teachers. The home school program allowed Eva's students to get hands-on practical experience teaching physical education and sport while fulfilling a need of home school parents by providing a weekly place for them to gather. Eva, though, was not just about educating the next generation about how to be a great physical education and sport teacher. She was also a community builder, and one of my first "local" friends when I arrived in Greenville. Eva quickly became one of those lifelong best friends as I got to know her and her family. They welcomed me to Greenville and made sure I had a tailgate to go to on one of my first fall Saturdays in the football-crazy college town. Eva was well-connected in the community, and because of that she was a huge reason Greenville quickly felt like a welcoming place for me.

Soon after Eva and her husband welcomed their third child and first son into the world, she discovered a lump on her neck. It was a rare form of lymphoma, and over the next five months she would lean into her faith and humor and display a grace that inspired many as she fought for her life. Eva graciously fought with her family by her side and ultimately passed away on January 1, 2013. What I and so many of her friends and family experienced after was a grief that is hard to describe to anyone that has not been through the loss of a loved one. I recall Dr. Grimsley, who this book is also dedicated to along with Eva, stopping by my office soon after she passed away. He told me: "There's always one death in your lifetime that really gets you and changes you forever. I had a friend that passed, and our friendship was much like yours and Eva's. I have since lost three brothers and that one was still the hardest." So, what does all this have to do with community and sport? Grief is another stage in life that everyone likely will have to go through at some point in their lifetime, and being in community is extremely helpful in getting through that natural stage of life.

Grief is a natural emotion-filled response to any loss, whether it's the death of a friend or family member, the end of a relationship, or any significant life change. At one time or another, everyone unfortunately experiences grief. Grieving is well-documented to negatively impact both mental and physical health, as well as overall well-being. It is linked not just to increased depression and anxiety, but also to the risk of a stroke or heart attack, disrupted sleep, immune system changes and the risk of blood clots.[25] The grieving process is unique to everyone, and how long the process takes can vary. However, research tells us that it is also a time when community and belonging are vital.

In their research entitled, *What Determines Supportive Behaviors Following Bereavement? A Systematic Review and Call to Action*, scholars Emma L. Logan, Jennifer A. Thornton, and Lauren J. Breen stated: "The provision of helpful, timely social support is one of the strongest determinants of positive psychosocial outcomes following bereavement. Although a multitude of factors (e.g., attachment to the deceased or cause of death) may complicate the grieving process, very few of these can be modified after the fact to the extent that social support can. However, bereaved people often do not receive the quantity or quality of social support that they would like." Further research also tells us that that the informal support that community can provide can be especially impactful during times of grief and bereavement.[26] A compassionate community approach has been well accepted for end-of-life care, but it needs to also be considered as a needed supportive mechanism for the grieving.[27]

So what? Why should sport managers care about grief? Because grief is a life stage and transition almost everyone will experience, and being in community can help mitigate the negative impacts of grief and aid in the healing process. The research is also clear that being in supportive communities is one of the malleable things that can counteract negative mental and physical health outcomes. Not surprisingly, this is why you often see marathons and half marathons being done in memory of someone or a moment of silence at a ball game in honor of someone who has passed; the supportive community that sport can provide is powerful and impactful, especially for those grieving. A year or so after Eva passed, I ran a half marathon with my sister and Eva's cousin. Eva's mom and aunt also completed it, and training with others was an important part of the grieving process for all of us. To provide another sport example, this is also why a local tennis and pickleball club hosts an annual tournament called Playing for Pearsall. The tournament is played in honor of Nick (son) and Greg (father) who both lost their life two years apart due to mental illness. The event is set up to benefit the North Carolina National Alliance on Mental Illness.[28] The event is a reminder of how important it is for the grieving to be in community, and how the community that sport provides

Christopher J. Stanfill, Ph.D. · 1st
Executive Director | Mobility Worldwide
2w ·

Today I am alive and on Sunday, I finished my fourth marathon.

I set out to run a marathon this year to celebrate the power of community and how community can help eliminate some of the darkest places we experience.

At the end of the day on Sunday, I felt accomplished, tired, and sore. But most importantly, I felt deeply loved.

My community saved my life and I live each day thankful for the love people show me and that they've welcomed me into their lives.

You are not alone and you are loved. While it may be hard to believe at times, I've learned first hand that these facts are always true.

Congratulate me by following the link below and follow Sprout Society on Instagram to learn more about the power of community.

Loneliness almost killed me. Community saved me.

#mentalhealth

https://lnkd.in/eGY9Ud9p

"Loneliness almost killed me. Community saved me." Community through sport isn't just about competition; it's about belonging, healing, and hope as demonstrated in this LinkedIn post.

can play an important role in addressing the loneliness and mental health crisis associated with loss.[29]

While I was writing and finalizing this book, a former classmate of mine posted on LinkedIn that he had completed his fourth marathon. With his permission and encouragement to further the conversation about community, the following is a verbatim from his fundraising page. (Warning: this message talks explicitly about suicide):

"On August 20th, 2017, I found myself in the most immense pain I'd ever felt. There were no broken bones or serious burns. I had not fallen, torn a ligament, nor was experiencing any kind of internal injury.

My soul and mind had reached a breaking point and one that manifested into a pain so deep that all I could do is scream.

Curled up on the couch and needing the pain to end, I could only see one way out: ending my life. And then series of events occurred that brought me out of darkness.

It was an unsolicited text message from someone that knew I needed help and showed up with pure empathy. It was hearing the voice of my niece. It was thinking about the earth shattering horror I would cause my mom. It was remembering there were people who love me. It was remembering that I'm needed. It was remembering that my life matters.

As I was finding a way out of this pain, I still needed a release. I needed to force this energy outside of my body. So, I ran.

I opened up the door and ran as fast as I could. Then I would walk or even stop and sit for a while, but would eventually start running again. I needed my body to feel something different and break apart from the emotional pain. I thought that taking my body to its physical limits would rid itself of the suffocating feeling of hopelessness.

When I exhausted myself, I sat in a field of grass, closed my eyes, and started the true pathway of trusting that I am loved.

Today, I know I am loved. The people that have brought me along the way carry me every single day. While my journey continues to have its own high and lows, the grounding force of those around me always pulls me through.

Every step of the 26.2 miles in October will remind me of what brought me to this life of joy and hope: You.

Loneliness almost killed me. Community saved me."

A community that develops around sport can be life-giving and life-saving for many.

Aging and Community

If you could not relate to parenthood or grieving yet, you can relate to aging. Given this is something that starts on the day you were born, it is the most compelling case regarding the importance of being in community at various life stages for every individual. One of the reasons we have sport opportunities for youth is because they can provide a needed arena for socialization. Other than potentially church, sport is typically a child's first exposure to community and group support. Given the results of a national sample of parents of children six to twelve years old, it is important we have sport and other community-building opportunities for children. A 2024 C.S. Mott Children's Hospital National Poll on Children's Health found that close to one in five parents (nineteen percent) said their child had no friends or not enough friends, while ninety percent said their child would like to make new friends.

Based on the research, this trend does not seem to get better with age. In fact, a 2021 research article entitled *Worldwide Increases in Adolescent Loneliness* found that overall, lack of friends and loneliness among teenagers increased significantly between 2012 and 2018. This study, which was based on worldwide data of fifteen- and sixteen-year-olds, revealed that in thirty-six out of thirty-seven countries, feelings of loneliness among teenagers rose sharply during this period, with the increase more pronounced for girls than boys.[30] The researchers proposed that the increase in social media and smartphone usage likely contributed to this. Pediatrician and adolescent medicine specialist Dr. Michelle Escovedo explained: "Humans are very social, and adolescents in particular," and added, "Having peer relationships is innately a very important part of their development."[31]

The pandemic only exacerbated this trend. A 2021 Harvard research study, *Loneliness in America: How the Pandemic Has Deepened an Epidemic of Loneliness*, found that during the pandemic, sixty-one percent of Americans aged 18-25 reported feeling lonely frequently, almost all the time, or all the time, compared to twenty-four percent of Americans aged fifty-five to sixty-five. One of the key recommendations from that work was, "Building not just our physical but our social infrastructure at every level of government and in our communities. We need to begin reimagining and reweaving our social relationships in health care, schools, and many other institutions."[32] Obviously, sport is among those many other institutions that can and should take note. Pre-pandemic, twenty-seven percent of adults aged fifty to eighty years old reported feeling isolated in 2018, while a 2023 report from the University of Michigan's National Poll on Healthy Aging found that thirty-four percent of adults in that age group reported experiencing loneliness or feeling socially isolated in the past year.[33]

Because of the more evident health impacts, older adults traditionally come to mind regarding the detrimental effects of loneliness, social isolation, and social connectiveness. For example, John Hopkins researchers concluded that the risk of developing dementia over a nine-year period was twenty-seven percent higher among socially isolated older adults compared with older adults who were not socially isolated.[34] However, the loneliness epidemic has seemingly hit young individuals from fifteen to twenty-four years old especially hard. For that age group, over the past two decades there has been a seventy percent stark decline in time spent with friends, from roughly 150 minutes per day in 2003 to forty minutes per day in 2020.[35] The evidence is clear that anyone aging, that is everyone, needs to be in community.

Conclusion

Building community through sport is not just a theoretical concept, but a practical necessity that addresses fundamental human needs and societal challenges. It highlights an important justification for sport, and something that all sport managers should understand and be well-versed in promoting. As emphasized throughout this chapter and the entire text, the desire to belong and be part of a community is deeply embedded in our genetic makeup and has significant implications for our health and well-being. The U.S. Surgeon General's report on loneliness equates the health risks of social isolation to smoking fifteen cigarettes a day, stressing the urgency of fostering social connections while providing a timely and important opportunity for sport managers.

Sport provides a unique platform for individuals to experience community and consequently reap the psychological safety, improved health, and well-being outcomes that accompany individuals who belong to community. The COVID-19 pandemic has further emphasized the importance of community, as the absence of being in community during lockdowns emphasized our innate need for connection. By creating inclusive and supportive environments and communities for individuals at various life stages, from parenting and grieving to aging, sport can play a crucial role in almost every individual's life. It is now up to current and future sport managers to see that a sense of community is fostered through sport. Sport managers can play a pivotal role in creating healthier, more connected, and resilient communities. If the five factors (Common Interest, Administrative Consideration, Leadership Opportunities, Social Spaces, and Equity in Administrative Decision) that comprise the Sport and Sense of Community theory, and will unfold in the following chapters, are better emphasized in sport settings, our efforts can make a lasting difference in the lives of individuals and the broader society.

Discussion and Reflection Questions

1. How can sport managers effectively bridge the gap between academic research and practical application in their work? Why is it important for sport managers to understand and apply theoretical frameworks in their community-building efforts?
2. Why is the current time particularly significant for understanding and promoting community building through sport? How did the COVID-19 pandemic highlight the importance of community in sport?
3. How can sport managers address the needs of different life stages (e.g., parenting, grieving, aging) through community-building initiatives? What are some specific examples from the chapter that illustrate the impact of community support during these life stages?
4. Consider the examples of community-building initiatives mentioned in the chapter, such as the Friday morning runs at Awaken Coffee, the Playing for Pearsall tournament, or someone completing a marathon in honor of a loved one. What is an example of a sport community-building event or program that you have participated in or is hosted within your hometown? Is or was it effective in fostering a sense of community for you? Why or why not?
5. Reflect on the U.S. Surgeon General's report on loneliness and other social trends provided in the chapter. What can sport managers do to mitigate the effects of loneliness and social isolation in their communities and help justify the importance of sport in our society?

CHAPTER 4

Common Interest: A Shared Mission, Goal, or Purpose

"You can make more friends in two months by becoming interested in other people than you can in two years by trying to get other people interested in you."
—Dale Carnegie

"Sport is a universal language that brings people together, no matter their origin, background, religious beliefs, or economic status."
—Juan Antonio Samaranch

As I got off the plane, the shocking chill of a windy February day in Boise, Idaho was an unexpected jolt to my body. The warm terminal was a short walk away, but it gave me enough time to question my decision to work the 2009 Special Olympic World Games. I had taken a break from my comfy studies and slow mornings in Austin, Texas as a doctoral student to gain some international sporting event experience. Having worked in the sport industry for a few years, I developed a personal philosophy to always say 'yes' to an adventure. I also recognized that work experiences were key to setting myself apart and providing me with opportunities to learn from others in the industry. At that point I had little experience with the Special Olympics, but I knew it was a well-respected sport organization with the mission to provide sport experiences and opportunity in a variety of Olympic-type sports for children and adults with intellectual disabilities. There is something to learn from everyone in every place, and I doubted I would ever have an opportunity to see an international sporting event in Idaho again. So, I confidently agreed to work with the event management company that was charged with hospitality and hosting corporate partners at the event. The World Games are the highest level of competition for Special Olympics. And like the Olympics Games, the World Winter Games and World Summer Games are held every four years in an alternating every-two-year schedule. In the summer of 2023, 6,500 athletes took part and were joined by over 3,000 coaches and support staff at the World Games. The event was supported by over 18,000 volunteers from 126 countries in Berlin, Germany, and Turin, Italy hosted the smaller winter World Games, with 1500 athletes, in February of 2025.

As I entered the airport terminal, both the questioning of my decision to work the 2009 event along with the shocking chill subsided. I was greeted by a local Special Olympics event volunteer who handed me a hand-knitted blue-and-white scarf. It was just what I needed. Not only because I was living in Texas and did not own a winter scarf, but also because it was the warm welcome signifying that this was something I wanted to be a part of, especially as I soon noticed that these blue-and-white scarfs were everywhere in Boise in support of the event. There was something different about that event, and the collective interest in hosting Special Olympic athletes from around the world, that brought people together. There was something special about that unique blue-and-white scarf that was handed to me, and the distinctive patterned scarves I saw draped around countless others as I made my way through the airport terminal. That hard-to-describe feeling was a sense that I was a part of something bigger than myself and had a shared interest with every person I saw who also was wearing a blue-and-white hand-knitted scarf.

In 2009 the Special Olympic World Games organizing committee decided to start a scarf project at the suggestion of a longtime volunteer. Their goal was simple: they wanted 2,500 homemade one-of-a-kind knitted scarves. The only standard features were the required dimensions and colors. The initial plan was that one scarf would be knitted by a volunteer for each of the athletes representing over 100 different countries that would participate in the Special Olympic World Games. The organizing committee and volunteers wanted each of the athletes who arrived in Boise to not only have something warm, but to know each scarf had a story behind it and was made by a person who was supporting them. They wanted to foster a sense of community and make sure each athlete knew they were being backed by a larger group of people. But it was not just the athletes who would proudly end up with a scarf.

The scarf project was the first of its kind for the Special Olympics. Coats & Clark, a Charlotte, North Carolina-based company, helped kick off the project by donating 2,000 skeins of yarn in their official 2009 Special Olympic World Winter Games colors of warm white and delft blue. Willing knitters could then pick up the yarn free of charge at a designated location to make the scarves for

A 2009 Special Olympics volunteer relaxes with a few of the thousands of hand-knitted blue and white scarves gifted to athletes in Boise, ID. What started as a simple goal became a global movement of generosity. These scarves became a powerful symbol of unity, warmth, and community for the Special Olympic World Games.

the athletes. The scarf project and the details of the initiative happened to be picked up and published by a magazine, *Crochet Today*. And then several social media outlets geared toward individuals with a Common Interest in knitting began sharing the story of the project, and it took off.

The response to the Special Olympics scarf project was more positive than anyone could have expected. The Boise-based volunteers reported receiving up to 700 packages a day with scarves in the months leading up to February event.[1] All of the scarves mailed in or dropped off at the event organizing committee headquarters were unique and handmade from individuals committed to showing the Special Olympic athletes they were supported. Many of the scarves arrived by mail at the organizing committee's offices with handwritten personalized notes indicating that they were knitted in memory of a Special Olympic athlete who is no longer with us or a loved one who was, or still is, a Special Olympic athlete. Each scarf had its own unique story about why it was carefully knitted together and why someone had donated their time to create it. All were from kindhearted knitters, both young and old, that wanted to donate their time and talents to be a part of a larger community supporting athletes with intellectual disabilities.

The result of the scarf project was that 60,000-plus scarfs arrived in Boise from fifty different U.S. states and twelve countries. Organizers and volunteers wanted to foster a sense of community for the athletes, but instead of just having a scarf or two for each athlete arriving in Boise, they ended up receiving almost twenty-five times their initial goal. So, in addition to giving them to the athletes, volunteers and organizers started handing them out to others who would be a part of the World Games. Throughout the World Games, the city of Boise was full of blue-and-white scarves knitted by people all over the world. "This is a tremendous opportunity for our athletes to proudly wear an outward sign of support from people who believe in the Special Olympics Movement and to demonstrate that they are all interconnected in one family of encouragement, inclusion and acceptance," said Bob Gobrecht, managing director of Special Olympics North America. "Through our partnership with Coats & Clark, we hope to build on the Scarf Project that was first introduced as part of the 2009 World Winter Games in Boise and bring this sense of community to our athletes throughout the United States."[2]

With sport as the backdrop, I watched as a sense of community was fostered by the scarf project. First, through the Special Olympic event and the gesture of receiving a handmade item, a community among the athletes with intellectual disabilities was created. Second, the city of Boise was brought together through hosting the event. Residents, volunteers, fans, and tourists passing through the city could not help but see these blue-and-white scarves everywhere. The event created a Common Interest for anyone in Boise leading up to, during, and after the event concluded. And finally, an amazing community of knitters (that I did not know existed prior to this experience) were brought together by a love for knitting and support of the Special Olympic movement. A simple yet fun add-on project dreamed up by a Special Olympics volunteer sparked something special, and it was a powerful and moving example of how, with sport as the background, a Common Interest can bring people together. Since that experience at the 2009 Special Olympic World Games, my research has remained focused on this idea of community building and understanding that "spark." Why had that one event felt so different than others, and why am I still talking and writing about the 2009 event years later?

In my research to uncover the factors that foster community, I have concluded that a Common Interest is one of the main necessary factors. If sport is going to have any positive impact on life quality, it is going to happen through fostering a sense of community. Community that can be found through sport is not solely limited to the athletes or participants; rather, sport can be used to create community for many other stakeholders that share a Common Interest in sport. This can include, but is not limited to, fans, parents, volunteers, residents of host cities, and those employed in the sport industry. A Common Interest in sport and a well-managed sporting environment can create and build community. The focal point of the community, or one's identification with the community, does not matter. That is, it does not matter if you are an active participant, or more tangentially a passive consumer who lives in the city hosting a sporting event, or someone who shows up to work the event. What matters is each individual's experiences and the recognition that they share a communal interest with others.

A Community of Scholars and Sport Officiating

Of the five factors (Common Interest, Leadership Opportunities, Social Spaces, Equity in Administrative Decisions, Administrative Consideration) that create a sense of community in sport, I initially thought that Common Interest was going to be the most difficult to write up and provide examples for. While I was contemplating potential examples for Common Interest, I received an email from a colleague, Jacob Tingle, indicating that a research article we had worked together on had been accepted. That colleague and I worked together more than two decades ago at Trinity University, when we were both young assistant athletic directors trying to navigate our careers in the sport industry. And now, as not-as-young professors in sport management, we had become research collaborators in the area of sport officiating. Without realizing it at the beginning, Jacob and I had slowly formed a community of scholars surrounding our shared interest in researching sport officiating. The now-Dr. Jacob Tingle was a former college basketball official, so his interest in the topic was clear.

My interest in sport officiating developed over time and grew more specifically when I was invited to work on a paper with an Australian colleague, Dr. Pamm Kellett-Phillips. After reading work by Kellett and Shilbury (2007) on umpiring abuse,[3] I began to recognize that my research on community building could provide a framework that could help address the global referee shortage. Sport officiating, refereeing, or umpiring is not portrayed as the most glamorous role to start with, and with the scandals surrounding the occupation, especially the FBI investigation and eventual conviction of NBA professional referee Tim Donaghy in 2007 for a point-shaving scandal, sport officiating was even more stigmatized. Not surprisingly, the sport world has been faced with a global shortage of referees since around that time. It is also a period when video technology has created more scrutiny for sports officials, and when social media and popular culture is able to amplify and quickly promote any violent act toward a sport official with the click of a few buttons.[4] Because of these images and high-profile scandals, many assumed that fan abuse was keeping individuals from refereeing. What Kellett and Shilbury's research highlighted, though, was that it is was a Common Interest in sport officiating and the reframing of fan abuse with other officials that was keeping referees retained.

In an article entitled, *Umpire Participation: Is Abuse Really the Issue?*,[5] the researchers found that it was not the fan abuse that was contributing to the shortage of referees. Rather, the umpires appreciated the social world that was created with other umpires and often centered around discussing the games and the fan abuse. The umpires in their study highlighted the importance of the social interactions among umpires as being fundamental to why they continued to be a part of officiating. Simply, umpires found community with other umpires that was positioned around their Common Interest in sport officiating. This community provided support for them to reframe the fan abuse. For example, in their study an amateur field umpire explained: "If you happen to stick around after training you will see little pockets of umpires having a drink and having a joke and having a laugh. It's absolutely fantastic. I'm still an active member in our cricket club and that runs a fairly vibrant social atmosphere, but hmm, this is right up there with the best atmospheres that I've been involved in. Yeah, the mateship is fantastic. I've been over here five years, and people are very, very friendly."[6] With me being immersed in the community building perspective and researching how community developed, it became evident that understanding community building was fundamental to the management of referees.

In academic papers and presentations, scholars are expected to provide comments on future directions or a call to action for others to explore. Kellett and Shilbury's (2007) article ended with such a future direction in stating, "It is time for sport managers to begin to consider the reasons why people take up umpiring, and continue to umpire, and to develop strategies that leverage that understanding for recruitment and retention." (p. 226) Ironically, enough, while presenting some community-building research at an international conference Kellett was in the audience. We had never met at that point, but in ending my presentation and suggesting my own future direction I discussed how understanding community building could positively impact referees and sport officials. It was just a sentence or two in a thirty-minute presentation, but after the presentation Dr. Kellett (nee Phillipps) introduced herself and said she would like to follow up.

It was during this chance meeting that the intersection of my research interest in community development and Kellett's interest in addressing the sport officiating shortage initially started me on the path of having a secondary research line focused on sport officiating. Kellett and I would publish a specific paper, *Creating Communities that Lead to Retention: The Social Worlds and Communities of Umpires,* on the topic. Our Common Interest in researching referees would later bring us both to work with Dr. Jacob Tingle and further explore this line. A small community of scholars developed around this Common Interest, and we have since added others interested in researching sport officials. Many of us are still researching the sport officiating experiences because of that Common Interest and the community that formed. Our small community of sport scholars researching the sport-officiating experience provided support at the group level.

Personally, I am still researching sport officiating today because of that community, and it has only become more evident to me that community is central to retention because of the work that has been done with sport officials. And there is no better example of how community leads to retention in the sport setting than the clear purpose that community serves in the sport-officiating realm. As the global shortage of referees has become more apparent in the sport industry, more and more competitions are being canceled because of the lack of referees, and disappointed athletes and their parents are taking notice, the answer lies in understanding the role that community plays in sport officials' retention. The National Federation of State High School Associations (NFHS) reported that approximately 50,000 individuals have discontinued their service as high school officials since the 2018-2019 season.[7] And it is not just high school sports feeling the impact. "There is a crisis facing youth sports: a referee and umpire shortage. The game officials who keep the peace and make the calls during youth sports competitions are hard to come by these days. Many referees and umpires are blaming the parents and coaches for the diminishing interest in refereeing youth sports. While there is a shortage of referees across all levels of sport, including high school and college, the impact is felt the most at the youth level."[8]

The answer to solving the referee shortage is, in my opinion, for more sport managers to understand the importance of creating a sense of community and belonging for individuals. Every individual has that need to belong and an innate desire to be a part of a larger, more stable social structure. But despite the importance of community, finding places to belong in today's world can be elusive. What the current sport officiating research continues to demonstrate is that the social benefits and creation of community are vital components of both referee recruitment and retention.[9] By focusing on increasing a sense of community for sport officials, the global shortage of referees can be addressed. Research and data continue to point to the fact that fostering a sense of community for referees is the best avenue to increasing sports official retention and creating a more inviting atmosphere that entices prospective officials. Additional research also has positioned sport officiating as an ideal extension of one's former athletic career and an ideal leisure time alternative to playing sports.[10] That is, "athletes are distinctly primed for becoming referees; yet the global referee shortage indicates this transition, or shift is not happening often enough" (p.556). Perhaps more importantly, though, there is a clear growing line of research indicating that the community often created around the Common Interest in sport officiating can improve the overall psychological well-being of individuals who officiate.[11]

Phillips and Fairley[12] put forth that sport officiating as a serious leisure activity, as well as the socialization and camaraderie among other officials, is what enhances their lives, giving the sport-officiating role meaning and making it enjoyable. Tingle and colleagues[13] focused specifically on the overlooked aspect of mental health needs among female sport officials, but also noted how refereeing could be "a positive outlet that allows individuals to escape from daily stressors" (p. 390). Combined, researchers have provided clear evidence that sport officiating can be a source of community for those with a Common Interest in refereeing, and that experiencing this sense of community can lead to positive social and well-being outcomes. From a sport scholar's perspective, it also has been clear that out of a shared interest in researching sport officials another community developed. In 2024, Drs. Tingle and Phillips joined forces with two other scholars to author a much-needed textbook entitled, *Managing and Developing Sports: Officiating Excellence*.[14] As I look through the contributors to that book it is also clear how Common Interest is fundamental to building community. I have not only worked alongside and published with many of the contributors of that text, but I also feel like a part of a community. I know that support is available at the group level for us to continue that work and research on the sport-officiating experience.

Common Interest and Fandom

Common Interest in the case of sports officials is somewhat clear, but Common Interest may not be immediately evident in every situation. I was on a return flight from Phoenix, AZ where I had just finished volunteering at the 2024 Final Four alongside some ECU Sport Management graduate students when I realized how Common Interest and community building may not always be apparent in the moment. The students and I had the opportunity to see whether UConn, Purdue, Alabama, or the NC State men's basketball team was crowned the national champion. Although ECU is about ninety miles from Raleigh, the home of NC State, and I am a UNC alum, I could not help but feel connected to the NC State fan base that made the trek from my home state. As I flew to Phoenix in my ECU purple polo shirt that stuck out in a sea of red-and-black Wolfpack gear, I quickly realized that when there is a Common Interest, in this case representing my home state, a sense of community can develop. Prior to that trip, many of my colleagues and friends were asking me who I would be cheering for after the Final Four teams were decided, and basketball fans only had the Huskies, Boilermakers, Crimson Tide, or Wolfpack to pick from. I responded with a "whoever," or "it doesn't matter" shrug when the question was originally posed.

That mentality and non-commitment to a specific team quickly faded, though, as I made my way through the Raleigh-Durham International Airport to fly to Phoenix. I almost stopped at a local shop in the airport terminal to purchase a red-and-black NC State Wolfpack t-shirt that I would likely never wear after the 2024 Final Four weekend. It was that innate need to belong that caused that crazy thought to even enter my mind. What would an ECU professor and UNC alum even do with a NC State t-shirt? Of course, I had to cheer for the Wolfpack because of the Common Interest that I did not initially realize existed. The students who travel to work the Final Four also felt that connection. While we may have initially traveled to Phoenix with the "I do not

A group of ECU students unexpectedly found themselves supporting their in-state rival, the NC State Wolfpack, at the 2024 Men's Final Four at State Farm Arena in Glendale, Arizona. Photo courtesy of Erin Wool.

care who wins" mindset and attitude, I think we were all (quietly as we were there to work) pulling for NC State because of that connection and Common Interest. Unfortunately, NC State lost in the Saturday night semifinal game. When the national championship game ended on Monday night with UConn beating Purdue, my students and I found ourselves sitting with two individuals wearing NC State gear. The confetti that poured down from the roof in State Farm Arena covered the floors and the stands as event organizers quickly assembled a stage on the basketball court for the awards ceremony. We all committed to staying and soaking in the experience no matter who won. As we waited to watch the "One Shining Moment" video in the arena, a small group of us with some connection to North Carolina formed—away from the much larger crowd of elated UConn fans in the arena.

The Emergence of Pickleball as a Common Interest

Another more evident example of how Common Interest is fundamental to community building has been seen with the emergence of pickleball. For the

A group of players gather to watch a match at a city-hosted tournament, but their biggest win? The friendships they've built through sport. From grandparents playing with college students, to parents balancing competition and childcare, pickleball brings people together, proving that a shared love for the game is the perfect foundation for belonging. Photo courtesy of John King.

fifth consecutive year in a row, pickleball has been the fastest-growing sport in the nation. Pickleball participation nearly doubled in 2022, increasing by 85.7% and by an astonishing 158.6% over three years.[15] Carmen Sanz explains that the sport is one that unites. "Pickleball is more than just a game; it's a community builder. Its inclusive nature means that friends, family, and even strangers can hop on the court for a friendly match. This accessibility fosters a sense of belonging and togetherness that is often absent in more exclusive sports."[16] Although pickleball was invented in 1965 and regularly played in schools and retirement communities throughout the 1990s, it really gained momentum during the COVID-19 pandemic. This occurred because it was not only easy to play by people of all ages, but it was also an affordable, low-cost, accessible sport that could be safely played outside while maintaining the recommended social distance during the pandemic.[17]

Pickleball is a community builder because a diverse group of individuals can form a community around their Common Interest in the sport. At a local park, you can see a grandmother and grandson competing against a very athletic college student and middle-aged individual who is trying to stay

Senior Sport Studies major Emma Phibbs (left) high-fives HHP faculty member Dr. Andrea Buenaño after a match. Photo courtesy of Kathryn Adkins, ECU Brinkley-Lane Scholar, Class of 2028.

physically active. There are few other sports like it. I also have observed new parents setting up a pack-n-play at the local courts so they can play a few games of pickleball with friends while their young child is within eyesight and safely confined to a temporary play area. It is the common and shared interest in the sport of pickleball that is a starting point for community to develop. Although I am a mid-career middle-aged adult, I have found community through pickleball at a local park a few weekday mornings at eight. This community includes individuals who I typically would not cross paths with, as many are retirees who are two and three decades older than me. But they have welcomed me and others on the pickleball courts a few weekday mornings a week because of our common and shared interest in playing pickleball, so I have felt a sense of belonging there. It is the Common Interest in the sport that is fundamental to community development, and many have observed no better example of the importance of Common Interest than with the growth of pickleball. It is a social sport.

In fact, in response to an exponential growth in reported mental health issues on college campuses, one solution may be providing an outlet that, like a shared interest in pickleball, could help address this pressing issue. A recent U.S. News survey has reported that about seventy percent of students have struggled with their mental health since starting college, yet only thirty-seven percent of respondents searched for mental health resources at their college.[18] But the concern on college campuses is not limited just to students enrolled at universities and colleges. Higher education faculty and staff report almost matching rates of severe depression, anxiety, and stress as college students do.[19] Because professors feel a responsibility toward student suffering and faculty-student interactions are key to student success,[20] providing an outlet with a Common Interest, like playing pickleball, may provide a solution. In the Fall of 2024, a group of sport management students and faculty proposed a pickleball club on ECU's campus with the goal of increasing student and faculty/staff interaction and providing a community or place for campus members to belong. The idea was built upon fostering an environment where the shared interest in playing pickleball would bring people together. Such a faculty and student program will not eliminate mental health issues on college campus, but it may foster a community that provides support at the group level, which may be what both students and faculty are missing as campus programming is typically geared at students or employees, not both. In the Spring of 2025, this idea evolved into the first intergenerational pickleball tournament, where a twenty-year age gap was required between doubles partners. The event was held on "reading day" (the day before final exams start) to provide students with a fun opportunity to interact with others.

Needing to belong is fundamental to the human condition. The first factor in creating an environment where a sense of community can be fostered is Common Interest. Although a Common Interest may not be immediately evident, it is clearly a necessary factor to experiencing a sense of community. To reiterate, the importance of Common Interest is not just for athletes or participants, but sport should be managed and positioned so that the Common Interest factor is well-defined for all and not limited to a few athletes or sport fanatics. If we discover a common and shared interest in something bigger than ourselves, then a well-managed sporting environment can create and build community. So, when you find yourselves being pulled towards cheering for a team, feeling a sense of pride in a city or location, or feeling connected to others, know that it is because of a Common Interest, a key community building factor. And any satisfying feeling you experience is an outcome of being in a healthy community.

Conclusion

Common Interest plays a powerful role in fostering a sense of community through sport. The 2009 Special Olympic World Games scarf project which united athletes, volunteers, and knitters worldwide in a shared mission of support and inclusion, is one example. This initiative, along with the importance of growing a community of sports officials and the widespread appeal of pickleball, demonstrates how common and shared interests can bring together diverse groups of people, creating a sense of belonging and provide a needed supportive environment. The sense of community in sport and the important role that sport plays in community building is not limited to athletes but extends to fans, volunteers, and even entire cities. By emphasizing shared interests, sport can address broader social issues, such as mental health on college campuses, remedying the sport officiating shortage, and fostering inclusive environments that create awareness and advocate for individuals with disabilities. Ultimately, Common Interest is a fundamental factor in building strong, supportive communities, making sport a powerful tool for social connection and well-being.

Discussion and Reflection Questions

1. What made the scarf project at the 2009 Special Olympic World Games so successful in fostering a sense of community? What is another example of a similar initiative that was implemented at other sporting events to create a sense of belonging and support?
2. Emphasizing a common and shared interest is a fundamental factor when attempting to build a sense of community among participants, fans, and volunteers. What are other examples in the context of sport that are focused on bringing together individuals with a Common Interest?
3. As discussed in the chapter, sport can help address mental health issues on college campuses. What specific mechanisms or sport-related programs could enhance the effectiveness of sport in promoting mental well-being among students?
4. How can sport be used to include individuals from diverse backgrounds and foster a more inclusive environment? What are some potential barriers to inclusivity, and how can they be overcome?

5. How does the sense of community among sports officials help address the global shortage of referees? What strategies can be implemented to foster a sense of community and improve retention among sports officials?
6. Compare the community-building impact of sport to other forms of communal activities, such as arts or community service. What unique aspects of sport make it particularly effective in fostering a sense of belonging?
7. Reflect on a personal experience where a Common Interest, whether in sport or another activity, helped build a sense of community. How did this experience shape your understanding of the role of shared interests in creating connections?

CHAPTER 5

Administrative Consideration: People-Focused

"Leadership is not about being in charge. Leadership is about taking care of those in your charge."
—Simon Sinek

"People will forget what you said, people will forget what you did, but people will never forget how you made them feel."
—Maya Angelou

It was a Thursday; it was always a Thursday when I would meet a group of runners at a local pub. We would go out for a three or five-mile run and return to the pub to enjoy a beverage with any of the five to twenty-five runners who would decide to show on any given Thursday. Among the regular runners everyone recognized everyone, and when a new runner would show up, someone would hand them a route sheet or ask them their mile pace and then introduce them to whoever they may want to run with to complete the route and return to the pub. You could never predict who the "real runners" were versus those of us who were more there for the peer motivation and the feeling that we needed to earn the after-the-run beverage by running a few miles. But one Thursday when a new guy showed up wearing a "Fleet Feet" hat, I knew instantly that we had a real runner on our hands.

I knew about Fleet Feet from my time in San Antonio, TX while working at Trinity University. One of the assistant cross-country coaches had worked part-time at Fleet Feet in the offseason, and I learned that Fleet Feet was far from just a shoe store. It was a running shoe store, and because of its service and proper shoe fitting Fleet Feet was where every current athlete, wise former athlete, aging adult trying to stay healthy, or worker with a job that required hours on their feet would go. The store also had a knack for building a community for runners through their training program and group runs. Runners would often use their store as a starting point for runs or a meeting point to assemble their running partners. By just seeing the "Fleet Feet" hat, I

A group gathers at Trollingwood Brewery after a Thursday evening run. The care, concern, and intentionality of both formal and informal leaders are key to fostering community. Photo courtesy of Robin Ashley.

understood that the guy wearing it knew more about running than most. I had only moved to the area a few years prior, but I immediately started questioning him: "Wait, is there a Fleet Feet around here? Where's the closest one?" I do not recall his response, other than it was extremely vague and oddly unclear.

Fast forward a few weeks later, and the subterfuge started to make more sense. When he showed up that Thursday night at run club, Chris Loignon was on a scouting trip, hopefully to find a store location to bring a Fleet Feet franchise store to Greenville, NC. At the time, though, he did not officially know if the franchise would agree to support the location, and there were still many details to work out. But Chris was prudent and forward-thinking enough to try to get to know the people he could eventually be serving in the Greenville running community. So, the somewhat-covert operation of showing up at a local pub run was the best way to learn about that community.

To add even more irony to this story, I had recently written a teaching case study with colleagues, *RunTex: A community landmark run out of business*, which focused on a running shoe store in Austin, TX. The crux of that teaching case study was centered around Paul Carrozza, who had built the once-highly successful RunTex business. "The company's community-based and socially responsible approach helped establish RunTex as the epicenter of Austin's running community. Many assumed, due to the well-established recognition, that RunTex was a thriving business." However, after twenty-five years the company closed, and Carrozza admitted he had never intended to be a business owner. The case was a compelling assignment for sport management courses, because many leisure-oriented small businesses fail due to lack of strategic management. And the fact that many owners are motivated by a hobby or personal interest can also result in failure.[1] In the case of RunTex, the hobby motive acted as a constraint and ultimately led to the unexpected closure of the business after twenty-five years.

What I appreciated about RunTex, nevertheless, was its focus on community and service. Throughout the almost-four years that I lived in Austin, RunTex was a well-known staple in the community, and not just a shoe store for runners. Countless others benefited from the company's focus on community and service. "RunTex provided water coolers along the popular Town Lake Hike and Bike Trail free of charge, a daily service that was appreciated by the thousands of locals who regularly used the trail. Additionally, in 2012, after the city of Austin announced that it would no longer host the annual Trail of Lights, a popular display of Christmas lights and vignettes in Zilker Park, RunTex agreed to be the sponsor of the event. The conditions of the sponsorship required RunTex to raise nearly half a million dollars."[2] Most Austin residents felt like RunTex, as a company, was a good neighbor because of its focus on the community and willingness to serve its fellow community members. It is this same very community-oriented, people-first approach that most Fleet Feet franchises take.

Chris Loignon and his wife, Kendra, would eventually go on to open a Fleet Feet franchise in Greenville, NC with that same focus on community and service. In fact, within a few weeks of opening their store, they had donated new cross-country uniforms to the local high school team. But they did not just bring tangible running products to the area, they also epitomized an essential element to building and fostering a sense of community as they opened and grew their business. The second factor in the Sport and Sense of Community Theory is Administrative Consideration, or the expression of care, concern, and intentionality of managers, officers, and other organizational leaders. Or, as it has evolved to, the people-focused factor. For a community to thrive, the people making things happen in any setting need to be genuine in their approach to others. Consideration, unfortunately, is often taken for granted, but it is clear from the data that it is essential to foster community. Chris, on that scouting trip and first pub run in Greenville, did just that by learning about local runners and finding out how his business could serve the community. Chris's wife Kendra also had that gift and mission in mind. They both genuinely got to know people in the running community, cared about others, and were intentional in their efforts.

The Loignons and Fleet Feet Greenville, NC exemplified Administrative Consideration because of their people-first approach. Each month the small business owners highlight and donate to a community partner. In 2022 alone they donated almost $35,000 to local non-profit organizations. More important than the dollar amount was the care, concern, and intentionality behind the store owners' actions.[3] Administrative Consideration is embedded in the culture and mission of their small business and that has created a sense of community for Greenville runners. Their stated mission is "At Fleet Feet Greenville NC, We 'Run For You,'" and their vision statement, based on the acronym S.E.R.V.E., is: Serve humbly; Educate customers; Run together; Value the act of giving; Empower our community. The people-first mindset of those organizing and directing any group is necessary for community to thrive. The Fleet Feet Greenville, NC store has been named a Top 50 Best Running Store by Running Insight.[4] The owners also received the Greenville-Pitt County Chamber of Commerce's 2022 Small Business Leader of the Year award, and Loignon was honored by *Business North Carolina* as a 2024 Trailblazer for thriving business owners and professionals under the age of forty who champion their communities.[5] Anyone who lived in Greenville prior to the opening of Fleet Feet likely will tell you that they did not just build a business; they helped build a running community. Their consideration and people-focused approach is a big part of that success.

Formal Sport Administrators – Keno and Gallo

Several other formal sport-related examples of the importance of Administrative Consideration also stand out. One is from my hometown, and another comes from the UNC Athletic Department. Both involve legendary administrators who understand the importance of considering others. William "Keno" Beezer, a beloved former director of the Moshannon Valley YMCA (for thirty-seven years) and a baseball scout for the Montreal Expos and Major League Scouting Bureau for much of his career, is the stand-out example from my hometown. Keno was instrumental in founding the Philipsburg YMCA, and he ran the after-school sports program for area youth. Keno had the gift of a brilliant memory, a knack for storytelling, and the ability to speak to the winner in someone before they had any idea a winner might exist in them. Under his tutelage and the care, concern, and intentionality he demonstrated toward countless others, he created a sense of community for many young people who participated in the after-school games.

Keno quickly became a family friend as I entered my high school years. I just wanted to make the varsity softball team, so Keno would help me and a classmate find extra time in a batting cage at the local YMCA when it was not being used. We showed up, and Keno genuinely cared for us and wanted us to succeed. And that meant we kept showing up, because of the community and culture that Keno built. My classmate would end up getting drafted by the Detroit Tigers in the tenth round of MLB draft, and I would eventually make the high school varsity softball team and earn a scholarship to play at Division II school. Reflecting back, those outcomes were not the most important factor in our careers or lives. Rather it was that we, like countless others, had a place to belong because of the authentic care and concern that Keno displayed to all.

In fact, Keno's brilliant memory, storytelling, and genuine care for others are similar to the characteristics of Larry Gallo, a longtime UNC athletics administrator. Anyone that crossed his path will likely tell you that Larry Gallo built a legacy of being a friend to all.[6] Senior Associate Athletic Director Martina Ballen stated, "Larry Gallo cares about people." He's always been known for reaching out with a phone call, text, or handwritten note to coworkers celebrating something or offering to help them in some way. Although I only spent one year as a graduate student at UNC, I'll never forget being the recipient of one of those phone calls. Gallo was on my admission graduate program interview panel. At the time of that call, his compliance intern was a dear friend of mine. So, our paths crossed, and he knew who I was, but never did I expect him to reach out about a potential job opportunity. One of his colleagues on a NCAA committee at the time was hiring, and he wanted to let me know he had recommended me for the job. Why? I have no idea, but he saw something in me that I did not see in myself, and he cared enough to know I would be looking for a job. He went the extra mile, and despite only being at Carolina for a year, I knew I was a part of the Carolina family when I got that call.

It is a mantra that you often hear about in organizations— "We are family." But Larry Gallo is one of those people who, with care, concern, and intentionality, makes everyone feel as though they belong and helps truly foster a community within Carolina athletics. Although I did not get that job, I did get an interview and was taught a valuable lesson about the importance of Administration Consideration when trying to build community. A few years later I would return to work in campus recreation at UNC, mostly because of the sense of community that was created through Larry Gallo's actions.

Informal Administrative Consideration: People First

Pickleballer Joyce

One weekday morning after a drenching evening of rain, I made my way to the pickleball courts at a local park to meet some friends to play. As I arrived, I noticed four of the eight outdoor courts were completely dried and ready to be played upon. I exclaimed to one friend I was meeting, "Wow, these look great even after all that rain." Her reply characterized the importance of informal consideration within a community. "Well, Joyce has a servant's heart and has been out here for an hour." Joyce, despite our age difference, was one of the first people I felt warmly welcomed by when I started playing pickleball at the local park on early summer mornings. Perhaps it was because she has a wickedly powerful swing with pinpoint accuracy and she welcomed any new player she knew she could handily beat, but that day it became clear her intent was more sincere and altruistic. As I took more time to survey the court area, I noticed there was a leaf blower, towels, and four other courts with well-defined wet spots from the rain the night before.

Joyce only needed to speed up the drying of one court for her to enjoy playing pickleball that morning, but she had that consideration for others to make an effort to dry three more of the courts, so that when her fellow morning pickleball players would arrive, the courts would be ready to go. It is that type of consideration, along with the sincere inquiries that she and others make about players' lives outside of pickleball, that builds a community. It is important to recognize that people do not show up to any sport setting without outside stress. Yes, some people may see sport as an escape from the monotony of daily life, but for many it is their chance for connection to community and the feeling that there is support at the group level. That is a powerful tool that sport can offer, but community will not happen without the intentionality of others demonstrating care and concern. Joyce, unlike Keno or Gallo, did not have a formal title or expected leadership responsibilities. But nonetheless she still played a key role in building community on the local pickleball courts and exemplifies why the Administrative Consideration factor is a key component.

Anyone who has bought shoes at a Fleet Feet in Greenville, been through an afterschool program at the Moshannon Valley YMCA, worked in UNC Athletics over the past couple of decades or played pickleball at Elm Street Park one weekday morning will likely talk about the Loignons or Keno Beezer or Larry Gallo or Joyce from pickleball, and about the community that they helped build for so many. Simply put, for community to develop you must have a culture of leaders and administrators that genuinely care and are intentional in their approach to demonstrating that. The Loignons, Beezer, and Gallo all held formal administrator roles: owners, director, senior associate athletics director. However, when it comes to community building, informal administrators and leaders and their consideration of others also can make a significant impact as well.

A Culture of Administrative Consideration

Importantly, Administrative Consideration should not rest just on one single individual. Rather organizations and businesses, much like Fleet Feet Greenville, can help cultivate Administrative Consideration to build and strengthen community. Two specific organizations that have capitalized on and recognized the importance of this factor in community building are CrossFit and Pickleball for Incarcerated Communities.

The CrossFit Movement and CrossFit Coaches

The final examples of formal Administrative Consideration do not involve a specific person, but rather the role of a coach or leader in an organization. Another striking case of Administrative Consideration and why it is one of the necessary factors for community building comes from the sport and fitness organization CrossFit. Researchers have found a stronger sense of community among CrossFit participants compared to other gym users, which result in greater exercise/fitness initiation and adherence, a higher perceived value of services and greater progress toward one's fitness goals.[7] When I asked about her commitment to five o'clock in the morning workouts, Diane Majewski, a longtime member of CrossFit, explained why it worked for her and the important role CrossFit coaches play in creating a welcoming environment. Majewski stated, "CrossFit is built on the idea of community. From the very beginning the coaches welcome you. You start by taking foundational courses that are taught by one of the coaches. They have a script, but it's very personalized as they really get to know you." She then added with a laugh, "Basically, they teach you all the moves and the language, so when you go to a class you don't feel like an idiot."

Diane further explained how the CrossFit coaches really listen to what she is saying about injuries and goals and then provide good feedback. "So, I'm not judged. They're very enthusiastic, very knowledgeable and professional. They're invested in you as a person, they care about who you are as a person. They help us find our goals and figure out what's a reasonable goal, and they want to see us succeed. The number-one goal for me is to not injure myself, and they also know that. They know they have to push me a little bit harder because they know I can do more, but they also know I'm thinking in my head, 'Don't do too much because you don't want to get injured.' So, they'll nudge me a little bit. They're very, very caring, very in tune with what you're doing, and they're paying attention. They're invested in it. Because they don't want anyone to get injured, they want to see people do well, they want everybody to feel good about the experience, and they want everybody to come back."

As Majewski mentioned, CrossFit was built upon creating community. The coaches and their consideration play a key role in fostering a supportive environment. The CrossFit website explicitly emphasizes the idea of everyone belonging in the CrossFit community. "CrossFit welcomes and unites people of all ages, abilities, and goals around a methodology that is accessible and effective for all," the website says. "We train, persevere, and progress together. We build strong local communities that drive unparalleled progress and a deep sense of belonging."[8] Without question much of the growth of CrossFit can be attributable to Administrative Consideration and growing the business with this idea at its core.

In 2000, Greg Glassman and Lauren Jenai co-founded CrossFit in Santa Cruz, California. The first CrossFit gym, or "box," and CrossFit.com, its official website, both launched that year. The first "box" was opened in a small warehouse, where it attracted a diverse group of early adopters while the official website provided daily workouts and created a virtual community for

CrossFitters worldwide. By 2005, the first CrossFit-affiliated gym outside California was opened in Seattle, Washington. This affiliation model allowed gym owners to operate independently and yet benefit from the established CrossFit brand and approaches. Thirteen CrossFit-affiliated gyms would follow suit in 2005, and the movement gained momentum. "This year also saw a shift in CrossFit's online presence. The website began publishing educational articles, reaching a broader audience, and expanding its virtual community. Glassman emphasized the importance of sharing ideas and best practices for the benefit of all CrossFit practitioners."[9] The formula, with community at the core and a commitment to best practices from considerate coaches, worked. CrossFit now has over 15,000 affiliated gyms worldwide in 150 countries.[10]

Pickleball in the Prisons: The Pickleball for Incarcerated Communities League

"The man himself," was heard inside the MacDougall-Walker Correctional Institution, a maximum-security prison, from one of the residents of the facility. Four prisoners were warming up, and their pickleball coach had just arrived. MacDougall-Walker launched its pickleball efforts in 2017, and at least half of the state's correctional facilities in Connecticut now offer pickleball. Pickleball for Incarcerated Communities coach Angelo Rossetti just started coaching the inmates a year prior, but it is clear he has some fans within the facility. Rossetti has been praised by many because of his empathy and non-judgmental approach. He does not see the athletes who he is coaching as inmates or prisoners, rather he sees them as people, and it is clear to the inmates that he respects them. As one of them said, "You feel like you're constantly being judged at every turn. So, it's like: 'Nobody cares. Why should I care?' So, you see one person show a little empathy, that little empathy went a very long way, and I'm grateful for that every day."[11]

Coach Rossetti is just one of the many Pickleball for Incarcerated Communities League coaches who takes this approach. They provide another great example of the importance of Administrative Consideration. According to the Pickleball for Incarcerated Communities League website, the league was "founded out of the belief that organized sports can be a powerful tool for restorative justice. Founded by a passionate group of individuals, including formerly incarcerated individuals, pickleball enthusiasts, and social activists, PICL (Pickleball for Incarcerated Communities League) emerged from a

First-year student, Roz Burgess, and first-year assistant professor, Dr. Ollie Taniyev, acknowledge and encourage one another after a great play during the 2025 inaugural "Better Together Intergenerational Pickleball" tournament. The sport of pickleball is gaining momentum in a variety of settings, from prisons to college campuses. This image highlights the positive interaction between a student and faculty member, illustrating the concept of Administrative Consideration. Photo courtesy of ECU Sport Management major, Maria Ferreira Santana.

collective vision to bring hope, skill development, and a sense of community to those behind bars. Understanding the challenges faced by incarcerated individuals, we recognized the potential of pickleball, a rapidly growing sport celebrated for its accessibility and adaptability. Our mission became clear: introduce pickleball programs into correctional facilities offering a holistic approach to rehabilitation that encompasses physical activity, skill acquisition, mental well-being, and social reintegration."[12]

It is evident that the program is working, and the large reason why is the program's Administrative Consideration at the organizational level. Simply, the Pickleball for Incarcerated Communities League has coaches who care about the mission. It is an effective program that has created a community. Sarah Gersten, Director and co-founder of Pickleball for Incarcerated Communities League, stated "One of the biggest benefits I see to the PICL (Pickleball for Incarcerated Communities League) program is reducing that sense of loneliness and isolation," while Eulalia Garcia, the programs and treatment director for the Connecticut Department of Correction, added that she's seeing the impact of the pickleball program. "We've seen more positive interactions with other individuals from our participants that are participating in pickleball; we've seen a healthier outlook on their future. It's something that they value, that they look forward to, that brings them happiness and motivates them to be better."[13] It's unmistakable that the positive interactions are a two-way street and that consideration behind those that lead the Pickleball for Incarcerated Communities League is a big part of its success.

Administrator Consideration at the Organizational Level, Social Responsibility and Sport

The Color Pink and Football

Since 1979, when opposing football players have walked into University of Iowa's Kinnick Stadium they have been greeted by a sea of pink. The Kinnick Stadium visitor's locker room is painted pink, the walls are pink, the floors are pink, and even the toilets are pink. Opposing teams are obnoxiously greeted with the color pink everywhere. Why? Former head coach Hayden Fry, who had a psychology degree, believed that the color pink would have a calming effect on opponents, potentially making them less aggressive and more relaxed.[14] In his memoir, "A High Porch Picnic," Hayden Fry elaborates on his thinking and the psychology behind the pink locker rooms. Fry knew that the psychological strategy of gaining a mental edge over his opposing team with a pink locker room worked in many instances. Fry stated in the book, "When I talk to an opposing coach before a game and he mentions the pink walls, I know I've got him. I can't recall a coach who has stirred up a fuss about the color and then beat us."[15]

The tradition or tactic, however you view it, has been a source of controversy and sparked debates and criticism for reinforcing gender stereotypes. This especially was the case in 2005, when Kinnick Stadium was being renovated, and efforts were made to add even more pink. This move drew significant backlash from some faculty members and students, who argued that the pink color perpetuated stereotypes of femininity and weakness. Former University of Iowa law professor Erin Buzuvis publicly criticized the locker room, stating that it implied that being "weak like a little girl" or "effeminate" was undesirable.[16] Despite the debate, many Iowa fans and university officials have defended the tradition, and the pink locker rooms have remained. The controversy, though, highlights the significance of the NFL and its breast cancer awareness campaign that began a few short years later in 2009. It also provides an example of how Administrative Consideration, defined as the expression of care, concern, and intentionality of managers, officers, and other organizational leaders, can be implemented or demonstrated at the organizational level.

The NFL's initiative, known as "A Crucial Catch," was launched in partnership with the American Cancer Society. The primary goal was to raise awareness about the importance of annual screenings, especially for women over the age of 40, throughout National Breast Cancer Awareness Month every October. This initiative also meant that the color controversially used by former Iowa football coach to weaken opposing teams by subjecting them to the color in their visiting locker room would now purposefully be placed on NFL fields. Pink ribbons were stenciled on the playing field and pink coins were used during games, while players, coaches and referees wore pink game apparel to raise awareness. The campaign was launched with sincere motives and demonstrated Administrative Consideration. That is, NFL administrators intentionally made efforts to show care, as breast cancer was and is one of the leading forms of cancer affecting women.

For a period of time, then, the NFL's Crucial Catch worked for the NFL as a way to demonstrate Administrative Consideration. Around 2013, though, controversy and skeptics started to weigh in regarding the program. Critics raised concerns about the transparency and allocation of funds and questioned how much of the money raised was actually going towards cancer research. The dollars from each piece of merchandise sold are divided up by the company that makes the merchandise and the company that sells the merchandise (50.0%), which is often the NFL and the individual teams. "In the end, after everybody has taken their cut, only 8.01% of money spent on pink NFL merchandise is actually going towards cancer research."[17]

Along with financial scrutiny of the NFL's Crucial Catch, many critics believe that the initiative was a public relations effort to attract female fans and combat the negative image of the NFL, rather than a genuine effort to fight cancer. October is both Breast Cancer Awareness month and Domestic Violence Awareness month, and the latter is an issue the NFL has been repeatedly criticized for amid allegations that the league has mishandled domestic violence charges among its players.

Today, almost every sport organization has some type of corporate social responsibility (CSR) plan because sport fans are interested in their favorite team's efforts to promote good in their communities. This promotes community building and fan consumption,[18] as it aligns with the Administrative Consideration factor. Corporate community initiatives are a segment of corporate social responsibility that focuses on community social issues, where sport organizations often partner with non-sport community groups.[19] Both corporate social responsibility and corporate community initiative efforts show that an organization cares about its stakeholders and local community. "Sports are unique as they can act as a powerful tool to connect people that transcend across race, religion, political beliefs, or socioeconomic status when mobilized in the right way. When connected with sports, CSR has a significant effect on brand reputation, engagement, and loyalty, all ultimately and directly impacting a team's bottom line."[20]

Major League Baseball's Boston Red Sox are credited with starting the first major social initiative in sport, the Jimmy Fund. Since 1953, the Boston Red Sox have partnered with the Jimmy Fund to raise awareness and funds to support the Dana-Farber Cancer Institute's efforts to prevent, treat, and defy cancer.[21] Then in the 1970s, the NFL partnered with the United Way, founding the first leaguewide foundation. Two National Hockey League (NHL) teams, the Calgary Flames and Vancouver Canucks, would follow suit by creating team foundations in the 1980s. However, it was not until 2005 when the National Basketball Association (NBA) launched its NBA Cares program and established the first formalized large-scale nationally marketed CSR program among the major sport leagues. "NBA Cares is the league's global social responsibility program that builds on the NBA's mission of addressing important social issues around the world."[22] Primarily, the NBA Cares program has focused on education, health and wellness, community development and social justice. Because sport organizations often connect with individuals on a much deeper level than most corporations do, this often puts those organizations in a unique position to advance positive social change. A growing number of athletes, sport organizations, and sporting events are being positioned to address various causes (e.g., Relay for Life, NFL breast cancer awareness, Coaches vs. Cancer tournaments, etc.) and this is one way Administrative Consideration can be expressed at the organizational level to build community.

Why Administrative Consideration Matters

Belonging, as defined by renowned positive psychologist Martin Seligman, stems "from belonging to and serving something beyond yourself, and then recognizing that you are in relationships with others who intrinsically value you."[23] This idea is heavily supported by numerous researchers studying servant leadership. Servant leadership is a leadership philosophy where the leader's primary goal is to serve others. Scholars have further elaborated, "Servant leadership is a holistic approach whereby leaders act with morality, showing great concern for the company's stakeholders and engaging followers in multiple dimensions, such as emotional, relational and ethical, to bring out their full potential and empower them to grow into what they can become. Servant leadership has been linked through various mediators to positive individual and collective outcomes, including behavioral, attitudinal, and performance."[24] Servant leadership is embedded in the Administrative Consideration factor, and in all the examples in the previous stories. A servant leader prioritizes the needs of followers and does so with great care and empathy, with a commitment to the growth and success of others and the community. Whether it is formally designated leaders like the Loignons, Beezer, Gallo, and CrossFit Coaches, or no-title informal leaders like Joyce from pickleball or administrators leading a social cause for their organization, their presence and consideration is key to building strong community.

Ultimately, though, community building can be even more simplified with the Administrative Consideration factor, which is seen when people doing administrative and behind-the-scenes work in an environment display care for those inside and outside the group. Whether administrators are designated formally or informally or whether they express it through words, actions, or simply trying to recall your name, Administrative Consideration cultivates an environment where healthy community can thrive. In the business world, we know that managers who have one meaningful conversation per week with each team member develop better high-performance relationships than through any other leadership activity.[25] In sport settings, we know that one coach, administrator, or manager making an effort to have meaningful conversation and relationships can build community.[26] While there are countless individuals that likely could help define Administrative Consideration, the ones who set the tone and model to others the people-first approach and leader consideration stand out the most. The benefits of this approach? A positive, healthy community and an environment where individuals feel that they belong and where others want to join in.

Conclusion

Administrative Consideration, or a people-focused approach, plays a critical role in fostering strong and resilient communities. Through various examples, such as Fleet Feet Greenville's Chris Loignon, YMCA Director Keno Beezer, UNC Senior Associate AD Larry Gallo and organizational level efforts such as CrossFit and the Pickleball for Incarcerated Communities League coaches, the genuine care, concern, and intentionality from leaders in cultivating a culture of Administrative Consideration can significantly impact the well-being and cohesion of a community. Whether through formal roles or informal actions, the presence of considerate administrators fosters a sense of belonging and support, which is essential for community development. The importance of corporate social responsibility initiatives, such as the NBA Cares and the NFL's Crucial Catch, demonstrate how organizations can show consideration towards their stakeholders and local communities. By prioritizing Administrative Consideration, both at the individual and organizational levels, communities can thrive, creating environments where individuals feel valued and motivated to contribute. This people-first mindset is crucial for building positive, healthy, and enduring communities.

Discussion and Reflection Questions

1. How do the examples of Keno Beezer, Larry Gallo, and CrossFit coaches illustrate different aspects of Administrative Consideration? What common traits do they share?
2. Discuss the story of RunTex. What lessons can be learned about the potential pitfalls of running a community-focused business without strategic management?
3. Analyze one of the examples of effective Administrative Consideration. How does the person or organization promote a sense of community while effectively running their business? What is an example of something that they do that could be modeled by other sport organizations?
4. In what ways can informal leaders, like Joyce from the pickleball courts, contribute to community building? How can organizations recognize and support these informal leaders?
5. Consider the mission and vision statements of Fleet Feet Greenville, NC. How do these statements reflect the principles of Administrative Consideration discussed in the chapter?
6. What role does servant leadership play in fostering a sense of community? Can you think of other examples where servant leadership has positively impacted a community or organization?
7. What impact does a people-first approach have on the employees in these organizations? Can you think of an example of an organization or administrative leader who values this approach, and how it has impacted their stakeholders?

CHAPTER 6

Creating Leadership Opportunities: Empowering Others

"A community is like a ship; everyone ought to be prepared to take the helm."
—Henrik Ibsen

"Great leaders do not create followers, they create more leaders."
—Tom Peters

It was pitch black out and I could hear, but not see, a group of men counting off in cadence. "One-two-three" echoed across the open field. It was not just dark, but it was cold too, and not the conditions that would inspire many to get out of bed and exercise outdoors in the elements. This was different though; this was a dedicated group of men that are part of F3 ENC. These men set their alarm clocks very early to meet others for a workout, usually at 5:30 a.m., on a weekday in a local park. F3 ENC is part of a larger F3 network, and it is basically a free workout group for men with the stated mission: "to plant, grow and serve small workout groups for the invigoration of male community leadership."[1] The F3 ENC group started when an ECU recreation professor, Dr. Nelson Cooper, heard about F3 Nation from a family member living near Charlotte. F3 stands for Fitness, Fellowship, and Faith. The organization was started in Charlotte, NC in 2011 with a few men and rapidly expanded to a larger current network of 4,368 free, peer-led workouts for men in forty-eight different states and seventeen countries on five continents around the world.[2] To grasp the exponential growth of F3 and the community it has provided, it is important to understand the story behind one region and those men who I heard counting in the distance one cold morning.

The story of how and why F3 ENC started—with five men in January of 2015 meeting two times a week to workout—and flourished to 334 men with fifteen different weekly workout times by 2024, exemplifies the importance of Leadership Opportunities in building a strong and thriving community.

After learning about F3 from his wife Mary Ann's cousin, Dr. Cooper, known as Coop to his many students, colleagues, and friends and Papa Smurf to his fellow F3 members, started a conversation with his neighbor about the group. Coop was a beloved recreation science professor, and when I interviewed at ECU in 2010, he was one of the many people who I initially met.

Often on academic interviews, the search committee will schedule meetings across campus with others who you might collaborate with or find yourself working alongside if you are lucky enough to end up with the job offer. After my scheduled meeting with Coop on that job interview, it was clear that as an ECU recreation professor, Coop was in his element. He loved his job and had a drive to serve and help direct college students on their career path and life journey. He loved helping to create other leaders. After I took the job at ECU our paths would occasionally cross on campus, and I would joke with Coop that I was fooled into thinking that we were going to get to work together. Yet we were in different departments and buildings. At the time, I was in Exercise and Sport Sciences and Coop was in Recreation and Leisure Sciences. We would leave those impromptu meetings on campus with a head nod and assurance that we were going to find a way to work together. Our research interests and life philosophies were too similar to not collaborate eventually. We both believed we could better serve students by working together and breaking down the imaginary sport-versus-recreation barrier.

When I first learned about F3 ENC, I knew this was the opportunity to work with and learn from Coop. In the Spring of 2015, any time our paths would cross I became more specific about wanting to learn more about this group that he helped start. Coop's daughter, Bailey, was part of a study abroad trip I led in the summer of 2015, and it was soon after that trip that Coop was diagnosed with ALS (amyotrophic lateral sclerosis). In September of that year, as classes were starting back up, Coop graciously sat down to chat about F3 ENC. One of the key components of F3 that Coop relayed to me is that the only thing that F3 Nation really wants from participants is for them to give the mission of F3 away to others so that community and male leadership thrives.

Even though the ALS had started to impact his speech, and he had begun using a wheelchair, Coop made the time to do an interview and talk with me about F3. He wanted to make sure F3 was given to others. He, like me, knew there was something powerful to learn about this group. He said what he discovered through F3 was "if you give to your body, you will quickly find yourself giving to your soul, and then before you know it, you'll be giving to others. And that really illustrates the 3 Fs of fitness, fellowship, and faith. Give

Dr. Nelson 'Coop' Cooper and his wife, Mary Ann, cheer on a runner at a local CoopStrong race. Coop, who helped start F3 ENC, believed in good leadership *and* followership. His legacy continues to inspire others through an annual CoopStrong event. Photo provided by Bailey Hanson and attributed to the Daily Reflector.

to your body, you'll give to the gift of fellowship of yourself and others, and then in faith you'll give more generously to others."

As ALS began to clearly impact Coop's body, the generosity of his time and the impact of F3 became even more valuable. Personally and professionally, Coop went on to explain his interest in the study of leadership. What F3 encouraged was leadership among men, he explained, but also the importance of followership. Most good leaders would likely agree that in order to be a good leader, you must also know how to follow. F3 provides an opportunity for both, Coop said. One of the key components of F3 workouts is that they are always peer-led. All participants will lead a workout on a rotating basis.

For example, in 2023 for F3 ENC, 144 of the 323 men who attended F3 led a workout at least once.

F3 as an organization is different, in that it provides Leadership Opportunities for everyone. This type of shared leadership is the third key component of creating a community. Creating either formal or informal opportunities for everyone to lead in some capacity has continued to emerge from the data as another vital factor in a healthy community. F3, and this shared leadership structure, ideally demonstrates the impact of creating Leadership Opportunities for members. In the research article entitled, *Sport as Medicine: How F3 is Building Healthier Men and Communities*, one member of F3 ENC stated, "It's funny because I really see F3 now as a leadership group instead of a fitness group." Another member added, "If we have them Q [lead] a workout, which I always say is like giving them a piece of F3, like sharing in the ownership, then we have like an eighty percent retention rate."

It is well-accepted among management and organizational researchers that shared leadership and input and contribution from multiple members enhance organizational performance,[3] but it is also clear that making sure individuals have opportunities to lead and provide direction is crucial to creating community. Thus, much of the success of F3 ENC is likely attributable to the leadership opportunity provided to its members. Because of that structure that fosters leadership opportunities a women's group known as FiA, Females in Action, was started in 2016 in eastern North Carolina. FiA is the counterpart to F3 that initially started when female F3 fans decided to follow the template F3 started. "Today, the FiA momentum is so great it operates with no "leader" in the traditional sense. FiA is led by all the women who show up and contribute to its success and growth - as well as their own."[4] FIA has grown to include 6,000 women in twenty-four states.

FiA ENC was added to that movement because of Coop's leadership and desire to provide opportunities to build up other leaders, leaders like my dear friend I met through FiA ENC, Shannon Williams. Shannon got more out of being a member of FiA ENC than she expected. She also got the opportunity to lead. Shannon was initially invited to a FiA ENC workout by a friend, and she admittedly was struggling with her health; she carried some extra weight and was borderline diabetic at the time. When asked to recall her first workouts and knowing she would be asked to lead one, she relayed, "I was intimidated at the thought of leading because I thought everybody was in better shape than I was. I was so impressed by what others were doing. And they seemed to have it together," she added with a laugh. The laugh was because as she knows now, those that seem to have it all together often do not. She continued, "Those leading knew what they were doing and were confident in what they were doing. At some point, I was like, 'Other people think I've got this, and they think I can handle leading.' People were always encouraging and trying to make me feel welcome and to feel part of the family. They were excited that I was there. It could be intimidating, but it's an environment where we (other FiA members) want to build up each other's confidence and make everyone feel that they are capable of leading."

Shannon went on to tell the story of one workout, where she was struggling to complete a run. A fellow participant ran up to her and said, "We're gonna go run from this telephone pole to this pole and then we're going to walk. And then we're going to run to that next telephone pole. Before I knew it, I was training for a 5K and did the couch-to-5K program! My FiA friends helped me to build up my endurance and encouraged me even when I wanted to stop. They believed in me and that I could do it." She continued, "When it came time to lead, at first, I felt a little uncomfortable. I guess I just wanted to make sure that I knew how to do the exercises—the names of the exercises, and that I was doing it correctly—and just wanted to be a good leader who encouraged others. Over time I saw other people that were stepping up and were starting to lead workouts. I felt like, you know, 'Hey, I can probably handle this.' I knew that I would have the support of other people and that they would assist me. In fact, one of them co-led with me the first time I led a workout, because it can be intimidating. So, you know the first time you are leading you're not on your own; you have someone that's gonna co-lead with you and kind of help guide you along as well." Shannon also pointed out that the organization does not just provide opportunities for women to lead workouts. She added, "If you don't want to lead a workout, you may lead a book drive or a food drive." So, as the FiA website touts, the organization is truly led by all the women that are a part of it.

CoopStrong

Years after that first FiA ENC workout, Shannon now leads regular workouts for the group. But that is just one example of a single leader that spun off that initial F3 ENC early-morning workout in 2015. Another cause inspired by Coop is CoopStrong, a charitable fund of The Community Foundation of NC East that was founded in Greenville, NC in honor and memory of Nelson Cooper. CoopStrong seeks to support families living with ALS, the

Creating Leadership Opportunities | 83

Dr. Nelson 'Coop' Cooper (center) surrounded by supporters at the annual CoopStrong 4-miler. Held each March to celebrate Coop's birthday, the yearly CoopStrong 4-Miler features a run, walk, ruck, virtual race, and 1-mile fun run for participants. CoopStrong is a non-profit organization formed to honor the memory of Nelson Cooper, a beloved husband, father, professor, and friend who passed away from ALS in May 2017. The event continues to bring supporters to together. Photo provided by Bailey Hanson.

ALS Association of North Carolina, and the research of Dr. Richard Bedlack of the Duke ALS Clinic. The organization also offers scholarships to Recreation and Park Management students at ECU. To keep the legacy of Nelson Cooper alive and support these causes, CoopStrong hosts a variety of fundraising events throughout the year. Numerous individuals from F3 ENC and FIA ENC, along with Coop's wife, son, and daughter, stepped up to lead the organization. On March 24, 2017, CoopStrong held its inaugural CoopStrong 4-Miler. This annual event offers a four-mile road race, four-mile ruck, or one-mile "fun run." In its inaugural event, the CoopStrong 4-Miler had a total of 395 participants ranging from five to sixty-six years old. That 2018 event raised approximately $15,214. The event continues to be held annually and continues to create opportunities for more people to lead.[5] Coop's daughter, Bailey, became one of those leaders, as she helped organize the event. She eventually would complete her signature honors project on research related to the motives surrounding the charity sporting event—something I know would have made her father immensely proud.[6] Knowing Coop's work and passion for recreation, F3, and community building, it is an ideal and fitting way to annually honor his life. It is also a great example of the importance of Leadership Opportunities to community building.

University Campus Recreation Sport Clubs

Another outstanding example of creating Leadership Opportunities in sport comes from earlier in my career, when I became the director of sport clubs at UNC-Chapel Hill. I had spent most of my career working in intercollegiate athletics up until that point. I was committed to this idea of sport providing educational opportunities for individuals at the collegiate level. I even focused my graduate studies on college athletics, did an internship at the NCAA, and was an assistant athletic director at a NCAA Division III school. I had not only been a college athlete, but I had practical work experience at all three NCAA levels and the NCAA headquarters. As a first-generation college student, I knew college sport provided me with an important opportunity, and I had a great appreciation for the whole idea of sport being educational.

To be honest, when I applied for the job, I did not know much about the university campus recreation or even intercollegiate sport clubs. I knew I wanted to be an athletics administrator. Well, I thought I wanted to be an athletics administrator. When the job for the Director of Sport Clubs at UNC posted, in my opinion, it described what an athletic director would do at a small college, and I welcomed this challenge. I wanted to use my skills to organize and administer sport for college students, so I thought it could be a good fit. And I no longer wanted to spend years doing minor unchallenged tasks within NCAA sports to get to that point. I was ready for a new challenge, and from my reading of the job description, working in university sport clubs was that next needed challenge.

Coincidentally enough, the campus recreation division at UNC happens to fall under the Exercise and Sports Science department, where I received my Master's in Sport Administration and, two years prior, taught courses as a graduate assistant in the department. I inquired about the job initially because I wanted to get back to Chapel Hill, but more importantly because it provided an opportunity for me to really be an administrator and oversee sport at a very young age and early in my career. Up until that point, I was well versed in NCAA and intercollegiate college athletics, where an athletic

A group of students take a break while volunteering at local sporting event. Similarly to university campus recreation sport club programs, volunteering can provide students an important opportunity to lead. These Leadership Opportunities and experiences are fundamental in fostering a strong sense of community, as they bring people together and create lasting bonds. Photo courtesy of ECU Sport Management major, Maria Ferreira Santana.

director oversees roughly fifteen or more different teams. Sport clubs within university campus recreation were very different in that one person was the administrator of fifty-plus different club teams, and all the club teams were student-led.

At the time, UNC Sport Clubs offered fifty-three different sport club options, and the sheer number of teams was intimidating to me. However, it was something that I felt would provide me with more opportunity and experience. Because of that tie to an academic department, UNC and that sport club position also offered me the chance to teach again, as I was able to negotiate the opportunity to teach an Introduction to Sport Administration course.

In that job and through teaching that introductory course, it became clear to me that sport clubs provided amazing, yet overlooked, opportunities for the students. NCAA athletics often receives all the spotlight, and all NCAA student-athletes are rightfully touted as leaders as they balance academics and high-profile sport. I do not want to take anything away from NCAA scholarship athletes, not only because I was one, but because of my firsthand knowledge that it is not as easy or glamorous to be a NCAA student-athlete as many outsiders may perceive. Yes, there are perks, but there are also countless hours in mandatory study halls, practices, traveling, and injury treatments, and the list goes on. Almost all current and former student-athletes will tell you that just the "athlete" part of student-athlete is like having a full-time job. It is difficult to balance being an NCAA student-athlete and a student, but unless an individual is designated as the team captain, there are few opportunities to lead.

In comparison to NCAA sport, the campus recreation sport club system and its structure provides far more Leadership Opportunities for students and therefore is much more productive and beneficial. In campus recreation sport clubs, the teams are truly led by students. The students are the coaches, or in some cases, they hire the coaches. Students run every aspect of the team, from practices to travel to fundraising to budgeting. Coming from an NCAA background it was impressive, but I found myself at first questioning whether students should have that responsibility and be trusted to run their own teams. Remarkably when students were provided with Leadership Opportunities they thrived, and the sense of community among them grew stronger. This underscored the whole idea of why sport and education are so intertwined and demonstrated what sport should look like if it is truly supposed to be educational and a source of Leadership Opportunities.

Many will tout a team captain on a high-profile team as a leader, but in reality, elite athletes are taking instruction and direction from a coach. In NCAA college athletics, athletes are directed by a coach or coaches: A coach plans practice, tells them what time to be where, when to study, what drills to do. In the campus recreation sport clubs, a student leads. The student or team will determine who the coach will be, when practice is, where and who they will compete against, how they will get there, who will serve as referees or judges, where they stay, what they will eat, etc. This structure fosters a stronger sense of community for the participants.

At UNC over 2,000 students participate in sport clubs, and although there is someone with the title of director of sport clubs, the program is led by 200-plus different club presidents, vice presidents, social chairs, fundraisers chairs, and other positions. The titles and structures vary by club, but the one thing they all had in common was that the students created the structure and the positions, and they truly led. And you know what? It was impressive. When people are given an opportunity to lead, they either step up or step out.

Ultimately, what happens is that community thrives when those Leadership Opportunities are provided or dissolve when no one steps up. For a sense of community to develop, it is necessary to create formal and informal Leadership Opportunities for people.

All healthy and strong communities have opportunities for their members to somehow contribute to a larger and more stable social structure and lead. In healthy communities, individuals are empowered to use their skills, talents, and gifts. Although it is not as hands-on as club sports, NCAA athletics does provide formal Leadership Opportunities for students as well, opportunities like the SAAC. "A student-athlete advisory committee (SAAC) is a committee made up of student-athletes assembled to provide insight on the student-athlete experience. The SAAC also offers input on the rules, regulations and policies that affect student-athletes' lives on NCAA member institution campuses. Presently, there are separate national SAACs for NCAA Divisions I, II and III. NCAA legislation mandates that all member institutions have SAACs on their respective campuses. Further, NCAA legislation requires that all member conferences have SAACs."[7] This NCAA legislation seems to take a page from the business sector.

In business, surveys and polls continue to link greater employee engagement to many important organizational outcomes like positive employees' attitudes, lower absence and turnover levels, and importantly, to higher profits within the organization.[8] When a company increases ways employees can be engaged, everything gets better. The same is true with sport organizations. Whether it is F3, FiA, a club sport, or NCAA sport, it is important that organizations find ways to better engage members and participants. If building strong and healthy community is a goal, the organization needs to recognize that the best way to do this is by creating Leadership Opportunities and then providing the support for members to be successful in those opportunities. While the previous examples focused on the participants, another area where a sport organization can create Leadership Opportunities is among their fans.

Fan Leadership Opportunities

In the article, *Developing Sport Communities via Social Media: A Conceptual Framework,*[9] Beth Cianfrone and I discuss how social media managers should be encouraged to continue to create Leadership Opportunities for fans. "In an online setting, this could be created through electing an online community member each year to serve various roles. Informally, allowing online community members to start, lead, and participate in discussions within established forums would also provide needed opportunity for community members to take on a leadership role," our report said. The ability for fans to share knowledge creates an empowerment opportunity, and an opportunity for the organization to display some trust and respect towards their fans.[10]

Wrexham Association Football Club

Wrexham Association Football Club, commonly known as Wrexham A.F.C., is a professional soccer team based in Wrexham, Wales that also has tried to create Leadership Opportunities within their organization. The club gained notoriety in 2020 when the purchase of the club by actors Ryan Reynolds and Rob McElhenney was profiled in the docuseries *Welcome to Wrexham*. Reynolds and McElhenney demonstrated a strong commitment to involving fans, and consequently, began to develop a community around the sport club. They reinvigorated fan-focused initiatives such as a fan ownership scheme, seeking supporter representation on the board and promoting transparency in club operations. This highlights the importance of providing fans with formal and informal Leadership Opportunities. These initiatives allowed fans to have to have a stake and voice in the club's operation. Wrexham A.F.C. fans also have representation on their board, to ensure that their perspectives and interests are considered in the decisions of the club. The empowerment and knowledge sharing that comes with creating fan Leadership Opportunities will foster community.[11]

Manning Theory

Manning theory, or later known as staffing theory, also illuminates some of the findings related to creating Leadership Opportunities and its importance to building community. The theory is credited to authors Roger G. Barker and Paul V. Gump, who explored the relationship between the number of people in a setting and the roles available within that setting. Specifically, in their text entitled, *Big School, Small School: High School Size and Student Behavior*,[12] Barker and Gump conducted surveys in schools of varying sizes, from fifty to 2,300 students. They found that smaller schools, despite having fewer resources, provided essential settings that encouraged active participation. For example, students from small schools participate in more extracurricular activities than students from large schools. The students from small schools were also found to participate in "non-class" settings to a greater extent, and the proportion of students holding positions of importance and responsibility was greater than students from large schools. This provided students with a greater opportunity for satisfaction of needs relating to competence, challenge, activity, and group affiliation. Finally, students in smaller schools were reported to have greater internal personal motivation, as well as external outside pressure and influence from peers or teachers toward participation.

Essentially, Baker and Gump's text suggests that environments with fewer people relative to the number of roles available can lead to greater individual participation, satisfaction, and skill development. In sport organizations, manning theory has been applied to understand and improve youth sport programs. For example, Hill and Green's (2008) research set forth how manning theory applies to youth sport settings:

> "When compared with participants in overmanned settings, participants in optimally manned and undermanned soccer teams will be less likely to miss training sessions and competitive matches; take on a wider variety of roles, including roles more central to the team's success; have coaches, parents, spectators, and other participants who are more accepting of all players in the team, particularly athletes with lesser skills; be presented with more participation opportunities such that weaker players will be included in play and receive extra training to correct inappropriate or less skilled play; and feel an increased sense of competence, belonging, satisfaction, and enjoyment." (p. 189)

Hill and Green's work alluded to the idea that an undermanned or optimally manned environment within sport may better lend itself to producing social rewards for the participants. Thus, the lack of structure within sport clubs when compared to varsity athletes may create a "manned" environment that ultimately produces greater social rewards, among which, one might posit, would be a sense of community.

Because each player gets more playing time and a more active role in the game, which can enhance their experience and development, the researcher demonstrated that youth teams with fewer players (and thus fewer substitutes) tend to provide a better social climate with greater internal and external influence (peer and coach) to participate. This not only enhanced their sport experience and development, but also led these athletes to enjoy the experience more. A right-sized environment, in terms of number of participants and duties, will naturally lead to increased Leadership Opportunities for participants. Thus, Leadership Opportunities are fundamental to creating an environment where community can thrive.

Why Leadership Opportunities Matter

This notion of an ideally manned environment is directly related to the Leadership Opportunities factor in the Sport and Sense of Community Theory. There is an optimal size of a community that requires participants to be active, engaged, and able to take on leadership roles. If the community or organization is overstaffed or overmanned, it will discourage participation and lead to dissatisfaction within the community or organization. This is because individuals or community members have less control and responsibility.[13] Overall, this work on manning, staffing, and undermanned environments provides support for the importance of creating Leadership Opportunities, which lends itself to greater engagement and social rewards for the participants.

In "Leading with Care in a Tough World: Beyond Servant Leadership" authors Bob DeKoch and Phillip G. Clampitt suggest that "Ninety-five percent of team members come to work every day desiring to do good work and contribute." And that means, "Only five percent or less come to work every day and don't care if they do a good job."[14] Understanding this is key to building community, and to the Leadership Opportunities factor. In an effort to build better and stronger communities, it is important to understand that most people are naturally intrinsically motivated, that they want to do good work, contribute, and belong. If these individuals are valued and empowered to do so, through creating Leadership Opportunities, a healthy environment can grow and thrive. It is also important to acknowledge that many people can be reluctant to lead, which makes it even more important for communities to foster a supportive environment that recognizes the interpersonal risk, image risk, and risk of being blamed for something that potential leaders must assume. That is, many potential leaders fear a leadership role will harm friendships and relationships with colleagues, harm their image with peers, or lead them to be criticized for a group failure. Organizations and groups that recognize the risks and nurture the leadership contributions of more of their members will be contributing to both individual and organizational growth and ultimately building community.[15]

Conclusion

The examples provided regarding Leadership Opportunities show that an environment that offers leadership, removes obstacles, and acknowledges the risk for potential leaders while fostering a sense of trust and collaboration will thrive. The stories of individuals like Dr. Nelson Cooper and Shannon Williams illustrate the profound impact that Leadership Opportunities can have on both personal development and community strength. This is why Leadership Opportunities were so important to allow F3 ENC, FiA ENC, and university club sports to thrive and provide a sense of community for their members. Further, it is important to underscore that providing both formal and informal leadership roles and opportunities will not only enhance organizational performance but also build a robust and engaged community.

Manning theory further supports this idea that environments with optimal Leadership Opportunities not only lead to greater satisfaction and skill development, but also to stronger, healthier communities. Ultimately the success of F3 ENC, FiA ENC, and similar organizations lies in their ability to create and nurture Leadership Opportunities for all members. This approach not only drives individual growth but also ensures the sustainability and vitality of the community as a whole. Fostering Leadership Opportunities is essential for building strong, resilient, and thriving communities. If ninety-five percent of your community members are showing up desiring to do good work, contribute, and belong, you must find or create Leadership Opportunities for them for that community to continue to thrive.

Discussion and Reflection Questions

1. How does the concept of shared leadership contribute to the success of community organizations like F3 ENC and FiA?
2. What are the benefits and challenges of peer-led leadership models in community groups and organizations?
3. According to the chapter and author, why does creating Leadership Opportunities enhance the sense of community among members?

4. How does manning theory explain the importance of Leadership Opportunities in building strong communities?
5. What lessons can be learned from the growth of F3 ENC and FiA that can be applied to other community-building initiatives?
6. How do personal stories, like that of Shannon Williams, illustrate the impact of Leadership Opportunities on individual growth and community development?
7. Give an example of how sport organizations could create more Leadership Opportunities for their athletes and/or fans?

CHAPTER 7

Social Spaces: A Place Where Everyone Knows Your Name

Making your way in the world today
Takes everything you've got
Taking a break from all your worries
Sure would help a lot
Wouldn't you like to get away?

Sometimes you wanna go
Where everybody knows your name
And they're always glad you came
You wanna be where you can see
Our troubles are all the same
You wanna be where everybody knows your name
—Cheers theme song by Gary Portnoy and Judy Hart Angelo

While many of you likely read the words that started this chapter, those who lived in the 1980s and 1990s probably sung the words instead. The catchy words are from the theme song to *Cheers*, a popular American comedy sitcom television series that ran for eleven seasons from 1982 to 1993 and earned twenty-eight Primetime Emmy Awards from a record of 117 nominations. The television show centered around a former relief pitcher for the Boston Red Sox who owned the bar, Cheers. When I think of the Social Spaces factor, I instantly think of the Cheers set and that catchy "where everybody knows your name" theme song. Norm and Cliff were two popular characters on the shows, and the Cheers bar served as the social space for them and countless others who would regularly wander into the bar. My previous research defined a social space as "a common physical space where individuals can interact."[1] In addition to the Cheers set, I often also reference the Wrigley Regulars and Holly Swyers' work[2] in my research when referring to a social space and its importance.

Swyers is an anthropologist who conducted ethnographic research on Chicago Cubs fans in an attempt to capture and better understand the importance of having a physical space (i.e., the bleacher seats of Wrigley Field) that allows community to develop. In order to do ethnographic work, a researcher must immerse themselves in the culture being studied. Ethnographic work is a lengthy time commitment and process; over a season, Swyers participated in the culture of being a Chicago Cubs fan at Wrigley Field, observing and conducting informal interviews to help guide her work. The sum of that work pointed to the importance of having an assigned physical space for sports fans to develop culture and community. What much of the research reinforced was that for athletes, this often means a social space is typically something outside of the playing field or courts. Common Social Spaces among athletes often include a locker room, a teammate's apartment or home, or even a designated pub or bar. These Social Spaces are the same for referees and sport officials, who will often meet up after games at a designated location.[3] While fans create Social Spaces in the stands or anywhere that they can see their beloved team on TV, whether it is a local establishment or someone's home, a physical space is needed to build community. Because sport fandom often provides an opportunity for social interaction and creating both physical spaces (and more recently virtual spaces), many of the following examples and cases will focus on Social Spaces in sport settings. The overarching point, though, is that these Social Spaces are a fundamental factor in community building for all in and around sport, not just fans.

Tailgating – A Fall Weekend Tradition

It was a cool fall Saturday in Austin, TX when an Australian visiting scholar called me. She had decided to go out for an early Saturday morning run around the University of Texas at Austin's campus and could not wait to tell me what she had observed. Even though she was a sport management researcher, she was taken aback by the scene. "There are people with campers, setting up chairs, tents, and these huge barbeque pits and grills. And they even have TVs set up, complete with electricity," she told me. The excitement and disbelief in her voice was memorable. As she ran around campus, she saw the infamous tailgates being set up as the parking lots opened on game day for the Longhorns. According to Betway Insider, "Tailgating is more than just a pre-game ritual – it's a time-honored tradition that has become an integral part of the football experience, especially in the NFL and at college games across the United States. But this unique cultural phenomenon goes beyond merely preparing for the game, it's also about *building community*, celebrating team spirit, and creating lifelong memories. "[4] (emphasis mine)

Although tailgating is a fundamental part of sport in the U.S., it is something most visitors, especially international visitors, would be taken aback by, especially when they see the magnitude of the set-up for tailgates. This is particularly true in Texas and specifically, Austin. Texas, as a state, is known for its storied high school football programs that were highlighted in the book (and later TV series based on the book), *Friday Night Lights*.[5] The area outside Darrell K. Royal-Texas Memorial Stadium in Austin has been ranked the second most popular tailgating spot among U.S. colleges. According to a 2024 report and poll, "If you attend a tailgate party at UT, expect a vibrant, Texas-sized celebration of Longhorn pride. Tailgating at the University of Texas is a cherished tradition, reflecting the school's deep football culture and community spirit. As a result, the University of Texas has 590,000 annual searches, 24,000 social media posts, and twenty-nine percent positive social sentiment (posts mentioning the college's tailgating parties in the past year.) This places them at number two, second to the University of Alabama, with a popularity score of 1.8248 out of 3."[6]

Because many U.S. professional and college sport facilities are surrounded by large parking lots, tailgating typically takes place right outside stadium and arena entrances as soon as the parking lots are officially open. Tailgating provides sport fans with an opportunity to bond with others and form a sense of community. So what happens on game days is that parking lots turn into tailgating lots, but most importantly, parking/tailgating lots become a Social Space for many fans.[7] According to Notre Dame anthropologist John Sherry, tailgate lots are microcosms of society. "What we really found was a real active and orchestrated effort in community building," said Sherry. "People have tailgated in the same place for years, they have tailgated through generations, they have encountered strangers who have passed through and adopted them to their families and became fast friends. They have created neighborhoods."[8] Or better yet, tailgating lots ideally display the importance of Social Spaces in community building.

Fans set up a tailgate, complete with everything needed to gather and socialize before a game. Photo courtesy of ECU News Services.

The History of the Tailgate

Even though every college football fan is likely to argue that their team invented tailgating, history tells us tailgating started in ancient Greece and Rome with fall harvest celebrations. The first American tailgate likely took part not surrounding a football game, but rather during the first major battle of the Civil War. This first American tailgate was one to remember and gives a unique perspective to the idea of opposing teams "battling it out" while fans are nonchalantly entertained by the action. "On July 21, 1861, residents of Washington packed picnic baskets and loaded into carriages and buggies for a day in the Virginia countryside. Rather than listening to the bucolic sounds of nature, they followed the sounds of artillery to watch from afar the first major showdown of the Civil War at the First Battle of Bull Run. The onlookers hoped the visiting squad would score a quick victory in what became known as the "picnic battle." Positioned miles from the action, spectators gazed through opera glasses and complained of the obstructed views from the smoke and trees."[9]

As absurd as that first American tailgate may seem today, tailgating is one of the most time-honored and revered American traditions. And it probably is the most visible and accurate representation of the importance of Social

Spaces in building community and a sense of belonging. Although college football games are far from actual battlefields with life and death stakes, sport fans tailgate with a passion that can be hard to describe to outsiders. In fact, tailgating has become such a rich part of sporting tradition and so clearly important to community building that sport marketers have had to be creative and figure out how to build upon the concept to create a Social Space for a broader global audience.

Virtual Tailgates and Baseball on the Big Screen

Because fans no longer need to live in a specific country or region to view sporting events, online sport forums have become increasingly popular due to their ability to provide a social space. In a research article entitled, *Virtual Tailgating: A Q-Methodology Analysis of Why Sports Fans Visit Online Sports Forums,* Boyles and colleagues explored the motivations behind why sport fans participate in such online sport forums. They concluded that three types of fans existed: tailgaters, trivia seekers, and bandwagon fans. Tailgaters, not surprisingly, use online sport forums to meet and socialize with other fans, and ultimately, they feel a sense of community as a result of this Social Space. It should be noted that these online sport forums often create a Social Space for fans during the offseason when the next competition seems far off.[10]

Similar to a traditional tailgate experience, individuals appreciate the opportunity to socialize with other fans in online forums. As sport becomes more global and actual attendance at sporting events becomes impractical for many fans, alternative Social Spaces surrounding sport are naturally becoming more popular. In Fairly and Taylor's work, *Bringing Baseball to the Big Screen: Building Sense of Community Outside of the Ballpark*, they demonstrate the impact of an alternative Social Space to the actual stadium. Their study focused on Boston Red Sox fans who attended cinemas in New England to watch live games. The game was displayed on a movie theater screen but was the same as someone watching at home; attendees saw the same commentators and commercials that they would have seen at home. The only difference is that the cinema experience was a collective experience with other fans. Through intentionally creating a Social Space for fans, community could be built. Today, fan watch parties and bars and pubs continue to host sport fans for important games. In doing so they create an opportunity for social interaction and thereby, a Social Space.

A father and his sons enjoy a Pittsburgh Pirate Major League Baseball game at PNC Park. Experiencing a sense of community through sport can happen for spectators, fans, and residents of host cities as well as for athletes. Researchers have demonstrated this sense of community can occur in virtual setting and at watch parties. Thus, expanding the potential to build and nurture community beyond narrow geographical boundaries.

The Jungle – Left Field

"Dad, you're on SportsCenter!" Brian Dilday's kids shouted the morning after he caught ECU's baseball Dwanya Williams-Sutton's home run ball in a megaphone during a March 2018 game. Dilday, an elementary school physical education teacher and volunteer youth pastor, is one of the most vocal and visible legends in the left field section of the area known as "The Jungle" at East Carolina University's home baseball games.[11] The Jungle is a legendary Social Space that aptly exemplifies the role a physical space can provide in community building. Before the current Clark-LeClair Stadium was built, two ECU fans, Tony Brown and Charlie Martin, sat in the unshaded metal bleachers at then-Harrington Field. They continued to do so in the scorching heat until they noticed a couple of men sitting under a seemingly cooler and shaded grove of large pine trees. As Bethany Bradsher documented in the

Social Spaces: A Place Where Everyone Knows Your Name | 99

More than just an outfield section –The Jungle is legendary. ECU baseball fans pack this infamous Social Space, bringing energy, chants, and a one-of-a-kind atmosphere known throughout college baseball. What started as a nickname for the thick outfield brush has grown into a rowdy, spirited community where fans of all ages come together to cheer on the Pirates. Photo courtesy of ECU News Services.

book *Never Take this for Granted: Around the Diamond with College Baseball's Most Devoted Fan Base*, it started out as an escape for two fans from the radiating heat. Brown and Martin were loyal fans and found their way to the shaded section beyond the center field fence where they could walk right up to with a cooler of beer. Somewhere along the way, the area was labeled The Jungle. "The nickname came from the trees and the kids (and some adults) who liked to climb up in the limbs for a better view of the action."[12] Because the area was surrounded by thick outfield brush, truly making it a "jungle", the name was fitting. As the space developed and grew with rowdy fans that developed a uniquely fun, yet usually civil banter with the opposing players, the name took on new significance.

Section 204 and the Advantages

The Jungle is not just about watching baseball; it is about building a community and the importance of a Social Space. ECU fans of varying ages come together, creating an energetic and spirited atmosphere with chants, cheers, and interactions with players. It's a place where friendships are forged and a uniquely supportive community is built.[13] But it's not the only place in Clark-LeClair Stadium where a social space has been created. Bradsher also highlights section 204 in her book, where one fan discusses how "204 became a family within a family." The physical space of section 204 provided an area

Lane Hoover, an ECU baseball player, faced several challenging injuries during his college career. Despite these challenges, he found immense support from fans who opened their homes, took him to church, and welcomed him before every game. The Social Spaces around ECU baseball created a community that provided Lane with vital support and a sense of belonging. Photo provided by ECU News Services.

for fans to learn about other fans, their jobs and outside interests. And when someone is in need, they are there for one another. Bradsher also writes about how one specific ECU player, Lane Hoover, benefited from this support at the group level.

Bradsher wrote, "Between two major accidents and the havoc COVID played on college baseball, Lane had a more tumultuous college career than most, but more than the pitfalls and even more than his many awards, post-season highlights moments, and 186 total runs scored, the Hoover family will hold on to the fans. . ." Bradsher then went on to describe the support Hoover received from fans that opened up their home to nurse Lane back to health after one of those accidents, a family that took him to church, and the left field megaphone crew, who welcomed him before every game. The Social Spaces created around ECU baseball have helped form a community, and there are countless other examples of how this social interaction and community building leads to support at the group level and a strong sense of community. Lane Hoover got to reap the benefits of that support created by these physical spaces, where social interaction can thrive. In Bradsher's book, Lane Hoover's mother sums it up perfectly: "The way they treated Lane, oh man, I get emotional thinking about it."

Clem's Cafe

While these examples of Social Spaces with fans often started out as informal get-togethers and turned more formal, it is important to recognize how serendipitously a social space can form for participants and athletes in sport settings. In 2024, I was fortunate enough to work with a team of individuals from ECU, Special Olympics International, and the Peru Special Olympics in a two-way sport diplomacy exchange. The goal of the exchange was pretty simple: We wanted to learn more about inclusive sport, build relationships, and ultimately try to improve sport in the disability space. After twelve U.S. delegates had the opportunity to visit and explore inclusive sport in Peru, as part of that exchange in the summer of 2024 our ECU team was charged with hosting a group of twelve Peruvian delegates from the Special Olympics. While the goal was simple, the logistics with the language barrier and details coordinating multiple partners and site visits were not always smooth. Everything was in place for a great inbound exchange when, a few short days before the delegates from the Peru Special Olympics were to arrive, we realized that the campus dining facilities would be closed.

The closure of the on-campus dining facilities meant we were not going to be able to provide easily accessible buffet-style meals with lots of choices for our guests throughout their ten-day exchange in Greenville. We quickly adjusted by arranging for lunch and dinner with local restaurants, but breakfast was more challenging. Everyone's culture is different, and everyone's morning routine is different. Some people need to have their slow mornings and a lot of people, especially people like me and the Peruvians we were hosting, needed to have their coffee. What my colleagues and I decided to do was to create a space in the dorms where our guests could have breakfast. Our thought was that we could set up a space much like a continental breakfast area at a hotel. So, we brought all the necessary things from our offices and homes like coffee

Members of the Special Olympic Peru delegation gathered here not just for breakfast, but for connection, conversation, and plenty of laughs (often while helping Clem fine-tune his Spanish). This impromptu Social Space proved that true community is built where people feel seen, heard, and valued. Photo courtesy of Clem Clouston.

pots, toasters, and mugs. We collected everything we could think of that our guests would need to make breakfast and coffee on their own, at their own pace and time, in the mornings.

We thought we planned the breakfast setting out perfectly, but it really took on a life of its own. Clem's Café, and a great example of a Social Space, would emerge. This was mostly due to a Special Olympics International staff member who was on-site for the exchange. Clem Clouston, the Senior Manager for Global Youth Development and Content Development, had come to help facilitate the exchange, and he was also staying near the designated makeshift breakfast spot. After the first morning Clem, with his gregarious personality and entertaining desire to learn Spanish, created a Social Space. The breakfast spot organically developed into Clem's Cafe within the first two days of the exchange, and my colleagues and I would receive updates each morning about the breakfast foods that we had stocked the night before.

There were some hits and misses with our makeshift breakfast options, but photo updates told the most important story. It was not the food or the coffee; it was the Social Space that defined the experience. By day three of ten we were receiving morning photos of the delegates having coffee and socializing. The smiles on their faces were full of joy, and it was clear that they looked forward to their morning discussions and laughs as they tried to help fine-tune Clem's Spanish. That temporary breakfast spot soon became known among the group as "Clem's Café," and some of our guests even personalized the paper coffee sleeves with markers and their artistic efforts. Clem's Cafe became a Social Space where everyone could interact and enjoy one another, a place where, like the Cheers theme song lyrics say, everyone knew your name.

In order for a community to be built, having a space where individuals can interact, share ideas, share laughs, and communicate is vital. For the exchange, Clem's Cafe became a Social Space that we did not even know that we needed. But that space really made the exchange more powerful and more meaningful to all those involved. Our experience proved that with just a little bit of effort, managers can create a Social Space in their sporting environments, even if in the case of the exchange, we inadvertently created a Social Space. Sometimes you have to be creative, but the most important thing is to have a physical (or virtual) space where people can interact, exchange ideas, talk, and laugh–a place where they know everybody will know their name.

Working with Vets, the Necessary Safe Social Spaces

With a brilliant smile, Gabriel "Gabe" George, who is missing an arm, cracked the timely one-liner, "I'd give you a hand, but I only got one," as I along with five others sat down for a discussion panel entitled *Working with Vets*[14] at the inaugural 2024 PickleCon event in Kansas City. The first thing I noticed about Gabe was not his missing arm, but rather his zest and eagerness to share what he has witnessed through serving as the Pickleball Director for Military Adaptive Court Sports. Despite our group being the first panel discussion of the morning, Gabe was wide awake, and his enthusiasm was contagious as the rest of us sipped on our travel mugs full of coffee. Joining Gabe on the panel were other military veterans, including a seasoned family practice physician, the executive director of Protect the Game, the founder of The Community

Creator, and the founder of Superlative Pickleball Travel and Resort Services. The common thread throughout our discussion was the need for a safe social space for veterans.

Luke Wade, a self-identified serial entrepreneur and the founder of The Community Creator, Facility Ally, and KC Crew Rec Sports & Special Events, kicked off the discussion. "When it breaks down to working with veterans, at the end of the day what we're doing is creating a community where we feel safe to come into that community. I do it with the VFW (The Veterans of Foreign Wars). I helped them create a cornhole tournament, and we created an Esports league for them called Combat-Tested Gaming. We had over a thousand members join the Esports league in about four months. And again, at the end of the day it's just veterans who like to play games that want to connect with other veterans. So, if you're using pickleball for that, it's the same concept. You just want to create something that veterans feel welcome into and feel safe. So that's what I would say to focus on. The number one thing in working with veterans is just creating a safe space for them. It helps to have other veterans involved already to get them in, but really, you're just creating a community for veterans to feel safe."

Gabe then followed up with a description of the Military Adaptive Court Sports program he directs, where he meets with veterans once a week for six weeks and teaches them the game of pickleball. "This is effective. It's not medicinal, but it is therapeutic. Physical injuries are always there, you can see those. But most of our attendees are from someone diagnosed with PTSD (post-traumatic stress disorder) or [they] don't even know that they have it and just they literally sit in the house for ten years without going out. Then it takes another veteran to invite them around to a safe space where they know it's around other veterans. And now they come out and you see people open up. And then they're smiling. They're talking. They're laughing."[15] Military bases provide an established community for military personnel, and it is not surprising that military reintegration, or the process of returning to family and community life after a deployment, can be a challenge. A supportive community can be difficult to find, but sport managers can help fill that gap by recognizing that sport can be used to create a Social Space.

Third Place

When I first started to recognize and research Social Spaces as being vital to community, one of the first things that I recalled was work related to a "third

Not home or work, a local establishment serves as a third place for many. A group of friends gather and create a Social Space after a weekly run.

place" and the growth of Starbucks. Third places can be defined as "public gathering places that ultimately contribute to the strength of community."[16] Sociologist Ray Oldenburg is credited with coining the term. In his article, *Our Vanishing 'Third Places'* Oldenburg states, "Third places are nothing more than informal public gathering places. The phrase 'third places' derives from considering our homes to be the 'first' places in our lives, and our work places the 'second.'"[17]

I first came across the term "third place" while reading a book by Starbucks CEO Howard Schultz. When Starbucks opened its first store in Pike Place Market in Seattle in 1971, it was a place to connect to sample and learn about Latin American coffee beans. It was not until 1987 that Starbucks added seating. "Customers lingered in stores, even if they had no one to meet, for the simple experience of being met with a friendly face and taking a moment to pause in the day."[18] Starbucks built its brand on being a third place,[19] and much of its growth was attributed to the fact that many found Starbucks a friendly place that was not home or work. "The idea of Starbucks as a third place became part of its corporate mythology. Starbucks aimed to create a welcoming environment for coffee drinkers and employees with comfortable seating, jazz music and the aroma of freshly brewed coffee. Employees who brewed and served Starbucks coffee, whom Starbucks called baristas, handwrote customers' names on their drink orders."[20] People needed to have a Social Space where they felt a sense of belonging. And Starbucks provided it….at one time.

The company changed, and perhaps evolved, over time. In 1995 Schultz added: "If you look at the landscape of retail and restaurants in America, there is such a fracturing of places where people meet. There's nowhere for people to go. So, we created a place where people can feel comfortable."[21] The company resisted offering drive-thru service throughout the 1990s because of this company mantra about being a third place. By 2005, almost fifteen percent of Starbucks' approximately 7,300 stores were drive-thru locations.[22] Today, seventy percent of Starbucks locations have a drive-thru option.[23] At one time also, the company prided itself on being a third space or social space for the estimated 15 million Americans who were self-employed.[24] In an attempt to address the re-imagining of Starbucks, which seems to be removing seating and added drive-thru options, Schultz noted: "I've never thought of the third place just as a physical environment. For me, the third place has always been a feeling. An emotion. An aspiration that all people can come together and be uplifted as a result of a sense of belonging. This is the cornerstone of our business, yes, but "belonging" is also a basic human right, which should be afforded all members of a society."[25] While I somewhat agree with Schultz that a third place can evoke feelings and emotions, it is important to recognize that a place to socialize is vital to the whole concept of a third place. Sport can be a third place for many, and if sport managers desire to build community, they need to be intentional about creating Social Spaces.

Why Social Spaces Matter

What this evolution of Starbucks and influx of drive-thrus has done is left us with fewer Social Spaces, and sport has continued to fill that gap. It is important to know that Social Spaces do not necessarily have to be physical spaces, as the virtual tailgates previously described demonstrate. Rather, researchers have found that online communities and support groups, like virtual tailgates, are just as impactful.[26] In fact, online sport communities created via social media, if intentionally built and designed,[27] can serve as social spaces and third places. John Bale's work on sport places and spaces reinforced this. Bale described three environments for fans to consume a game. The first space is the actual stadium where the game is being played live. This is often financially constraining due to ticket prices and the cost of traveling to the event. The second space is viewing the televised game at home, which is more accessible and even preferred by some fans. Third, viewing the game at a pub, bar, or movie theater, is what Bale referred to as the third place for sport fans. Viewing the game in a third place can fulfill an individual's social needs, and with the right crowd it can emulate the social experience that fans at the actual event are experiencing.[28] As Oldenburg said, "Life without community has produced, for many, a lifestyle consisting mainly of a home-to-work-and-back-again shuttle. Social well-being and psychological health depend upon community."[29] Thus, it is not surprising that savvy sport marketers are finding ways to strategically connect consumers and fans inside stadiums and online through social media.[30] Whether it is in-person through events outside stadiums or virtually, like virtual tailgating,[31] many loyal fans appreciate the socialization and social interaction that a physical or virtual Social Space can provide. Thus, Social Spaces help fill an innate need to belong.

Conclusion

Creating Social Spaces is integral to building and fostering a sense of community. From the iconic Cheers bar to the vibrant tailgating scenes at college football games, these physical spaces provide a venue for individuals to interact and share experiences and give people a place to belong. In sport settings, these third places will often extend beyond physical locations and evolve to virtual spaces in online forums. Importantly, these Social Spaces are essential for creating and maintaining social bonds, whether in a stadium, a pub, or even a makeshift breakfast spot like "Clem's Café," which organically and authentically developed. These environments enable people to connect on a deeper level, supporting each other and building lasting relationships. To maximize the impact of sport, it is important to reiterate that having a Social Space, like a locker room, teammate's home, or local bar or pub, is important to everyone, not just to the athletes. Creating and fostering Social Spaces is a vital factor in building community.

Discussion and Reflection Questions

1. How does the concept of Social Spaces contribute to community building and social interaction? What roles do physical spaces like bars or tailgating areas play in fostering a sense of belonging?
2. In what ways do virtual Social Spaces, such as online sport forums, emulate the social experiences of physical gatherings?
3. The chapter discusses the role of locker rooms and bars or pubs as Social Spaces for athletes. How do these spaces support team cohesion and morale? What are the potential benefits and drawbacks of such designated spaces?
4. How can sport marketers leverage the concept of Social Spaces to enhance fan engagement and community building? What is an example of a current way a sport team or organization is utilizing this concept?
5. Define and identify your "third place," as popularized by Starbucks. What are some traditional Social Spaces you've been a part of in sport? What role does this concept play in modern society, and how does it contribute to individuals' sense of belonging?
6. How do Social Spaces contribute to the psychological well-being and social support of individuals, according to the chapter? Reflecting on your own experiences, how have different Social Spaces (both physical and virtual) influenced your psychological well-being and social support?

CHAPTER 8

Equity in Administrative Decisions: The Importance of Clarity and Transparency

"The difference between equity and equality is that equality is when everyone gets the same thing, and equity is when everyone gets the things they deserve."
—Activist DeRay Mckesson

"It's simple but transformative: Clear is kind. Unclear is unkind. Feeding people half-truths or bullshit to make them feel better (which is almost always about making ourselves feel more comfortable) is unkind."
—Brene Brown[1]

"We need to have a policy on the cheerleaders that run out on the floors with the big flags," Sue Donohoe, then-vice president of NCAA Division I Women's Basketball, said to me. I was an intern under her supervision at the NCAA headquarters, and we were working on the NCAA Division I Women's Basketball Tournament Final Four Championship manual. "Really?" I replied, "We have to have a policy on that?" I did not know it at the time, but in her response, Sue would teach me about another key to community building, Equity in Administrative Decisions. This factor encompasses the idea that for a sense of community to be fostered among members of a sport community, it is important for sport managers to ensure that all policies and procedures are perceived to be equitable and fair. In other words, community members need to feel that administrative and organizational decisions are just and evenhanded for community to be built.

Donohoe was not just any sport manager. She was a women's basketball legend and Class of 2021 Women's Basketball Hall of Fame inductee. Her legendary career went beyond her playing days, and she was named by *The Chronicle of Higher Education* as one of the "Top 10 Most Powerful People in College Sports" at the height of her administrative career. Sue also was not a typical administrator or mentor to me; she was not a buttoned-up reserved executive.

She was someone who loved basketball, was a phenomenal leader, and never took anything for granted. Sue was probably the first person I met along my career path who really demonstrated to me how important it is to have fun and enjoy your job, but also to make sure you are being fair to all. Whatever we do for work, whether we want to admit it or not, we spend a good portion of our lives at our jobs. On average we spend forty out of 168 hours a week at work. Donohoe's philosophy and perspective were very straightforward. She felt like she had the best job in the world, enjoyed the work she did, and loved to crack a joke at her own expense. One of my fondest memories of Sue was how she would pass time in airports. She would use her creative mind to tell potential stories about passengers passing through the airport terminal. Inevitably, in describing the most weary 'likely just got off a red-eye flight' tired-looking woman who was struggling along with a suitcase in tow, she would claim in a self-deprecating way that it was a former vice president of NCAA Division I Women's Basketball.

Sue Donohoe was very well-respected and great at her job, but she never lost her perspective or her sense of humor. Everyone had fun when Sue was around; she was always joking around and making other people laugh. She had an incredibly stressful task each year to put on the NCAA Division I Women's Basketball Championship, but she made sure everyone on staff knew not to take our jobs too seriously. An immense amount of planning and details went into every event, and she was better at "dotting your I's and crossing your T's" than anyone could imagine. Even though we had a tremendous task at hand to put on a major sporting event, her agenda was modest. Donohoe wanted every person who walked into that arena to say, "Wow, that was a really great experience." That was it, and yet she knew that creating a great experience happened in the details, and she understood how impactful our policies and decisions could be on that experience. Because of that, I spent countless hours on that tournament manual during my yearlong stint as the NCAA Division I Basketball Championship intern. There was a policy for everything, even those big flags, so each team, fan, or any observer could clearly see that every effort was made to make sure all the details were fair and equitable.

NCAA Women's Basketball and Equity

Sue Donohoe was a key figure in the growth of women's basketball, and ensuring fairness and impartial treatment was fundamental to that growth. She led an effort in 2008 to help fans, coaches, and media better understand the selection process for the NCAA tournament. Having been a naïve observer of the selection tournament process in 2002, it was eye-opening for me to see the work that went into selecting the teams. It was arduous work for the committee, but it also seemed very secretive and guarded at the time. Sue and others recognized there was no need for the selection of teams to be a guessing game for fans, and that more clarity and less subjectivity would help.

In February 2008, she invited a group comprised of media members and former coaches to attend a weekend workshop at the NCAA headquarters in Indianapolis. Applying the same data, procedures, and rules that the selection committee would use, the group participated in a mock exercise of selecting the teams. That created greater transparency and a better understanding of the selection process. Those who participated clearly saw the difficulties in the process, but also the NCAA and committee's commitment to being fair and equitable. Women's Basketball Coaches Association CEO Beth Bass said of Donohoe. "Her commitment to openness 'de-mystified' many NCAA processes and helped administrators, coaches and media alike gain a greater understanding of the NCAA's policies and procedures."[2]

Sue left that vice president role in 2011 and went on to become the executive director of the Kay Yow Cancer Fund until retiring in 2015. The Kay Yow Cancer Fund, named in honor of the legendary North Carolina State basketball coach, and 1964 ECU alum, is a nonprofit organization dedicated to fighting *all* cancers affecting women. Donohoe passed away in December 2020, but her legacy and commitment to fairness and equity continues. Ironically enough, during the 2021 NCAA Women's Basketball tournament, the first tournament after her passing, the importance of fairness and equitability would be highlighted in a viral video.

Sedona Prince's TikTok video – Tournament Discrepancies

During that 2021 March Madness tournament, University of Oregon all-star forward Sedona Prince made a TikTok video showing the women's weight room in comparison to the men's weight room.[3] Prince's social media post was viewed more than thirteen million times in a few days and resulted in major positive changes for future events. In fact, those changes would be documented in a 100-plus page external gender equity report submitted to the NCAA a few months later. Importantly, noticeable changes to the 2022 tournament occurred because of the viral video.[4] That external report submitted to the NCAA started with acknowledging Prince's video:

> On the night of March 18, 2021, University of Oregon basketball player Sedona Prince posted a video on social media contrasting the spacious room full of assorted barbells and other weightlifting equipment provided to the men's NCAA championship participants with the small, single tower of hand weights provided to the women's NCAA championship participants at the start of the NCAA Division I Men's and Women's Basketball Tournaments.[5]

It was a glaring example of just how important fair and equitable policies were for the mega-event and for any sport organization. Community is quickly diminished when there is a lack of equity.

Having been a part of the NCAA Division I basketball staff almost two decades prior, I must admit I was a bit surprised at the video. Because twenty years earlier, when I served as the Division I Basketball Championships intern under Donohoe and Greg Shaheen, I worked very closely with both the men's and women's staff, and we thought of ourselves as one unit. We met regularly as a Division I basketball staff because it was important to ensure the same standard and quality of the tournament. After all, we had the same goals and objectives, to put on a Division I basketball tournament. Not only that, but I was very familiar with the 2021 NCAA Women's Final Four Organizing Committee in San Antonio, where Prince's infamous video was shot.

San Antonio hosted the Women's Final Four in 2002 when I was on staff. I knew firsthand they had a commitment to growing women's basketball, and the-now Executive Director of the 2021 NCAA Women's Final Four Organizing Committee, Jenny Carnes, was an upstanding and well-respected professional, who was on the 2002 organizing staff as well. Carnes also happened to be a former All-American basketball player herself, and she had a clear and evident commitment to equity.[6] The San Antonio Sports Foundation has an outstanding reputation for hosting high-quality events because of the efforts of individuals like Jenny Carnes and the rest of the staff. It was a good reminder that what you see in a thirty-seven-second video clip is never the whole story. But nonetheless, it served as an important catalyst to get the attention needed for more changes and powerfully highlighted the importance of equity, transparency, and clarity in administrative decisions.

Spot Bonuses and Programs to Promote Equity

When I interned at the NCAA as a broke college student, I distinctly recall receiving a "spot bonus" for a project that I had worked on related to the upcoming women's basketball tournament. Spot bonuses are "relatively small, spur-of-the-moment gifts to employees, long used by some companies to recognize outstanding performance. Spot bonuses are not for the upper ranks. They are designed to motivate a broader-based group of employees: A $50 prize will have more impact on someone making a modest hourly wage than on someone with a six-figure salary."[7] It was not just any spot bonus that I received; it was a gift certificate to a local shopping center to buy a business suit for upcoming job interviews. The decision to give me that spot bonus was a prime example of Equity in an Administrative Decision, and it helped me feel a part of the community at the NCAA headquarters.

As a first-generation college student, I certainly did not own multiple business suits or have the means to purchase a new one. Rather than giving me a gift certificate to a local restaurant, my supervisor of the project thought through what an equitable reward would be. For me, an equitable reward that was greatly appreciated was being able to buy a new business suit as it was standard for the staff to wear for both the semi-finals and final games. For someone else, a nice dinner out or spa day would be more of a reward. Equity in Administrative Decisions like that well-thought-out bonus can make a difference in the community that develops. Along these same lines, community builders must constantly be thinking about how to be transparent and fair. And depending on your circumstances, such as socioeconomic class and physical abilities, fairness looks different for different people.

In several courses that I teach, students are graded on professionalism for in-class presentations. This will often include points for how well they are dressed and how professionally they present themselves. In order for this to be equitable for students who may not own or have the means to purchase professional attire, I make sure students are provided with information on ECU's Professionally Purple Closet and local thrift stores. The Professionally Purple Closet gives students the opportunity to build their professional wardrobes for free, while local thrift stores can provide clothing for a nominal price. According to an article on ECU's website, the Professional Purple Closet resulted from the vision of Dr. Amanda Muhammad, Department Chair of Interior

Dress for success, without the stress! ECU's Professionally Purple Closet helps students build their professional wardrobe for free, ensuring everyone has a fair shot at making a great first impression. Because confidence starts with opportunity.

Design and Merchandising who arrived at ECU in the fall of 2022. Her goal was to establish a campus-wide professional clothing closet that addresses the needs of ECU students, so that they had greater opportunities for success when they landed those sought-after job interviews. ECU's Professional Purple Closet began serving students in the fall semester of 2023.[8]

If I were to grade students on professionalism and consider their attire without providing this resource, it would not be an equitable decision. What Dr. Muhammad's decision and vision to start the Professional Purple Closet provided was a chance to give everyone equal footing, to avoid decisions based on socioeconomic status and whether a student already owned business attire or could afford to purchase it. Resources like this build a sense of community because there is a consciousness regarding fairness within the group. To build community in sport settings, decisions that promote transparency and fairness need to be at the forefront.

Hot Topic – The Black Swimmer

In an Introduction to Sport Management class that I teach, I always like to assign to students "hot topic" presentations. This requires students to find a topic from the current issue of the *Sport Business Journal,* present it to the class, and then ask questions and lead a discussion based on that article. I never know where these topics are going or where the students will take the discussion. During one hot topic presentation, a Black male student stood in front of the classroom and presented his article on a Black swimmer. The article highlighted how the swimmer didn't feel that they belonged in a swimming community, and they had numerous racial barriers to break down during their swimming career. After the student presented the article, he then threw a question out to the thirty students sitting in the class: "Have you ever felt like you didn't belong in a sport setting?" I wasn't sure what to expect, but as an educator I truly want to give college students the floor during this time and not interject.

I watched as almost everyone's head nodded in agreement to the question, "Have you ever felt like you didn't belong somewhere in a sport setting?" Quickly one hand shot up instantly. The student responded: "Definitely. I tried out for soccer a few years ago and I was the only Hispanic." Another hand shot up, "I'm always the only Black kid in my hometown playing sports." Another hand shot up. "I definitely don't feel like I belong in sport settings because of my stature," said a student who was under five foot tall. Another hand shot up with a smile, "I also don't feel like I belong because of my stature," said a much larger-framed individual. This went on as I watched the group of thirty individuals be very vulnerable with one another.

The student presenter then asked, "Well, what would you suggest you tell somebody who doesn't feel they belong?" Someone belted out, "I would just tell them to work harder." A few others jumped on that bandwagon. "Yep, you just gotta work harder and not give up." As the time on the presentation started to dwindle, I couldn't sit back and hold my thoughts anymore. The students clapped, and as the student who was presenting his hot topic sat down, I found my way to the front of the room and said, "That's a great example of the types of things that we need to be talking about." I then praised the students for their vulnerability, for their willingness to participate in the discussion and to give examples relevant to them. I pointed out that almost every person in the room felt like they did not belong in a sport organization at some point. I asked them to really remember that feeling, and I asked the class to truly tell me if they could have solved the problem by just telling them to work harder. The class moved to a different frame of thinking and concluded that if working harder would solve the issue, we would have no need for fair policies and procedures. That opened a discussion on the 2003 Rooney Rule and provided another example of the importance of Equity in Administrative Decisions.

NFL's Rooney Rule

Another example of how this factor, Equity in Administrative Decisions, works is the NFL's Rooney Rule. The NFL adopted the Rooney Rule in 2003 based on recommendations made by the league's Workplace Diversity Committee, now known as the Diversity Equity and Inclusion (DEI) Committee. It was named after then-chairman of the committee, Dan Rooney, the late owner of the Pittsburgh Steelers. The committee's initial focus was on the historically low number of minorities in head coaching positions. The policy originally required every team with a head coaching vacancy to interview at least one or more diverse candidates before making a new hire.[9]

When I ask students if they are familiar with the NFL policy, only a handful of them usually raise their hands. I then always must age myself and share that growing up, it was rare to see black head coaches and even quarterbacks, except for Warren Moon and Randall Cunningham. And the only females on the sidelines were the cheerleaders or occasionally sideline reporters. There were not any female coaches, athletic trainers, or strength coaches on the sidelines. In fact, it was not until 2023 and Super Bowl LVIII that two Black quarterbacks faced off. It was a historical and culturally significant moment when Jalen Hurts of the Philadelphia Eagles and Patrick Mahomes of the Kansas City Chiefs took the field in Phoenix, Arizona. The Hurts-versus-Mahomes moment on one of the biggest stages in sport has been documented in the Amazon Studio's film *Evolution of the Black Quarterback*. The series starts with Michael Vick narrating and recounting that historical moment, as well as his own. Vick, who faced a litany of troubles off the field yet came back to have a successful NFL career, starts the series and first episode, "In the Beginning," with a personal reflection. "Philly will always be a special place to me. That's where I got a second chance to show what I could do. And that's really the story of the Black quarterback. Someone gets a chance, and that changes everything."[10]

Initially, the NFL's Rooney Rule led to a significant increase in the number of Black head coaches in the NFL. Within three years, the percentage of Black head coaches rose from six percent to twenty-two percent.[11] Six years after the rule was initiated, in 2009, it was expanded to include general manager and other front office positions, and in 2020, additional measures were introduced.

> In 2020, team owners approved a system intended to reward teams for developing minority talent into potential head coach or general manager candidates. If a team loses a minority executive or coach to another team, they would receive a third-round compensatory pick for two years. In the event that they lose both a coach and a personnel member, that compensatory pick would be extended for a third year.[12]

Finally, in 2021 and 2022, the rule was further expanded to mandate that teams interview at least two minority candidates for general manager/executive of football operations positions. The definition of minority candidates was broadened to include women, and the rule was extended to also cover the quarterback coach position.[13] While there has been a visible increase in the number of racial minorities in coaching roles since the passage of the NFL's Rooney Rule, the impact of the rule extends beyond minority coaches. For example, that historical and highly visible Hurts-versus-Mahomes Super Bowl LVIII faceoff was noteworthy. Additionally, the number of female NFL coaches has more than doubled since 2022. In 2024, there were a record-setting fifteen female assistant coaches across the NFL. The NFL now boasts that it has more female coaches than any male professional sport league in the world.[14] While this is significant in itself, the NFL's Rooney Rule and other equitable administrative decisions are also noteworthy because of their impact on community building.

The Nine-Point Touchdown

It was a cool, crisp, beautiful fall day and I was playing on a co-ed flag football team at UNC. My team was made up of students and staff who worked in campus recreation, and we were in it to win it. The recruiting to field a competitive team started in August as soon as the leaves started to change colors on the maple trees surrounding the fields where we would play. "Now I can throw a football," I adamantly relayed to the flag football recruiter, who happened to be my peer in the campus recreation office. His face lit up. Apparently, that was what I needed to say to get on the team. My confidence in my ability to throw a football did not stem from my softball-playing days, but rather from the lessons I took in a tailgating parking lot. Throwing a round object is very different than throwing a football, and it is not something people usually naturally pick up. Because I have always enjoyed playing a game of catch, I would insist on those tailgating days that my fellow tailgaters teach me to throw a football. After all, many of them played high school football and were happy to teach me. Those lessons would pay off and ensure my roster spot on this intramural co-ed flag football team. I would later learn why it was so important.

In many co-ed flag football leagues, including NIRSA-affiliated programs, there is a rule where touchdowns scored by females are worth nine points, while those scored by males are worth six points. So, if a female player throws a legal forward pass and a touchdown is scored by any player, the point value is nine. As a result, there is a strategic advantage to finding a female who can throw and play quarterback. I would discover this strategic advantage very quickly in one of our first games. My teammate CJ was not just a very athletic student, but he was also a tremendously gifted basketball player. In fact, after playing two seasons on the junior varsity squad, he would earn a coveted walk-on spot on one of the best teams in college basketball for his senior year at Carolina. We were losing with little time remaining in one of our first co-ed flag football games, and I distinctly recall CJ saying, "Just throw it to me in the end zone. I'll get it."

The memory of CJ's athletic skill and my subpar effort is still etched in my mind. In the huddle, I pointed to the very general direction in the end zone where I would try to throw the football. The center hiked the ball, and I don't even think my eyes were open when I let go of it. I just threw the football as far and as high as I could while trying to ensure it would land somewhere in the end zone, if it made it that far. The football did make it to the end zone, and out of nowhere CJ grabbed what became a "jump ball" in the air as he seemingly levitated several feet above the defender. With that successful grab of the throw that was not even close to the general direction I was aiming for, my team scored a nine-point touchdown to give us the win and an important illustration. The nine-point touchdown rule is another example of the importance of Equity in Administrative Decisions in community building.

The co-ed scoring rule in flag football is designed to encourage more inclusive participation and ensure that female players have a significant impact on the game. Historically, co-ed sports have faced challenges related to gender biases and stereotypes, which can affect participation and enjoyment. Administrative decisions like this nine-point touchdown scoring rule, or any other rule modifications that are designed to address these issues by creating a more equitable playing environment, can positively impact community building. Because administrators can have a significant impact on the student experience in intramural sports by implementing such rules and modifications, they can build stronger communities by promoting inclusivity.[15]

The Right Call – KC Crew

In his LinkedIn bio,[16] Luke Wade, asks: "Have you played in mismanaged sports leagues or attended a crappy event?" He goes on to rhetorically answer, "I get it. I've been there. About ten years ago I was new to my city, driving all over looking for quality sport and events and trying to meet new friends. I went to several events that were nothing but walking from bar to bar. I'd show up for my softball league and the lights would be off with no one there. Turns out the games were canceled but no one notified all the players. I was SOOO tired of this. I just wanted to get out of my house, have some fun and meet some new people. I just couldn't find what I was looking for." What Luke did was start a softball league for his friends in downtown Kansas City, and that eventually evolved into KC Crew Rec Sports & Special Events. Since 2012, KC Crew has been Kansas City's largest adult social sport league and special events company. The company grew from softball to offering sand volleyball, basketball, pickleball, cornhole, and kickball, and as a result it has connected over 100,753 individuals through its leagues.[17]

Why the exponential growth for KC Crew? The answer to that is three-fold. First, the company understood the need for people to connect. Second, it recognized that sport managers need to provide the right environment. And third, it is evident that the company and individuals running the company recognized the importance of Equity in Administrative Decisions. As previously noted, there is a global shortage of sport officials. Remarkably, KC Crew has been able to recruit and retain enough sport officials to maintain their growth. Wade stated:

> I know it's different in youth sports, but we have sixty to seventy part-time officials that we're hiring and retraining every single year. I luckily have almost half of them that have been with me for over a year. We do adult sports, which is probably not as crazy as youth sports, because you got the parents yelling at you. But adult sports are just as crazy when somebody gets mad about a kickball game, right? And so, I think it really is on the organization running that event to make the change. Because we hire and train every single one of our employees. And when someone acts a fool to our referees, we kick them out. They're gone. So, it's got to come from an organizational level. Top down. Because you can't expect your officials to be the ones to do that. So again, I know it's difficult for youth because you're typically hired by a school or an organization who's in charge of that. But in my organization, we're hiring and training the people who are reffing our games we're putting on. And we kick people out all the time. And typically, at the end of the day, when you do that, everyone else is happy that you did that, as well. And so, it's really got to come from the top-down organizational level to not allow parents and people to act like that again. And we're able to keep staff and we have tons of staff, because they're constantly wanting to be in that environment with other people and [that] organizational level top-down mindset.[18]

So, without question, KC Crew displays Equity in Administrative Decisions by having clear and equitable policies and not hesitating to remove people that are not adhering to those policies.

KC Crew also has well-defined inclusion policies and league rules, and "anyone and everyone is welcome" to join their leagues. Their website clearly outlines that their goal as a company is "to provide awesome sport leagues and events where all of our participants and staff feel safe, accepted, and know they belong. For several years now, we have been working very hard as a company to educate ourselves and become more aware of gender roles. We currently offer non-gender specific (open) leagues for a variety of sports with a goal to bring more inclusive options for all!"[19] However, KC Crew takes it one step further and clearly spells out why every league is not open.

"KC Crew strives to promote equality and inclusivity throughout our leagues with respect to everyone's race, religion, age, gender expression or sexual orientation. We created different team options and rules for the comfort and safety of all our participants. It is not our intent to make anyone feel excluded from our leagues or events, which is why we provide so many options. Participants are encouraged to sign up for the option that will make them feel the most comfortable with the entire goal of having fun and meeting others in the community! If you aren't sure of a sport's gender requirements, you can find them in every league description when you go to sign up."[20] The KC Crew inclusion webpage then goes on to explain co-ed rules and why they exist for each sport. The very well-defined and transparent policies are prime examples of a company and organization demonstrating Equity in Administrative Decisions, and distinctly a reason why KC Crew has built a successful company and place for individuals to belong in the Kansas City area.

Why Equity in Administrative Decisions Matters, Inequity Theory

I have no doubt that the Division I NCAA basketball staff and Women's Final Four Organizing Committee did all that they could to ensure that all of those athletes fortunate to make it to San Antonio for the Final Four had an amazing experience. However, Prince's viral video gained momentum with thirteen million views because, in general, people tend to want things to be fair and equitable. Whether it is a personalized spot bonus, a program to provide professional clothing to job seekers, the NFL's Rooney Rule, a nine-point touchdown, or non-gender specific open leagues, these organizational decisions will positively impact not just the "in need of catching a break" recipients, but all members of the community. Because when the playing field is level, and everyone has the same chance of success, individuals will recognize there is support at the group level. This is what builds and creates a sense of community. Not surprisingly, it is one of the reasons Equity in Administrative Decisions is key to building community. Further, this element is supported by Inequity Theory,[21] which states:

> "Fairness is perceived when resources or outputs are allocated in proportion to the efforts or inputs. That is, when individuals feel a balance is met, in comparison with others, between their contributions and the rewards received, justice is perceived. When individuals do not feel this balance exists, there is a felt inequity and a stress or strain to resolve the inequity. When administrative decisions were viewed as fair and just, this contributed to

SOC (sense of community); however, when administrative decisions were not viewed in this manner it detracted from the participants' SOC (sense of community)."[22]

Early on in my research, after interviewing several female athletes, I recall joking that "if you want to know how many pair of free shoes any student-athlete gets, ask a volleyball player." It seemed like every volleyball player that I interviewed knew exactly how many pairs of shoes every athlete at their university received. It was not about the shoes; it was about being treated fairly. And it was not just volleyball players, although it seems that they did have a heightened awareness of equity or lack thereof, likely because their season overlapped with football and basketball. And if a track athlete received more shoes than a volleyball player, an explanation for the disparity was needed, or community building would be thwarted. Things do not have to be equal, which is a key difference between the term *"equality"* and "equity," but they do need to be equitable for community to thrive. Equitable means that if a track athlete burns through five pairs of shoes a season and a volleyball player only one pair, then most would agree a track athlete should receive more shoes. People want and need to be treated fairly, and policies need to be clear and transparent if community is going to thrive.

Several sport scholars have supported this idea. Researchers have found that NCAA coaches, administrators, student-athletes, and students believe distributing resources equally or based on program needs was fairer than distributing them based on program contributions.[23] Because this builds community, we know that it also impacts retention and satisfaction, as well as organizational outcomes like organizational commitment, evaluation of authority, organizational citizenship behavior, withdrawal, and performance.[24]

Conclusion

Equity in Administrative Decisions is crucial for community building and fostering a sense of community within sport settings. By ensuring that policies and procedures are fair, transparent, and considerate of diverse needs, administrators can create an inclusive environment where all members feel valued and supported. This approach not only enhances individual satisfaction and engagement, but also strengthens the overall cohesion and success of the community. Whether through thoughtful rewards, equitable resource distribution, or inclusive policies like the NFL's Rooney Rule and rules like the coed nine-point touchdown, prioritizing equity in decision-making is essential for building a thriving and supportive community within sport settings.

Discussion and Reflection Questions

1. In what ways did Sue Donohoe's efforts to improve the transparency of the NCAA Women's Basketball Tournament selection process illustrate the principles of equity? What were the broader implications of these changes for women's sport?
2. How did Sedona Prince's TikTok video influence gender equity in NCAA sports, and what changes resulted from it?
3. What is the NFL's Rooney Rule? How effective has the Rooney Rule been in increasing diversity within coaching and executive positions, and what are the potential limitations or criticisms of this policy?
4. How can sport organizations ensure that their policies and procedures are perceived as fair and equitable by all members?
5. How do spot bonuses and professional clothing programs illustrate the concept of Equity in Administrative Decisions?
6. How can the concepts of equity and fairness discussed in the chapter be applied to your own experiences or professional environment? What steps can you take to promote equity in your sphere of influence?

CHAPTER 9

Now What? Measuring a Sense of Community in Sport

"If you can't measure it, you can't improve it."
—Peter Drucker

"In God we trust. All others must bring data."
—W. Edwards Deming

Why do we need to have a measurement tool?

"Not another 'check' on an assignment. How do you always get 'check-pluses?'" I exhaustedly asked a classmate. I was in one of Dr. Laurence Chalip's courses at the University of Texas at Austin at the time. Dr. Chalip had a unique grading system for his graduate-level seminars: check-minus, check, and check-plus (and, I would later learn, "check/check-plus"). A check-minus was insufficient work, a check was adequate work, and a check-plus was good-to-excellent work. The check/check-plus was not quite a check-plus, but close. Measuring things like my effort on an assignment, through grading, was important to progressing through the class. I was probably like most students and would have been content with a check grade on my assignments, but the classmate next to me always seemed to receive check-pluses. She was working on her master's and was a few years younger than me, while I was working on my doctorate and trying to figure out how to be a student after taking a break for a few years. As we got to know one another through those weekly classes, we would trade notes and thoughts on the class and assignments. Throughout my time in Dr. Chalip's courses I would never, despite the effort and time I put in, receive a check-plus, and it bothered me.

The measurement and grading systems he used were not traditional, but being able to measure and quantify the things I was learning was essential. One of the great things about higher education is that often before we enter our professional career, we spend time in classrooms and have the opportunity to interact and learn from professors who have intensely studied a subject matter. Many are quite gifted at relaying thoughts and ideas to novice thinkers, who are just at the beginning of their careers. These new learners usually want to have an impact on the world, yet they are not really sure where they fit or how they can contribute. The college years are often a time when our thinking can be heavily influenced by professors and the knowledge that they have gained through studying a subject matter. I would never earn a check-plus from Dr. Chalip, but I did take away something more valuable—the understanding that you cannot improve anything if it is not evaluated and measured.

Dr. Chalip is a titan in the field of sport management. He is a well-respected, brilliant scholar whose thinking around sport has really impacted both the field and me personally. I was fortunate enough to cross paths with Dr. Chalip during my time as a student at Texas. I even served as his graduate teaching assistant, and he would eventually become a mentor of mine. He was, though, when I started my doctorate program, by far the most intimidating professor I had come across up until that point. His vocabulary and everyday vernacular are second-to-none. When he dropped words and ideas into conversations, I would try to mentally note to look them up later. Nonetheless he had a knack for explaining sport in a way that few others had, and I was fortunate to learn from him. He served on my dissertation committee, and in my last year at Texas I sat in on and helped with an undergraduate sport marketing course he taught. He was passionate about sport and yet highly critical of it. In his research and teaching, Dr. Chalip was able to frame ideas about sport in a manner that caused me to think critically about sport. I, too, am passionate about sport, but he would label me a Pollyanna when it came to my thinking.

Pollyanna, another thing I had to look up at the time. For those, like me, not familiar with a 1913 novel, the term comes from the book *Pollyanna* by Eleanor H. Porter.[1] A Pollyanna is a person who is excessively cheerful or optimistic, often to the point of being unrealistic. In the book, Pollyanna is known for her unwavering optimism and her ability to find something to be glad about in every circumstance, no matter how trying or difficult. As a future academician and researcher, I knew I had to be more concrete and critical in my thinking and work for it to be impactful, even though I hope I never stray too far from that Pollyanna image. I never want to be labeled as strictly a critic of sport; instead, I hope I am seen as an optimistic advocate for sport. I relay this to students and others all the time. I love sport for what it can be, not for what it is currently. Because of that influence from Dr. Chalip and being labeled a Pollyanna, I know that we cannot just simply accept that sport is good. We must find a way to critically analyze it and measure its impact.

In 2006, Dr. Chalip was named the North American Society for Sport Management Earle F. Zeigler Lecture Award winner. This is the most prestigious award given by the organization, and the recipient delivers a distinguished scholarly lecture based on their career works at the annual conference, which is then printed in the *Journal of Sport Management*. What Dr. Chalip delivered in that lecture and article, *Toward a Distinctive Sport Management Discipline*,[2] remains foundational to the sport and community conversation. Despite the fact that the article and lecture were written nearly two decades ago, his words, ideas, and thoughts continue to be relevant. Although sport, sport policy, and sport structures vary across levels and in national settings, Dr. Chalip's work put forth the five main legitimations for sport that are popularly championed globally to justify sport.

Those legitimations, or justifications for sport, identified by Dr. Chalip are: health, salubrious socialization, economic development, community development, and national identity. Dr. Chalip argued, "These legitimations are important not merely because they are commonly espoused, but also because they assert that sport bestows good public outcomes. They suggest that sport is not merely about play and entertainment but is also a means to some of our most revered policy objectives. Yet, the credibility of these legitimations remains suspect when so much of what we do in the design and implementation of sport programs, sport events, and sport systems is inconsistent with (indeed, often antithetical to) realization of the outcomes upon which our legitimations are based." Dr. Chalip goes on to highlight how the value of sport depends on the ways that sport is managed, and the "factors that facilitate and that inhibit optimization of sport's contribution to each must be identified and probed. Identifying and probing those factors will be aided by research that confronts popular beliefs about sport."

Even as a Pollyanna who experienced and witnessed how sport could bring people together, I conceded that Dr. Chalip had a valid point. We must be critical of sport if we are going to maximize its potential contribution to society. So, I set out to identify the factors that facilitate and inhibit community development within sport settings. The previous chapters laid out the five factors of the Sport and Sense of Community Theory, which was based on my work with well over 130 interview participants and exhaustive literature reviews. But I had a feeling this would only be "check" and not "check-plus" work. Why? Because theory must be refutable and testable.[3] However, good theory[4] is also useful and influences practice.[5] In order for the Sport and Sense of Community Theory to be useful and influential on practice, I knew we needed to find a way to measure it. As Peter Drucker, considered the father of modern business management, is credited with saying, "If you can't measure it, you can't improve it."[6] I know that we need to find ways to improve upon sport, and measuring a sense of community was a missing piece to that puzzle.

Finnish social researchers Timo Räikkönen and Juha Hedman, in an overview of the idea of sport building community, point out: "Beyond its surface-level narrative, sports play a significant role as social venues and shared places, providing opportunities for community cohesion and enhancing individual well-being. However, the prevailing discourse surrounding sports often fixates narrowly on quantifiable outcomes and commercialisation, focusing on metrics such as tournament victories and financial gains. This limited perspective fails to capture the holistic impact of sport, neglecting intangible benefits such as personal growth and community cohesion. By relying solely on easily measurable markers, sports' broader achievements and transformative power in fostering social connections and enhancing shared experiences remain underestimated and undervalued."[7] The well-documented innate need to belong or experience a sense of community is evident, but the question of how to measure it has been elusive.

When the Sport and Sense of Community theory was first published, a colleague from the field called me and said, "This needs to be a scale and measurement." She too knew that our field was at the point where we had to be able to quantify this mysterious and seemingly subjective outcome and benefit of sport. Before I knew it, that colleague, Dr. Shannon Kerwin, and another colleague, Dr. Matt Walker, were working alongside me on creating a scale. We had, at this point, a well-developed theory to work with, so formulating the items for measurement was the next logical step. The community psychology, education, and sport management literature provided strong support for each of the factors in the Sport and Sense of Community Theory,[8] and we had clear definitions for each of the factors. At that point seven factors of the theory existed:

Sport and Sense of Community

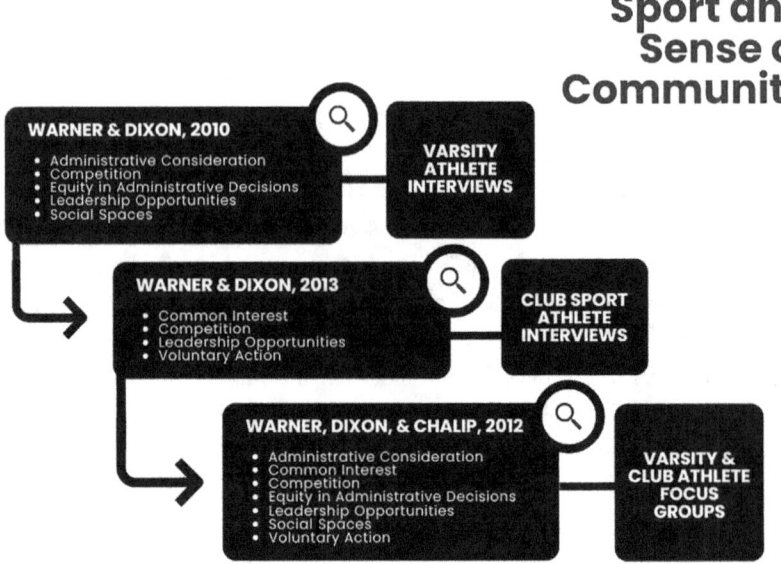

The Sport and Sense of Community theory was built upon the findings in three foundational qualitative research studies (Warner & Dixon, 2010; 2013; Warner, Dixon, & Chalip, 2012). As new knowledge and a quantitative tool emerged from the theory, evidence supported that the theory could be reduced from seven factors to a more parsimonious five-factor model. This allowed for the scale to be more broadly used across sport context. The 15-item scale, which is comprised of three-items per factor, provides a robust tool for practitioners to evaluate or diagnosis a sporting environment and pinpoint areas of improvement. Image created by Kathryn Adkins.

1. Administrative Consideration - The expression of care, concern, and intentionality of administrators.
2. Common Interest - Group dynamics, social networking, and friendships that result from individuals being brought together by a shared interest.
3. Competition - The challenge to excel against both internal and external rivalries.
4. Equity of Administrative Decisions - Decisions that demonstrate all community members are treated equally.
5. Leadership Opportunities - Informal and formal opportunities to guide and direct others in the community.
6. Social Spaces - A common area or facility in which athletes could interact with one another.

7. Voluntary Action - Self-fulfilling and self-determining activities resulting from little-to-no external pressure or incentive.

We would use the three steps outlined by DeVellis's Scale Development Theory and Applications text[9] to produce the initial scale. Based on previous literature and theory, the first step included identifying, grouping and categorizing, and then labeling potential items for the scale. This resulted in a large initial forty-one-item survey pool. Next, that pool of 41 survey questions was analyzed for both face and content validity evidence. Face validity tests whether the items superficially appear to measure what they are supposed to measure, while content validity assesses whether the proposed items cover the entire range of the concept they aim to measure. This was accomplished by thoroughly examining and evaluating the relevance of each item relative to the dimension it was intended to reflect.

Next, the items were reviewed by a panel of experts to determine each item's relevance to the dimension it was intended to reflect. This then resulted in a refined group of twenty-eight items representing a scale of seven factors. We then tested the twenty-eight-item scale with a youth sport population. This resulted in a valid and reliable twenty-one-item instrument with six subscales (i.e., Administrative Consideration, Common Interest, Competition, Equity in Administrative Decisions, Leadership Opportunities, and Social Spaces) to measure the sense of community in sport.

The resulting twenty-one-item Sense of Community in Sport scale provided practical support for six of the original seven factors. Voluntary Action was removed. That is, Voluntary Action was not supported by quantitative results. Although this may have been due to the age of the participants–given youth are dependent upon adults for transportation, information, and resources, so they could not voluntarily decide to belong or not–this factor was removed so the scale could be more broadly used across sport settings regardless of the participants' age. Thus, the scale was then refined and broadened in a later study on small-scale event volunteers. The refined scale now had fifteen items and was now more suitable to be used with other sport stakeholders, not just athletes.[10]

Statistical model testing of the data collected from sport event volunteers indicated all but one of the now-six factors, Competition, fit the measurement scale. Therefore, the three items regarding the Competition factor were dropped because this analysis indicated they didn't fit conceptually with the other factors. This means that while the researchers initially felt that Competition (similar to Voluntary Action in previous aforementioned work) might

More than just a race –it's a community gathering. Two volunteers at the annual Good Samaritan 5K work at the registration table, embodying the spirit of giving back. The experience of event volunteers isn't just about service; it's about connection, purpose, and belonging. Photo courtesy of Hope of Glory Ministries.

be a contributing factor to a sense of community, additional survey responses indicated to researchers that the Competition items were somewhat irrelevant and not connected to the other sense of community concepts. Given the Competition items did not "fit" with the group, the idea that Competition is a central part of developing community in sport was dropped. The resulting fifteen-item scale, comprised of five subscales with three items each included:

Administrative Consideration

1. Leaders of [club, sport organization, or event name] care about their volunteers
2. Leaders of [club, sport organization, or event name] support their volunteers
3. I feel comfortable talking openly with the leaders of [club, sport organization, or event name]

Common Interest

    4. I share similar values with other volunteers at [event name]
    5. I feel like I belong when volunteering for [event name]
    6. Volunteering provides me with friends who share a strong commitment to volunteering

Equity in Administrative Decisions

    7. Staff working for [club, sport organization, or event name] make decisions that benefit everyone
    8. Staff working for [club, sport organization, or event name] make decisions that are fair
    9. Staff working for [club, sport organization, or event name] consider everyone's needs when making decisions

Leadership Opportunities

    10. I have influence over what [club, sport organization, or event name] is like
    11. If there is a problem at [event name], I can help to solve it
    12. I have a say about what goes on at [club, sport organization, or event name]

Social Spaces

    13. When going to [event name], there are places where I can interact with other volunteers
    14. When going to [event name], I know I'll have an area where I can interact with other volunteers
    15. [club, sport organization, or event name] creates a place for me to interact with other volunteers

In summary, the study of small-scale event volunteers further empirically assessed, validated, and refined the Sport and Sense of Community theory and the development of a quantitative measurement of that theory. I viewed this fifteen-item scale as a diagnostic tool for sport organizations interested in community building. Based on the surveys conducted using the scale, organizations could measure and pinpoint areas of importance and improvement. Thereby, this work provided and demonstrated the much-needed utility and practical potential of the theory.

Sense of Community in Sport Scale Uses

Initially, the Sense of Community in Sport Scale was used in a youth archery setting and then refined in a study on sport volunteers at a small-scale event. The scale since has been adapted and used in variety of sport settings, including among event volunteers at the China Open 500[11] and among adaptive sport participants,[12] Canadian military recreation program participants,[13] female hockey players,[14] and campus recreation program participants.[15] In each of these studies, researchers used the Sense of Community in Sport Scale, or a slightly modified version, to capture the sense of community support and belonging experienced by the participants. In turn, this helped researchers relay to managers and leaders the strengths and weaknesses of the current environment and areas to consider for improvement if community building is their goal. To demonstrate some previous uses of the Sense of Community in Sport Scale, I will provide three examples. These examples include Andrew Pickett and his colleagues' work in a three different fitness contexts, Amy Kim and his colleagues' research among participants in local tennis leagues, and James Lowrey's work with esports athletes.

Fitness Context Findings

Pickett and his colleagues used a modified version of the multidimensional scale initially developed by Warner, Kerwin, and Walker to measure the sense of community among participants in three fitness contexts: CrossFit, traditional group fitness classes (e.g., yoga, cycling), and individual gym attendance. In their study, the researchers examined the influence of the sense of community on the perceived value of physical activity across different fitness contexts. Pickett and colleagues' findings demonstrated that the scale can be used as a diagnostic tool to pinpoint the strengths and weaknesses of an organization in terms of community building. Specifically, Pickett and colleagues observed that CrossFit participants reported the highest levels of belonging or sense of community when compared to traditional group fitness classes and individual gym-goers. Further, they were able to determine that Administrative Consideration, Equity in Decision-Making, and Social Spaces specifically made a strong difference among the participants in their study.

The results provided evidence that group fitness classes did not significantly differ from individual gym attendance in terms of the community and belonging that they reported. Overall, in terms of sense of community experienced by participants, individual gym-goers had the lowest levels of sense of community. From a practical standpoint, the researchers were able to provide recommendations on how managers in these fitness contexts could improve the sense of community experienced by participants. For example, the researchers noted that: "Based on this, fitness managers could create emotional value more effectively by creating an equitable social space for individuals to interact as peers. In particular, group fitness contexts could focus on more explicit interaction, such as small group activity, personal recognition of individuals and their goals, etc., which could lead to stronger felt SOC (sense of community) and increase the perceived value of the service provision. The value derived from administration, instead, comes in the form of higher quality and reputation for the facility. Thus, intentionality in creating social spaces should foster a greater level of community among participants." By providing these recommendations, the researchers demonstrated the value and importance of applying the Sense of Community and Sport theory and using the respective scale to gauge an environment in terms of how it could be improved.

Local Tennis Leagues and Community Findings - Health-Related Psychological Outcomes

In another example of the utility of Sense of Community in Sport scale, Kim and colleagues conducted a study to explore the relationships between the sense of community in sport, social support, and health-related psychological outcomes (depressive symptoms and happiness) among participants in local tennis leagues.[16] The researchers in this study used sophisticated statistical procedures, specifically multigroup moderated-mediation structural analysis with partial least squares structural equation modeling (PLS-SEM), to determine the relationship among these noted factors. Importantly, Kim and colleagues determined that the Sense of Community in Sport scale was positively associated with social support, indicating and confirming that sport communities can be influential sources of support. Additionally, the Sense of Community in Sport scale was negatively associated with depressive symptoms and positively associated with happiness. This provides evidence that a strong sense of community, as measured by the Sense of Community in Sport scale, can enhance psychological well-being. Kim and colleagues' study of the local tennis participants highlights the importance of fostering a sense of community through sport to enhance social support and psychological well-being. Their work explicitly provides quantitative data supporting the Sense of Community in Sport theory and scale. Notably, the research advances the idea that local sport leagues can play a significant role in promoting mental health through community building and social support mechanisms.

Esports Athletes, Community, and Mental Health Outcomes

Although esports, or competitive video gaming, likely first emerged in the early 1970s when Stanford University competed in the "Intergalactic Spacewar Olympics," the term "esports" was not coined until 2000,[17] and the movement has rapidly and exponentially gained momentum over the past two decades. Today, esports is a multibillion-dollar industry with a global audience and professional leagues. As a result, colleges and universities took note and esports has quickly become a part of the higher-education landscape. "The opportunity is ripe for institutions to connect with students in new ways and build new communities of engagement with esports teams and gaming facilities."[18] By 2024, more than 200 universities in North America boasted varsity esports programs in which students can compete and earn scholarships. In fact, approximately $16 million in scholarships were awarded to esports athletes in 2023 alone.[19] Colleges also are now offering academic courses to prepare students for careers in esports beyond just being an esports athlete. Because of the expected growth of the esports industry, colleges are building dedicated facilities and programs to prepare students, as well.[20]

Many attribute the COVID-19 pandemic to further accelerating the growth of esports. While traditional sporting events were canceled or postponed and people were spending more time at home, there was a notable increase in engagement with esports. Simply, individuals needed to have an alternative to both entertainment and social engagement during COVID-19 lockdowns. The surge in collegiate esports is a result of higher education institutions recognizing esports as an area worth investing in because of its potential to build community and bring people together. "Esports fosters a sense of community and inclusivity, appealing to a diverse student body. Unlike traditional sport, esports is accessible to a broader range of participants, including those who might not engage in conventional athletic programs." With this new idea that esports could build community on college campuses, it became important to be able to quantify the impact of esports.

In his research, "Protecting the New Student Athlete: Exploring the Mental Health Outcomes of College Esports Athletes and the Supportive Factors of Collegiate Esports Organizations,"[21] James Lowrey compared collegiate esports athletes to their non-esports peers. He was most interested in mental health outcomes and how supportive outcomes like community support, access to institutional resources, distributed leadership, and respect for diversity play a crucial role in these positive results. He used a modified version of the Sense of Community in Sport scale to determine community support. He concluded that collegiate esports athletes generally have better mental health outcomes compared to their non-esports peers, and that supportive factors measured did have key functions in these positive outcomes related to mental health.

Not surprisingly, and similarly to Kim and colleagues' work with local tennis leagues, Lowrey observed that community support was the most significant predictor of good mental health among collegiate esports athletes. Specifically, Lowrey concluded, "...colleges should focus on establishing collegiate esports organizations that place extra attention on cultivating strong feelings of community support....Instead, the modality of each participant's esports team did not significantly predict their mental health outcomes when it was included in a regression equation that also contained a variable of community support. While between-groups tests revealed that varsity esports athletes had improved mental health outcomes as compared to their club counterparts, the findings of RQ5 suggest that these improved outcomes are simply a function of the increased levels of community support that were observed among varsity esports organizations."[22] Thus, with the findings in the cases of a fitness context, local tennis programs and now esports, there is evidence of the usefulness of the Sport and Sense of Community scale.

Psychometrics of the Sense of Community in Sport Scale

The next step that will hopefully elevate this to check-plus work is to ensure and test the psychometrics. Psychometrics play a crucial role in scale development because they ensure the reliability and validity of a measurement tool. Through applying psychometric principles, we can assess whether the Sense of Community in Sport scale accurately measures the intended factors and constructs while producing consistent results across different contexts and populations. This process involves rigorous testing and analysis, including item analysis, factor analysis, and reliability testing, to refine the scale and confirm its effectiveness. To that end, I looked for support within my own community of scholars to help with the psychometrics. Dr. E. Whitney G. Moore is a highly skilled researcher in sport psychology and psychometrics with whom I was fortunate to start collaborating when she started at ECU in 2022. Ultimately, psychometrics analysis is needed to create a robust, trustworthy scale that not only measures Sense of Community in Sport but can also provide meaningful and actionable data needed to make informed decisions in the management of sport.

Quality of the Fifteen-Item Sense of Community in Sport Measurement Tool

The research previously described provides the conceptual foundation for the refined sense of community in sport scale with five factors (with three items each) that can be used across sport-related contexts and populations. Given this, the next step is confirming the quality of the measurement is equally good across important social groupings – race, team or individual sport participation, and gender– for each of the five factors and the overarching sense of community in sport. This is done by confirming that people answer the items consistently across groups. Then, having met this standard, if there are differences in the overall levels for the groups, we can be confident those differences are true for the groups, rather than due to differences in measurement quality. As part of an American Athletic Conference Academic Consortium research grant received in 2021, Brennan Berg and I collected data from 776 college athletes who completed the refined fifteen-item sense of community in sport scale. Moore analyzed the data and demographics (i.e., race and sport type) from that work to determine the psychometric or quality of the measurement.

Race, Team vs. Individual Sport, and Gender. First, the consistency of measurement across Black and White athletes was supported for both the five characteristics and the overall Sense of Community. The five characteristics and overall Sense of Community were all measured reliably for both White (composite reliability range = .79 - .95) and Black (composite reliability range = .88 - .96) athletes. The means for four of the five characteristics and overall Sense of Community were not significantly different across Black and White athletes. This indicates that a difference between Black and White athletes was not found to be related to individuals' responses about their sense of community.

Next, looking across sport types (i.e., teams vs individual), again the five characteristics and overarching Sense of Community measurement structure was supported. The five characteristics and overall Sense of Community were all measured reliably for both Team (composite reliability range = .85 - .95) and Individual (composite reliability range = .83 - .95) athletes. The means of the five characteristics and overall Sense of Community for individual and team sport athletes were not significantly different. That is, a difference between team sport and individual sport athletes was not found to be related to individual's responses about their sense of community.

Finally, the measurement quality was examined across gender groups (i.e., men and women). The five characteristics and overarching Sense of Community measurement structure was supported for both men and women. All five characteristic factors and the Sense of Community factor were all measured reliably for both men (composite reliability range = .88 - .96) and women (composite reliability range = .80 - .94). Next, the means of the five characteristics and Sense of Community factor were not significantly different for men and women. In other words, a difference among women and men was not found to be related to individual's responses about their sense of community.

Thus, these psychometrics provide additional evidence that the fifteen-item (five factors with three items each) Sense of Community in Sport Scale produces sound and reliable scores. While this can be very academic and confusing for someone who does not routinely collect and assess data, it is a necessary step to ensure the Sense of Community in Sport Scale is psychometrically sound. Or in other words, the scale will measure what it intends to measure. Importantly too, the inclusion of the measure and details are intended to help narrow the gap between academic theory and practice. For practitioners, it is vital to make sure they are using sound surveys and have an understanding that the data they collect is only useful if collected with a valid measure.

Conclusion

The development and refinement of the Sense of Community in Sport scale underscores the critical importance of measuring and understanding the multifaceted nature of community building within sport settings. By systematically identifying and validating key factors such as Administrative Consideration, Common Interest, Equity in Administrative Decisions, Leadership Opportunities, and Social Spaces, the Sense of Community in Sport scale provides a robust tool for researchers and practitioners alike. This tool not only aids in the empirical assessment of community dynamics and support but also offers practical insights for enhancing the sense of community among sport participants. As demonstrated through various applications, from youth sport to collegiate esports, fostering a strong sense of community can significantly impact participants' psychological well-being and social support networks. Moving forward, continued research and application of the Sense of Community in Sport theory and scale will be essential in optimizing the positive contributions of sport to individual and community development.

Discussion and Reflection Questions

1. What are the five key factors identified in the Sense of Community in Sport scale, and why is it important to be able to measure a sense of community in sport settings?
2. Provide an example of how these five factors can be managed to enhance community building.
3. Consider the dual role of being passionate about sport while also being critical of it. How can this balance be beneficial in your professional or academic pursuits?
4. Reflect on a time when you were evaluated or measured in an academic or professional setting. How did this measurement impact your performance and motivation?
5. What are the five legitimations (or justifications) that Dr. Chalip identified in his 2006 article? Which legitimation do you think is used the most for youth sport? What about for professional sport?
6. Discuss the implications of the findings from studies using the Sense of Community in Sport scale in various sport settings. How can these findings be utilized to better the experiences in various sport settings such as youth sport, local leagues, and esports?
7. If you were a sport marketer, how could you use the existing Sense of Community in Sport scale to improve sport environments in recreation and/or a professional sport?

CHAPTER 10

What's Next? A Call to Action and Community of Practice

As Dr. Jerry McGee slid his Rose Bowl Championship ring across the conference room table for me to inspect one rainy Friday afternoon, I realized that, despite already celebrating the completion of the first full draft of this book, I was not done yet. Just a week or so prior a friend asked me, "What's next?" when we were out celebrating another work week in the books and my confident proclamation that I had completed the first draft. With energy and self-assurance, I responded with the next steps in having some trusted colleagues review the draft and the publishing process. A week or so later, though, I would have a meeting with Dr. Jerry McGee, inspect that Rose Bowl ring, hear his story, learn of his connection to Dr. Leroy T. Walker, and I realized that the book was not done yet. For Dr. McGee, Dr. Walker and all the other legends who promoted and advocated for sport over the years, I needed to make sure that I did not end with "Now what?" but rather adequately and clearly answer the question, "What's next?."

From the Intramural Fields to Rose Bowl – Dr. Jerry McGee

Dr. McGee was an ECU Health and Physical Education graduate who went on to have a very successful career in higher education. From 1992 to 2015, he served as the President of Wingate University, and under his leadership Wingate was routinely recognized as one of the best small universities in the South. Upon his retirement in 2015, Dr. McGee was the longest tenured college or university president in the Carolinas. So why was a professor from the Department of Recreation Sciences and Sport Management meeting with him? Well, there were three specific reasons. First, Dr. McGee and I shared a mutual friend in Dr. Jimmie Grimsley, one of three individuals to whom this book is dedicated. Second, he was a member of the North Carolina Sports Hall of Fame and served as a very well-respected college football official. Third, he is a proud 1965 ECU alumnus.[1] Because of our mutual friend, my research interest within sport officiating, and my position as a recipient of a College of Health and Human Performance professorship (Dr. Leroy T. Walker Professorship), I was grateful to have the opportunity to meet with Dr. McGee.

I had the pleasure of working with Dr. Jimmie Grimsley when I first arrived at ECU. Grimsley used to share stories about his friend who was a big-time college football official and university president. I would learn that McGee, that friend, and Grimsley met during their sophomore year in college in the late 1960s. Along with another friend, Charles Jenkins, they would become lifelong friends who all earned doctorate degrees and had successful careers in higher education.[2] What was unique about Dr. McGee was that he started officiating intramural games while he was a college student and never stopped. In fact, Dr. McGee officiated more than 400 major college football games in thirty-six years, including the Orange Bowl, two Rose Bowls, the Army-Navy game twice and three games that determined the national champion. Probably most impressive to me was that for sixteen of those officiating years, he was President of Wingate University!

I think it is safe to say that he is the only university president to have served simultaneously in both roles. Needless to say, I think he will be the only one to ever serve in both capacities at such a high level. In our conversation, Dr. McGee shared how in 1992, when he was asked to serve as President of Wingate, he also was serving as a football official for a conference and had been doing that for some time. As McGee told the *New York Times* in 2008, "When I was talking about the job here, I said, 'I officiate football. I would like to continue to do that, but if it becomes an issue at Wingate, obviously, I'll quit.' They said, 'By all means, go ahead and do it, and we'll see how it works out.' Once we started getting that publicity, they said, 'Maybe you ought to keep doing that a little while longer.'"[3]

The publicity for Wingate was welcomed, and McGee continued in the dual role of university president and college football official for sixteen years. "Ending his career with a bang in his final game on Jan. 8, 2009, Dr. McGee was on the field for the BCS National Championship between No. 1 Oklahoma and No. 2 Florida. He watched as Tim Tebow led the Gators to a national title over fellow Heisman winner Sam Bradford and the Sooners, the program's second championship in three seasons."[4] In our conversation, I asked him if he missed officiating, and his response inspired this "What's Next?" chapter. It was clear he really understood that there was something powerful about continuing to be in a sport setting. McGee said, "There is a sisterhood and a brotherhood that sport has provided to so many. Sport has given me so much. I do miss it." With that, I knew that a call to action and the "What's Next?" was needed. Sport, too, has given me so much, and I have a sense of responsibility to make sure it does the same for others.

From the Humble Beginnings to the Olympic Stage - Dr. Leroy T. Walker

"How did this child who, so long ago, played stickball in the streets near the site of the Olympic Stadium get to march in this parade of the world? The distance from Walker's boyhood home on Parsons Street to that stadium in Atlanta is two miles. On the way there, his story covered six continents, seventy-eight years, and millions of dreams." [5] Also, in that conversation with McGee, in which I realized I had a final chapter and a call to action to write, I had the opportunity to ask Dr. McGee about Dr. Leroy T. Walker. A few months prior to our conversation, I was grateful and honored to be named the Dr. Leroy T. Walker Distinguished Professor. This professorship was named for the late Dr. Walker, who had a remarkable and storied career in sport and education. And because of their mutual passion for sport and both serving as college presidents in North Carolina, McGee knew Walker and I hoped could shed light on how the professorship in his honor was started. To my knowledge Walker had no formal ties to East Carolina, and I wanted to understand and learn more about Dr. Walker's legacy and the history behind the professorship.

Dr. Leroy T. Walker was the grandson of slaves, and the first in his family to attend college. After graduating in 1940 from Benedict College, Walker went on to earn a master's degree from Columbia University. Walker then served as both the football and basketball coach at North Carolina College (now North Carolina Central University), where he also developed the college's first track team. He would continue his education while coaching and earn a Ph.D. in exercise physiology and biomechanics from New York University in 1957.[6] Two short years later, Dr. Walker would have the opportunity to serve as a summer educational specialist in the U.S. Department of State's Cultural Exchange Program. This would take him to Ethiopia, Israel, Syria and Lebanon. "While working in Ethiopia, the small, African country that still was developing its Olympic involvement, officials noticed on his visa that Walker also was a track coach, and they asked him to work with some of their athletes. When he went to Israel, the same thing happened. By the next summer, both countries asked that Walker return for another stint, though it was not generally permitted by the State Department. He returned and was named head track coach for both countries, though that task may not be as daunting as it sounds."[7]

This propelled Walker's international coaching career. Ethiopia sent a total of nine people to the 1960 Rome Summer Olympic Games, while Israel sent twenty-three. He then served as consultant for the Trinidad and Tobago Olympic team during 1964 Tokyo Summer Olympic Games, the Jamaica teams during the 1968 Mexico City Summer Olympic Games, and the Kenya team during the 1972 Munich Summer Olympic Games. "Finally, after about five countries, America felt I had done enough internships," Walker quipped.[8] At the 1976 Montreal Summer Olympic Games, Walker made history as the first black coach of an American Olympic team.[9]

Dr. Walker went on to become one of the most decorated track coaches in the world and played a vital role in preparing and teaching many athletes to be the best they could be. Importantly, he always recognized the whole person, not just the athlete, and took that holistic approach into coaching. One of many former track stars that Dr. Walker coached, Edwin Roberts, stated: "What made him special as a coach is that he would take the initiative with his athletes to work with them not only as a coach but to guide them to be good citizens of the community and of their country. His emphasis was education. It was also that if you wanted to succeed in life, you had to put out 100 percent."[10]

It was that philosophy and mentality that landed Dr. Walker in University of North Carolina system president William C. Friday's office in 1983. Friday had led the restructuring of the entire UNC system, which included North Carolina Central University (commonly known as NC Central), in the early 1970s. Now a decade later, Friday was profoundly troubled about the future direction of NC Central, which many felt had an unstable administration with unmistakable dissension among faculty and trustees of the university. NC Central's academic Dean, Dr. Leonard Robinson, requested that meeting with Friday and invited Dr. Walker. Walker did not go to that meeting looking for a job offer to be the next chancellor. Rather Friday recalled, "For about forty-five minutes LeRoy took the lead in outlining, in clear detail, what was wrong with the institution" with what Friday called "an uncommon sense of devotion and concern."[11] (p.166)

Friday quickly knew he had found the next chancellor of NC Central University in Dr. Walker, and he called him after that meeting to offer him the job. While Friday was confident in his choice, there was a question. "But how would the academic community accept an untraditional selection for chancellor, even an interim chancellor, who came from the ranks of coaching and physical education? A 'jock,' as it were, taking the reins of a major university. It was a super choice. Friday recounted: 'What we had was a man who was widely known in the academic world, had a good relationship in the community, could pull people together, and everyone on campus trusted him.'"[12] (p.167) Walker went on to serve at NC Central from 1983 to 1986. The theme and slogan Chancellor Walker set for his administration and the upcoming diamond/seventy-fifth anniversary of the university was "Excellence Without Excuse: A Shared Responsibility."[13]

Walker became TAC (forerunner to United States Track and Field Association) president from 1984-88 and later served as senior vice president for sport of the Atlanta Committee for the Olympic Games. He would go on to become the first African American President of the U.S. Olympic Committee from 1992 to 1996. While carrying out his duties as United States Olympic Committee president and CEO, Walker continued to occupy an office on the NC Central's campus, where he was chancellor emeritus.[14] He famously led a 10,000-member group of the most talented athletes in the world in the final Olympic torch run to open the 1996 Summer Olympics Games in Atlanta. His goal was to ensure that American citizens felt ownership in the program, saying, "*We ought to keep them informed. We ought to let them know what the Olympic movement is all about and what's happening to the dollars that they give.*"[15] In 1996, Walker was named the first President Emeritus of the United States Olympic Committee.[16]

When I asked Dr. McGee why he thought Dr. Walker, with clear ties to NC Central and the Raleigh-Durham area, decided on East Carolina for a performance center and professorships, McGee's response was simple: "He cared." Walker's passion to help athletes was evident in the establishment of the Human Performance Center and three professorships that bear his name at East

Carolina. Former ECU Chancellor Richard Eakin said, "The Walker Center, thanks to our outstanding faculty in the School of Health and Human Performance and to the leadership of Dr. LeRoy Walker, has clearly demonstrated to the IOC (International Olympic Committee) the value of the services we provide to the world's athletes, coaches and sports administrators."[17] It was noticeable that Dr. Walker cared, and he proved that the theme he carried as the chancellor at NC Central decades prior, *Excellence Without Excuse: A Shared Responsibility*, is still fitting today.

Community of Practice - Excellence Without Excuse: A Shared Responsibility

What I realized, as I learned more about Dr. McGee and Dr. Walker, is that I am part of a community of practice. "Communities of practice are groups of people who share a concern or a passion for something they do and learn how to do it better as they interact regularly."[18] If you have completed this book, whether for enjoyment or because it was required reading for a course, I want to encourage you to consider yourself now part of a community of practice. The Sport and Sense of Community theory is based on extensive interviews and focus groups, stories, information, and knowledge all from people, who now like you, have either observed, witnessed, been a part of, or at least read about the power of sport to create community. What is next? My hope is that you will take the ideas outlined in this book and put them into practice—recognizing, without excuse, that sport can make a difference, and that we all have a shared responsibility to see it happen. When and if you do so, I hope this text provides you with a source of encouragement and support on *how* to create sport settings that can better society and improve individual's lives.

Through acknowledging the power of environments that promote a Common Interest, Administrative Consideration, Leadership Opportunities, Social Spaces, and Equity in Administrative Decision, sport can be a powerful tool. The societal reports and trends are well-defined, stating that we need to start building stronger communities and places for individuals to belong. Sport provides an opportunity, and we all have an opportunity and shared responsibility. Sport is not just a trivial activity; it is a powerful tool that can improve individuals' lives and have a tremendous impact on society. It is now up to each one of us to stay the course as we promote sport and its community-building potential to create a "better together" society for all.

Conclusion

The enduring impact of sport on personal and professional lives, glimpsed through the stories of Dr. Jerry McGee and Dr. Leroy T. Walker, exemplifies how dedication to sport and education can create lasting legacies and foster a sense of community. Dr. McGee's dual role as a university president and college football official, along with Dr. Walker's groundbreaking achievements in athletics and education, highlight the powerful synergy between leadership, sport, and community building. There is a collective responsibility to continue to leverage sport as a tool for societal improvement. By embracing Walker's "Excellence Without Excuse: A Shared Responsibility" philosophy, everyone can actively participate in creating more inclusive and supportive environments through sport. This call to action underscores the potential of sport to not only enhance individual lives but also to strengthen communities, ultimately contributing to a more cohesive and better society for all.

Discussion and Reflection Questions

1. Consider the challenges Dr. McGee faced in balancing his roles as a university president and a college football official. Now consider the challenges Dr. Walker faced with having a coaching and physical education background when he was offered the NCCU chancellor position. How do you think both Dr. McGee and Walker overcame the sport stigma (i.e., dumb jock stereotypes) to become successful university leaders at their respective universities? What career strategies can you adopt from Dr. McGee and Dr. Walker's experiences?
2. Both Dr. McGee and Dr. Walker understood the importance of education alongside athletic achievement. The U.S. is the one of the only nations in the world that has this emphasis and expectation of higher education institutions. Should this holistic approach continue? Why or why not?
3. What common qualities do you think made Dr. McGee and Dr. Walker effective leaders? How can these qualities be applied in your own life or in the organizations you are part of?
4. How do you interpret the slogan "Excellence Without Excuse: A Shared Responsibility"? Discuss how this philosophy can be applied in your future work.

5. Reflect on the concept of a community of practice as described in the chapter. How does being part of such a community influence individual and collective growth? Can you identify a community of practice you belong to?
6. The chapter ends with a call to action to promote sport as a means of community building. What steps can you take to contribute to this goal in your own community or professional field?

Acknowledgments

Writing this book has been a venture that would not have been possible without the support and enthusiasm of so many.

First and foremost, I would like to acknowledge my audience of One who has blessed me with opportunities, opened doors, put the desire to pursue this book on my heart, and most importantly, perfectly placed so many people in my path to ensure it was a challenge full of adventure (Proverbs 3:5-6).

To my family, who instilled in me a grittiness, curiosity, and work ethic to sustain me in any challenge or trial, you have always been my greatest pundits and supporters. This project would not have been nearly as enjoyable without your, "Wait, what are you doing? And where are you going now?" inquiries with a smile.

To my wise counsel, your guidance and wisdom have been a constant source of light and laughs. I am convinced that I have some of the best, most insightful friends and encouragers that anyone could ask for. You help me navigate the twists and turns of this project, my career, and my life and faith with ease, humor, and a sense of optimism that I am grateful to have in my corner.

I am deeply grateful to my friend turned editor, Bethany Bradsher, whose guidance and reassurance were invaluable in shaping this book. Your expertise, patience, and formidable pickleball play have made this a much more enjoyable process. It is more than fitting that we met through FiA, whose tagline is better together. We endured, with our FiA ENC community, many early morning runs in 2021, which only reinforced and nudged this project along.

I also would like to acknowledge the contributions of my research collaborators, ECU colleagues, and numerous sport management researchers and educators, whose dedication and knowledge were crucial in bringing this book to life. Because of you, I have a community of scholars and practitioners that

I can always turn to and be supported by. Your hard work and insights have been invaluable. I would especially like to thank Drs. Emily Sparvero, Andrea Bueñano, Marlene Dixon, Todd Fraley, Kindal Shores, and Jacob Tingle for graciously providing reviewer feedback and lending their expertise. I am grateful for your insights, ideas, and perspective. I would also like to thank Ronnie Woodward, Sharon Justice, and Kandy Houmard for proofreading the final draft. Each of you have made me a better researcher, writer, and teacher.

To all my former students and study participants, thank you for your willingness to share your experiences. Whether it was in a classroom discussion or as a research participant, your contributions have been essential to this work.

A special thank you to my fellow pub runners and pickleball enthusiasts, who provided a much-needed balance of work and play. Your camaraderie and shared moments of joy have been a source of inspiration.

To ECU's College of Health and Human Performance, UNC Press, and ECU's Office of Research, Economic Development and Engagement, thank you for your support of this research, the ECU Sport & Community Development Lab, and throughout the publishing process.

To my readers, thank you for taking the time to read this book. I hope we can make an impact on sport and in many lives through building better and healthier communities.

Lastly, when I think about community building and the warm welcome that I received in eastern North Carolina in 2010, three ECU legends come to mind that I want to acknowledge. All were once employed within ECU's Health and Human Performance college, and I was blessed to call them colleagues and friends. They all taught, loved students, and played a key role in the Greenville, NC sport scene. Mention any one of their names to someone who has been in Greenville for a while, and a smile will come across their face. This book is dedicated to the memory of Dr. Nelson "Coop" Cooper, Dr. Jimmie Grimsley, and Mrs. Eva Price.

Coop made me feel welcomed at ECU the very first day I ever set foot on campus. "If I get to work with people like him, ECU is where I want to be," I thought back then. After starting at ECU, our paths would occasionally cross, and we would talk about how we needed to work together on something and that our two programs (sport management and recreation management) needed to collaborate more. I did not get to work closely alongside Coop, except for a paper on F3 ENC, an organization he helped found. But I did get to work alongside two others like him in the department then known as exercise and sport science. Similarly to Coop, both Jimmie Grimsley and Eva

Price also welcomed me to Greenville, instantly made me feel at home in my new job, and were beloved by students. Both Jimmie and Eva worked within the physical education concentration and were extremely well connected and loved in the Greenville sport community. When I think about leaders who have built community via sport well and inspired others, I am overcome with gratefulness to have called each of them a friend. This book is dedicated to their memory and the legacy they each left behind in the students that they impacted.

Dr. Nelson "Coop" Cooper (1967–2017)

Nelson Cooper was a full-time instructor from 1995-2000 in the Department of Recreation and Leisure Studies in the College of Health and Human Performance. After earning his PhD, he returned in 2003 as an associate professor. Nelson's legacy is in the many recreation professionals he trained at ECU, and his passion for promoting leadership through sport was instrumental in establishing F3 (Fitness, Fellowship, and Faith) in eastern North Carolina. He was the loving father of two (Jefferson and Bailey – class of 2019 and 2020), husband to Mary Ann, and beloved instructor to many ECU students when he passed away at age fifty on May 18, 2017.

Dr. Jimmie Grimsley (1944–2015)

Jimmie initially attended East Carolina University on a football scholarship, where he received both his undergraduate and graduate degrees from East Carolina before earning his Doctorate in Education. His entire career was spent at East Carolina University, beginning as a Graduate Assistant and culminating as an Associate Professor Emeritus in the College of Health and Human Performance. Early in his tenure at ECU, he served as a tennis coach and soccer coach and later worked with future physical education teachers. Jimmie also was very active in the Greenville sport community, with stints on the Greenville Babe Ruth Board of Directors, the Greenville Little League Board of Directors, J.H. Rose Athletic Foundation, and the Bradford Creek Golf Advisory Committee and as the founder of the Pitt-Greenville Hot Stove Baseball League. He served as the official clock operator for both Pirate football and basketball games for over forty years. Dr. Jimmie Grimsley, ECU alumnus and faculty emeritus, passed away on January 28, 2015.

Eva Price (1978–2013)

Eva Price was a full-time teaching instructor from 2005-2013 in the Department of Exercise and Sport Sciences (now Kinesiology) in the College of Health and Human Performance. She was a well-known beloved instructor at Rose's Gymnastics and is credited with starting ECU's Homeschool Physical Education program. Eva's legacy is in the physical education teachers she trained at ECU, and her character and spirit can be seen within the many children she taught in the local community. She was committed to student success, saw the best in people, and had the ability to calm and/or bring great enthusiasm and humor to any situation. She was the loving mother of three (Lilyanna, Willow, and Rivers), wife to ECU assistant track coach David Price, and favorite instructor to numerous ECU students when she passed away on January 1, 2013.

About the Publisher:

Researchers in the ECU Sport & Community Development Lab focus on the use of sport as a platform for achieving positive outcomes. Although sport is an activity that most people have experienced at some point in their life and feel knowledgeable about it, there is limited meaningful, well-informed research regarding the role sport can play in improving life quality and building community. Given its popularity, the use of sport as a tool for positive community level impact remains high. The SCDL has specialized in research and creating experiences that will promote community building, economic development, and health outcomes.

The ECU Sport & Community Development Lab is committed to continuing to fostering community through sport initiatives. To support these endeavors and partner with us, please consider donating at http://give.ecu.edu/SCDLab or following us on Instagram (@ecuscdl). Together, let's build a better society and strengthen our communities through sport.

REFERENCES

2009 Special Olympics World Winter Games Scarf Project, 2014. https://www.youtube.com/watch?v=ZT5TNtuMtRQ.

Abeza, Gashaw, Norm O'Reilly, Benoit Séguin, and Ornella Nzindukiyimana. "Social Media Scholarship in Sport Management Research: A Critical Review." *Journal of Sport Management*, 2015. https://doi.org/10.1123/jsm.2014-0296.

Adams, J Stacy. "Inequity in Social Exchange." In *Advances in Experimental Social Psychology*, 2:267–99. Elsevier, 1965.

African American Registry. "LeRoy T. Walker, Educator, and Athletic Coach Born." Accessed October 7, 2024. https://aaregistry.org/story/leroy-t-walker-born/.

Altschuler, Sasha. "The Power of Social Responsibility in Sports – Sports Philanthropy Network." Accessed September 3, 2024. https://sportsphilanthropynetwork.org/the-power-of-social-responsibility-in-sports/.

American Psychological Association. "Stress in America 2023: A Nation Recovering from Collective Trauma," 2023. https://www.apa.org/news/press/releases/stress/2023/collective-trauma-recovery.

Aoun, Samar M, Lauren J Breen, Ishta White, Bruce Rumbold, and Allan Kellehear. "What Sources of Bereavement Support Are Perceived Helpful by Bereaved People and Why? Empirical Evidence for the Compassionate Communities Approach." *Palliative Medicine* 32, no. 8 (September 2018): 1378–88. https://doi.org/10.1177/0269216318774995.

Arkell, Stephen. "Examining The Impact of Campus Intramural Sports Participation on Students' Sense of Community Using A Pre-Test Post-Test Design," 2020.

Artavia, David. "Pickleball Is America's Fastest-Growing Sport. Why Is It so Addictive — and Divisive?" Yahoo Life, August 31, 2023. https://www.yahoo.com/lifestyle/pickleball-sport-addictive-divisive-tennis-171700283.html.

Associated Press. "Wearing a Different Hat When Saturday Comes." New York Times (Online). New York, United States: New York Times Company, October 18, 2008. https://www.proquest.com/docview/2221144289/abstract/A9474A856F1446A2PQ/1.

Associated Press Archives, L. A. Times. "Starbucks' Drive-Through Service Attracts the Regulars." Los Angeles Times, December 26, 2005. https://www.latimes.com/archives/la-xpm-2005-dec-26-fi-starbucks26-story.html.

Babiak, Kathy, Brian Mills, Scott Tainsky, and Matthew Juravich. "An Investigation into Professional Athlete Philanthropy: Why Charity Is Part of the Game." *Journal of Sport Management* 26, no. 2 (2012): 159–76.

Babiak, Kathy, and Richard Wolfe. "Determinants of Corporate Social Responsibility in Professional Sport: Internal and External Factors." *Journal of Sport Management* 23, no. 6 (November 2009): 717–42. https://doi.org/10.1123/jsm.23.6.717.

Bacharach, Samuel B. "Organizational Theories: Some Criteria for Evaluation." *The Academy of Management Review* 14, no. 4 (October 1989): 496. https://doi.org/10.2307/258555.

Berg, Brennan K., S. Warner, and Bhibha M. Das. "What about Sport? A Public Health Perspective on Leisure-Time Physical Activity." *Sport Management Review* 18, no. 1 (February 2015): 20–31. https://doi.org/10.1016/j.smr.2014.09.005.

Bergeron, Michael F. "Improving Health through Youth Sports: Is Participation Enough?" *New Directions for Youth Development* 2007, no. 115 (2007): 27–41. https://doi.org/10.1002/yd.221.

Betway Insiders. "Most Popular Colleges for Tailgate Parties." Betway Insider, August 29, 2024. https://blog.betway.com/nfl/most-popular-colleges-for-tailgate-parties/.

Bezboruah, Karabi. "Building and Strengthening Communities: What Works? What Doesn't?" In *Building Community and Family Resilience*, edited by Mike Stout and Amanda W. Harrist, 1–17. Emerging Issues in Family and Individual Resilience. Cham: Springer International Publishing, 2021. https://doi.org/10.1007/978-3-030-49799-6_1.

Bissinger, Harry Gerard. *Friday Night Lights: A Town, a Team and a Dream*. London: Yellow Jersey Pr, 2005.

Bowen, Daniel H, and Collin Hitt. "History and Evidence Show School Sports Help Students Win." *Phi Delta Kappan* 97, no. 8 (2016): 8–12.

Boyle, Kris, Jordan Mower, Tom Robinson, and Clark Callahan. "Virtual Tailgating: A Q-Methodology Analysis of Why Sports Fans Visit Online Sports Forums." *Journal of Sports Media* 14, no. 1 (2019): 137–54.

Bradsher, Bethany. *Never Take This for Granted*. Whitecaps Media, 2024.

Bright, Vanessa, Stacy Warner, and Claire Zvosec. "Refereeing as a Postathletic Career Option." *Journal of Sport Management* 36, no. 6 (November 1, 2022): 548–58. https://doi.org/10.1123/jsm.2021-0268.

Brown, Brené. *Dare to Lead: Brave Work, Tough Conversations, Whole Hearts*. New York: Random House, 2018.

Buenaño, Andrea L., and Stacy Warner. "Girls With Game: Sport and Community Development Strategies." *Case Studies in Sport Management* 12, no. S1 (January 1, 2023): S18–21. https://doi.org/10.1123/cssm.2022-0027.

Burns, Sean. "Expanding Esports in Higher Ed: Benefits and Guidance for New Esports Programs." EDUCAUSE. Accessed September 11, 2024. https://www.educause.edu/ecar/research-publications/2021/expanding-esports-in-higher-ed-benefits-and-guidance-for-new-esports-programs/introduction-and-key-findings.

Byers, Terri, and Trevor Slack. "Strategic Decision-Making in Small Businesses Within The Leisure Industry." *Journal of Leisure Research* 33, no. 2 (June 2001): 121–36. https://doi.org/10.1080/00222216.2001.11949934.

Cacciatore, Joanne, Kara Thieleman, Ruth Fretts, and Lori Barnes Jackson. "What Is Good Grief Support? Exploring the Actors and Actions in Social Support after Traumatic Grief." Edited by Manuel Fernández-Alcántara. *PLOS ONE* 16, no. 5 (May 27, 2021): e0252324. https://doi.org/10.1371/journal.pone.0252324.

Canavesi, Alice, and Eliana Minelli. "Servant Leadership and Employee Engagement: A Qualitative Study." *Employee Responsibilities and Rights Journal* 34, no. 4 (December 2022): 413–35. https://doi.org/10.1007/s10672-021-09389-9.

Carson, Jay B, Paul E Tesluk, and Jennifer A Marrone. "Shared Leadership in Teams: An Investigation of Antecedent Conditions and Performance." *Academy of Management Journal* 50, no. 5 (2007): 1217–34.

Carter, Beth. "Tailgate Parties Are a 'Powerful Impulse' and a Microcosm of Society." *Wired*. Accessed September 6, 2024. https://www.wired.com/2012/09/anthropology-of-tailgating/.

Chalip, L. C. "Toward a Distinctive Sport Management Discipline." *Journal of Sport Management* 20 (2006): 1–21.

Chalip, Laurence. "Towards Social Leverage of Sport Events." *Journal of Sport & Tourism* 11, no. 2 (May 2006): 109–27. https://doi.org/10.1080/14775080601155126.

Chu, Donald. *The Character of American Higher Education and Intercollegiate Sport*. ERIC, 1989.

Cianfrone, Beth, and S. Warner. "Developing Sport Communities via Social Media: A Conceptual Framework." *International Journal of Sport Management* 19 (2018): 44–56.

Clark, Sarah J, Susan J Woolford, Sara L Schultz, and Acham Gebremariam. "C.S. Mott Children's Hospital National Poll on Children's Health," n.d.

Coakley, Jay. *Sports in Society: Issues and Controversies*. 10th ed. New York: McGraw-Hill, 2008.

———. *Sports in Society: Issues and Controversies*. New York: McGraw-Hill Education, 2015.

———. *Sports in Society: Issues and Controversies*. 13th ed. New York: McGraw-Hill Education, 2021.

Colquitt, Jason A., Donald E. Conlon, Michael J. Wesson, Christopher O. L. H. Porter, and K. Yee Ng. "Justice at the Millennium: A Meta-Analytic Review of 25 Years of Organizational Justice Research." *Journal of Applied Psychology* 86, no. 3 (2001): 425–45. https://doi.org/10.1037/0021-9010.86.3.425.

Cooper, Bailey. "Sustainable Success: Motives and Small-Scale Charity Sport Events," 2019. https://thescholarship.ecu.edu/server/api/core/bitstreams/13e5be20-0770-4541-85e8-d25bbfe0329f/content.

CoopStrong. "Home," October 9, 2024. https://www.coopstrong.org.
Cunningham, George B., J. Fink, and A. Doherty, eds. *Routledge Handbook of Theory in Sport Management*. Milton Park, Abingdon, Oxon ; New York, NY: Routledge, 2015.
Dana-Farber Cancer Institute. "Boston Red Sox." Accessed September 3, 2024. http://www.jimmyfund.org/about-us/boston-red-sox/.
Deci, Edward L, and Richard M Ryan. "The" What" and" Why" of Goal Pursuits: Human Needs and the Self-Determination of Behavior." *Psychological Inquiry* 11, no. 4 (2000): 227–68.
Dekoch, Robert J., and Phillip G. Clampitt. *Leading with Care in a Tough World: Beyond Servant Leadership*. Garden City, New York: Rodin Books, 2022.
Delaney, Tim. "The Social Aspects of Sports Tailgating." *The New York Sociologist* 3 (2008): 1–10.
Demirel, Duygu Harmandar, and Ibrahim Yildiran. "The Philosophy of Physical Education and Sport from Ancient Times to the Enlightenment." *European Journal of Educational Research* 2, no. 4 (2013): 191–202.
Dixon, Marlene A, and Stacy Warner. "Employee Satisfaction in Sport: Development of a Multi-Dimensional Model in Coaching." *Journal of Sport Management* 24, no. 2 (2010): 139–68.
Dixon, Marlene A, Stacy Warner, and Christine M Habeeb. "Athlete Concerns: What Can Coaches Do?" *Journal of Issues in Intercollegiate Athletics* 15 (2022): 314–28.
Dixon, Marlene, Stacy Warner, and Jennifer Bruening. "More than Just Letting Them Play: Parental Influence on Women's Lifetime Sport Involvement." *Sociology of Sport Journal* 25 (2008): 538–59.
Dorsch, Travis E., Alan L. Smith, Jordan A. Blazo, Jay Coakley, Jean Côté, Christopher R. D. Wagstaff, Stacy Warner, and Michael Q. King. "Toward an Integrated Understanding of the Youth Sport System." *Research Quarterly for Exercise and Sport*, September 22, 2020, 1–15. https://doi.org/10.1080/02701367.2020.1810847.
Dorsch, Travis E., Alan L. Smith, and Meghan H. McDonough. "Early Socialization of Parents through Organized Youth Sport." *Sport, Exercise, and Performance Psychology* 4, no. 1 (2015): 3–18. https://doi.org/10.1037/spy0000021.
"East Carolina University – UNC System." Accessed July 1, 2024. https://www.northcarolina.edu/institution/east-carolina-university/.
ECU College of Health & Human Performance. "HHP Alumnus Pledges $333,000 to Establish First Endowed Distinguished Professorship." *HHP Visions: College of Health & Human Performance Alumni and Friends Newsletter*, November 4, 2010, Fall 2010 edition. https://issuu.com/chhp/docs/hhp_newsletter_fall_2010.

ECU News Services. "IOC Selects ECU's Walker Center." News Services, December 15, 1998. https://news.ecu.edu/1998/12/15/ioc-selects-ecus-walker-center/.

Edelmann, Charlotte M., Filip Boen, and Katrien Fransen. "The Power of Empowerment: Predictors and Benefits of Shared Leadership in Organizations." *Frontiers in Psychology* 11 (November 19, 2020): 582894. https://doi.org/10.3389/fpsyg.2020.582894.

Edmonds, Charlotte. "What Is the NFL's Rooney Rule?" *NBC Sports Philadelphia* (blog), January 19, 2024. https://www.nbcsportsphiladelphia.com/nfl/nfl-rooney-rule-explained/559718/.

Eitzen, D. Stanley. *Fair and Foul: Beyond the Myths and Paradoxes of Sport*. Lanham, Md: Rowman & Littlefield Publishers, 2006.

Ellis, Kevin, and Natalie Bradin. "Trailblazers 2024: The Seventh Annual Roster of under-40 N.C. Leaders Making Dynamic Local Impacts." *Business North Carolina*, October 1, 2024. https://businessnc.com/trailblazers-2024-the-sixth-annual-roster-of-under-40-n-c-leaders-making-dynamic-local-impacts/.

Elon University. "Elon University Campus Recreation Mission Statement." Accessed June 18, 2024. https://www.elon.edu/u/campus-recreation-wellness/about-us/.

Evolution of the Black Quarterback - Season 1, Episode 1, Prime Video. Vol. 1. The Beginning. Amazon Studios, 2024. https://www.amazon.com/Evolution-Black-Quarterback-Season-1/dp/B0D7S7XTKX.

"F3 Nation," 2024. f3nation.com.

Fairley, S., and B. Tyler. "Bringing Baseball to the Big Screen: Building Sense of Community Outside of the Ballpark." *Journal of Sport Management* 26 (2012): 258–70.

FiA Nation. "About FiA." Accessed September 1, 2024. https://fianation.com/about-fia/.

Fields, Lisa. "Why Loneliness Affects Young People More Often Than Older Adults." Cedars-Sinai. Accessed September 18, 2024. https://www.cedars-sinai.org/blog/why-loneliness-affects-young-people.html.

Fink, J. "Theory Development in Sport Management: My Experiences and Other Considerations." *Sport Management Review* 1 (2013): 17–21.

Flaherty, Colleen. "Faculty: 'Gatekeepers' of Student Mental Health?" Inside Higher Ed. Accessed August 21, 2024. https://www.insidehighered.com/news/2021/04/08/faculty-gatekeepers-student-mental-health.

Flannery, Mary Ellen. "The Mental Health Crisis Among Faculty and College Staff | NEA," March 7, 2024. https://www.nea.org/nea-today/all-news-articles/mental-health-crisis-among-faculty-and-college-staff.

Fry, Hayden, and George Wine. *Hayden Fry: A High Porch Picnic*. Champaign, IL: Sports Pub, 1999.
Gaddy, Charles. *An Olympic Journey: The Saga of an American Hero: LeRoy T. Walker*. Griffin Publishing Group, 1998.
Gaines, Cork. "A Shockingly Small Amount Of Money From Pink NFL Merchandise Sales Goes To Breast Cancer Research." Business Insider. Accessed September 4, 2024. https://www.businessinsider.com/small-amount-of-money-from-pink-nfl-merchandise-goes-to-breast-cancer-research-2013-10.
Gasparini, William. "Council of Europe and Sport: Origin and Circulation of a European Sporting Model | Digital Encyclopedia of European History," June 22, 2020. https://ehne.fr/en/encyclopedia/themes/material-civilization/european-sports-circulations/council-europe-and-sport-origin-and-circulation-a-european-sporting-model.
Greenville-Pitt County Chamber of Commerce. "Chamber Recognizes 2022 Small Business Leader of the Year," May 23, 2023. https://www.greenvillenc.org/news/single-news-page/?no_cache=1&tx_news_pi1%5Bnews%5D=320&tx_news_pi1%5Bcontroller%5D=News&tx_news_pi1%5Baction%5D=detail&cHash=d18acb74d922f5a1c4e953dad038145c.
Grobeck, Joe. "Iowa Pink Locker Room: How Hayden Fry Gave His Team an Edge." Fan Buzz. Accessed September 4, 2024. https://fanbuzz.com/college-football/big-ten/iowa-pink-locker-rooms/.
Guba, Egon G. "Reviewed Work(s): Big School, Small School by Roger G. Barker and Paul V. Gump." *The School Review* 74, no. 2 (1966): 241–46.
Gustafsson, H., S. S. Sagar, and A. Stenling. "Fear of Failure, Psychological Stress, and Burnout among Adolescent Athletes Competing in High Level Sport." *Scandinavian Journal of Medicine & Science in Sports* 27, no. 12 (December 2017): 2091–2102. https://doi.org/10.1111/sms.12797.
Habeeb, Christine, Stacy Warner, and David Walsh. "Managing Mental Health: Athlete Help-Seeking." *Sport Management Review* 25, no. 5 (October 20, 2022): 871–91. https://doi.org/10.1080/14413523.2021.2018836.
Harter, Jim. "In New Workplace, U.S. Employee Engagement Stagnates." Gallup.com, January 23, 2024. https://www.gallup.com/workplace/608675/new-workplace-employee-engagement-stagnates.aspx.
Hayhurst, Chris. "Collegiate Esports Programs Provide Academic Pathways." Ed Tech Magazine. Technology Solutions That Drive Education, August 26, 2022. https://edtechmagazine.com/higher/article/2022/08/collegiate-esports-programs-provide-academic-pathways.
Heinrich, Katie M, Taran Carlisle, Ainslie Kehler, and Sarah J Cosgrove. "Mapping Coaches' Views of Participation in CrossFit to the Integrated Theory of Health Behavior Change and Sense of Community." *Family & Community Health* 40, no. 1 (2017): 24.

Heinze, Kathryn L, Sara Soderstrom, and Jennifer Zdroik. "Toward Strategic and Authentic Corporate Social Responsibility in Professional Sport: A Case Study of the Detroit Lions." *Journal of Sport Management* 28, no. 6 (2014): 672–86.

Henderson, Karla A. "A Paradox of Sport Management and Physical Activity Interventions." *Sport Management Review* 12, no. 2 (May 2009): 57–65. https://doi.org/10.1016/j.smr.2008.12.004.

Huang, Alison R., David L. Roth, Tom Cidav, Shang-En Chung, Halima Amjad, Roland J. Thorpe, Cynthia M. Boyd, and Thomas K. M. Cudjoe. "Social Isolation and 9-Year Dementia Risk in Community-Dwelling Medicare Beneficiaries in the United States." *Journal of the American Geriatrics Society* 71, no. 3 (March 2023): 765–73. https://doi.org/10.1111/jgs.18140.

Huang, Kelly, and Marlene A Dixon. "Examining the Financial Impact of Alcohol Sales on Football Game Days: A Case Study of a Major Football Program." *Journal of Sport Management* 27, no. 3 (2013): 207–16.

Huber, Dave. "Color the Opposing Team's Locker Pink and … Risk a Lawsuit?" The College Fix, August 30, 2014. https://www.thecollegefix.com/color-the-opposing-teams-locker-pink-and-risk-a-lawsuit/.

Hums, Mary A., and Packianathan Chelladurai. "Distributive Justice in Intercollegiate Athletics: The Views of NCAA Coaches and Administrators." *Journal of Sport Management* 8, no. 3 (September 1994): 200–217. https://doi.org/10.1123/jsm.8.3.200.

Igbokwe, Nick. "What Is the Rooney Rule? How Effective Has It Been since Its NFL Inception?" Accessed September 2, 2024. https://www.sportskeeda.com/nfl/news-what-rooney-rule-how-effective-since-nfl-inception.

Imbrogno, Chris, Brianna L Newland, and Stacy Warner. "The Role of Community in Athlete Transgressive Behavior." *Journal of Issues in Intercollegiate Athletics* 14 (2021): 285–303.

Inoue, Yuhei, Brennan K. Berg, and Packianathan Chelladurai. "Spectator Sport and Population Health: A Scoping Study." *Journal of Sport Management* 29, no. 6 (November 1, 2015): 705–25. https://doi.org/10.1123/JSM.2014-0283.

Jewell, Jessica. "Greenville Named Sportiest City in the U.S." *WNCT* (blog), July 15, 2016. https://www.wnct.com/news/greenville-named-sportiest-city-in-the-u-s/.

Jia, Runyuan, Juan Antonio Sánchez-Sáez, and Francisco Segado Segado. "The Impact of the China Open 500 Event on Sense of Community: Comparisons of Volunteers' Pre- and Post-Event Perceptions." *Sustainability* 15, no. 8 (April 12, 2023): 6547. https://doi.org/10.3390/su15086547.

Kannan, Viji Diane, and Peter J. Veazie. "US Trends in Social Isolation, Social Engagement, and Companionship – Nationally and by Age, Sex, Race/Ethnicity, Family Income, and Work Hours, 2003-2020." *SSM - Population Health* 21 (March 2023): 101331. https://doi.org/10.1016/j.ssmph.2022.101331.

Kaplan, Hecker, & Fink, LLP. "KHF Gender Equity Review Phase I Report," August 2, 2021. https://kaplanhecker.app.box.com/s/6fpd51gxk9ki78f8vbhqcqhob00950xq.

Katz, Matthew, and Bob Heere. "Leaders and Followers: An Exploration of the Notion of Scale-Free Networks within a New Brand Community." *Journal of Sport Management* 27, no. 4 (2013): 271–87.

KC Crew. "Inclusion." KC Crew Sports and Events. Accessed October 5, 2024. https://kccrew.com/leagues/inclusion/.

———. "Leagues - Kansas League Sports Event | KC Crew." KC Crew Sports and Events, October 4, 2024. https://kccrew.com/leagues/.

Kellett, Pamm, and David Shilbury. "Umpire Participation: Is Abuse Really the Issue?" *Sport Management Review* 10, no. 3 (September 1, 2007): 209–29. https://doi.org/10.1016/S1441-3523(07)70012-8.

Kenney, Dan. "A Friend of a Friend-Jimmy Grimsley and Charles Jenkins -January 29." *Coach4aday* (blog), January 29, 2015. https://coach4aday.wordpress.com/2015/01/29/a-friend-of-a-friend-jimmy-grimsley-and-charles-jenkins-january-29/.

Kerwin, Shannon, Stacy Warner, Matthew Walker, and Julie Stevens. "Exploring Sense of Community among Small-Scale Sport Event Volunteers." *European Sport Management Quarterly* 15, no. 1 (January 2015): 77–92. https://doi.org/10.1080/16184742.2014.996581.

———. "Exploring Sense of Community among Small-Scale Sport Event Volunteers." *European Sport Management Quarterly* 15, no. 1 (January 2015): 77–92. https://doi.org/10.1080/16184742.2014.996581.

Khanam, Kazi Zainab, Gautam Srivastava, and Vijay Mago. "The Homophily Principle in Social Network Analysis: A Survey." *Multimedia Tools and Applications* 82, no. 6 (March 2023): 8811–54. https://doi.org/10.1007/s11042-021-11857-1.

Kihl, Lisa, Kathy Babiak, and Scott Tainsky. "Evaluating the Implementation of a Professional Sport Team's Corporate Community Involvement Initiative." *Journal of Sport Management* 28, no. 3 (May 2014): 324–37. https://doi.org/10.1123/jsm.2012-0258.

Kim, Amy Chan Hyung, James Du, and Jeffrey James. "A Social Epidemiological Perspective on Local Tennis League Participation: A Multigroup Moderated-Mediation Structural Analysis Using PLS-SEM." *International Journal of Sports Marketing and Sponsorship* 23, no. 2 (April 5, 2022): 437–61. https://doi.org/10.1108/IJSMS-02-2021-0046.

Kim, Minjung, Han Soo Kim, Andre Simmond, and Stacy Warner. "Strengthening Referees' Psychological Well-Being through Engagement and Authenticity." *Sport Management Review* 25, no. 2 (March 15, 2022): 254–74. https://doi.org/10.1080/14413523.2021.1930952.

Klein, Christopher. "Tailgating: How the Pre-Game Tradition Can Be Traced to Ancient Times." HISTORY, June 1, 2023. https://www.history.com/news/tailgating-history-football-game-traditions-rituals.

Komarraju, Meera, Sergey Musulkin, and Gargi Bhattacharya. "Role of Student–Faculty Interactions in Developing College Students' Academic Self-Concept, Motivation, and Achievement." *Journal of College Student Development* 51, no. 3 (2010): 332–42. https://doi.org/10.1353/csd.0.0137.

Kuh, George D. "High-Impact Educational Practices: What They Are, Who Has Access to Them, and Why They Matter." *Peer Review* 14, no. 3 (2012): 29–30.

Kumar, V, and Anita Pansari. "Measuring the Benefits of Employee Engagement." MITSloan Management Review. Accessed September 2, 2024. https://sloanreview.mit.edu/article/measuring-the-benefits-of-employee-engagement/?switch_view=PDF.

Lananna, Michael. "East Carolina's Jungle Rocks The Greenville Regional." *College Baseball, MLB Draft, Prospects - Baseball America* (blog), June 4, 2018. https://www.baseballamerica.com/stories/east-carolinas-jungle-rocks-the-greenville-regional/.

Lee, Audrey. "The State of Referee and Umpire Shortage in Youth Sports." Athletic Business, August 20, 2024. https://www.athleticbusiness.com/operations/personnel/article/15682076/the-state-of-referee-and-umpire-shortage-in-youth-sports.

Leek, Desiree, Jordan A Carlson, Kelli L Cain, Sara Henrichon, Dori Rosenberg, Kevin Patrick, and James F Sallis. "Physical Activity during Youth Sports Practices." *Archives of Pediatrics & Adolescent Medicine* 165, no. 4 (2011): 294–99.

Lewis, Tom. "Legendary Coach Dr. LeRoy Walker Passes Away at 93." USTFCCCA, April 23, 2012. https://www.ustfccca.org/2012/04/featured/legendary-coach-dr-leroy-walker-passes-away-at-93.

Lim, So Youn, Stacy Warner, Marlene Dixon, Brennan Berg, Chiyoung Kim, and Michael Newhouse-Bailey. "Sport Participation across National Contexts: A Multilevel Investigation of Individual and Systemic Influences on Adult Sport Participation." *European Sport Management Quarterly* 11, no. 3 (2011): 197–224.

Linabary, Jasmine. "Working in Diverse Teams." *Small Group Communication*, 2021.

Linder, Jannik. "Crossfit Growth Statistics Statistics: Market Data Report 2024," July 17, 2024. https://gitnux.org/crossfit-growth-statistics/.

Lowrey, James. *Protecting the New Student Athlete: Exploring the Mental Health Outcomes of College Esports Athletes and the Supportive Factors of Collegiate Esports Organizations*. Notre Dame of Maryland University, 2023.

Mahony, Daniel F, Harold A Riemer, James L Breeding, and Mary A Hums. "Organizational Justice in Sport Organizations: Perceptions of College Athletes and Other College Students." *Journal of Sport Management* 20, no. 2 (2006): 159–88.

Malani, Preeti. "Trends in Loneliness Among Older Adults from 2018-2023 | National Poll on Healthy Aging." University of Michigan, March 13, 2023. https://www.healthyagingpoll.org/reports-more/report/trends-loneliness-among-older-adults-2018-2023.

Marot, Michael. "Longtime NCAA Exec Donohoe Hands in Resignation." Lubbock Avalanche-Journal, October 26, 2011. https://www.lubbockonline.com/story/sports/2011/10/27/longtime-ncaa-exec-donohoe-hands-resignation/15202766007/.

Martin, Tiesha, Stacy Warner, and Bhibha Das. "Senior Games: Service-Learning with Older Adults in a Sport Setting." *Sport Management Education Journal* 10, no. 1 (April 1, 2016): 43–53. https://doi.org/10.1123/SMEJ.2015-0004.

Martinez, Eddy. "'Give Them Hope': A Pickleball Program inside a CT Prison Helps Incarcerated People Find Self-Worth." Connecticut Public, August 23, 2024. https://www.ctpublic.org/news/2024-08-23/pickleball-prison-ct-inmates-sports-rehabilitation.

Maslow, Abraham Harold. "A Theory of Human Motivation." *Psychological Review* 50, no. 4 (1943): 370–96.

McClung, Andrew. "Pickleball for Pearsall Carrying on Life and Legacy of Greenville Pickleball Player," June 28, 2024. https://wcti12.com/news/local/pickleball-for-pearsall-carrying-on-life-and-legacy-of-greenville-pickleball-player.

McGinnis, Michael. "Wrexham Red Dragons | How to Build and Grow the Fanbase." Wrexham Red Dragons Building Community. Accessed September 2, 2024. https://www.wrexhamreddragons.com/building-community.

McLeod, Kembrew. "The Case against Kinnick's Pink Locker Room." The Des Moines Register. Accessed September 4, 2024. https://www.desmoinesregister.com/story/opinion/columnists/2014/05/05/argument-against-kinnick-stadiums-pink-locker-room/8718293/.

McPherson, Miller, Lynn Smith-Lovin, and James M Cook. "Birds of a Feather: Homophily in Social Networks." *Annual Review of Sociology* 27, no. 1 (August 2001): 415–44. https://doi.org/10.1146/annurev.soc.27.1.415.

Merschel, Michael. "How Grief Rewires the Brain and Can Affect Health - and What to Do about It." www.heart.org, March 10, 2021. https://www.heart.org/en/news/2021/03/10/how-grief-rewires-the-brain-and-can-affect-health-and-what-to-do-about-it.

Meyersohn, Nathaniel. "A Major Shift at Starbucks Is Changing Its Personality | CNN Business." CNN, July 19, 2024. https://www.cnn.com/2024/07/19/business/starbucks-mobile-orders-third-place/index.html.

Mieleszko, Asia. "From Hang Out To Hurry: Why Starbucks Wants To Redefine 'Third Place,'" August 2, 2024. https://www.strongtowns.org/journal/2024/8/2/from-hang-out-to-hurry-why-starbucks-wants-to-redefine-third-place.

"Mission Statement - Duke University," July 30, 2005. https://goduke.com/sports/2005/6/30/mission-statement.aspx.

Moore, Mariah Rose. "You Belong in the CrossFit Community." CrossFit, February 6, 2023. https://www.crossfit.com/essentials/magic-of-the-crossfit-community.

Morris, Erin Leah. "The Impact of Structural Systems on Perceptions of Legitimacy and the Experiences of Female Hockey Players," 2016.

Moss, Gary. "Gallo Built a Legacy as a 'Friend to All.'" *University Gazette*, January 12, 2015, sec. Athletics. https://www.unc.edu/posts/2015/01/12/gallo-built-a-legacy-as-a-friend-to-all/.

Mueller, Caroline. "CrossFit History: Timeline & How It Started." Sports Foundation, January 13, 2024. https://sportsfoundation.org/crossfit-history/.

Mueller, Lynette. "Special Olympics Joins With Red Heart Yarns To Inspire Handmade Unity," February 23, 2011. https://omegareporting.com/special-olympics/.

Murthy, Vivek H. "Opinion | Surgeon General: Parents Are at Their Wits' End. We Can Do Better." *The New York Times*, August 28, 2024, sec. Opinion. https://www.nytimes.com/2024/08/28/opinion/surgeon-general-stress-parents.html.

Nai, Jared, Jayanth Narayanan, Ivan Hernandez, and Krishna Savani. "People in More Racially Diverse Neighborhoods Are More Prosocial." *Journal of Personality and Social Psychology* 114, no. 4 (April 2018): 497–515. https://doi.org/10.1037/pspa0000103.

Najle, Maxine, and Robert P. Jones. "American Democracy in Crisis: The Fate of Pluralism in a Divided Nation | PRRI," February 19, 2019. https://www.prri.org/research/american-democracy-in-crisis-the-fate-of-pluralism-in-a-divided-nation/.

National Football League. "The Rooney Rule | NFL Football Operations." Accessed July 1, 2024. https://operations.nfl.com/inside-football-ops/inclusion/the-rooney-rule/.

NBA Cares. "About Us." NBA Cares. Accessed September 3, 2024. https://cares.nba.com/about-us/.

Neal, Dan J., and Kim Fromme. "Hook 'em Horns and Heavy Drinking: Alcohol Use and Collegiate Sports." *Addictive Behaviors* 32, no. 11 (November 2007): 2681–93. https://doi.org/10.1016/j.addbeh.2007.06.020.

Niehoff, Karissa. "With Loss of 50,000 Officials, NFHS Organizes Consortium to Find Solutions." Accessed August 14, 2024. https://www.nfhs.org/articles/with-loss-of-50-000-officials-nfhs-organizes-consortium-to-find-solutions.

North Carolina Central University Student Newspaper. "The 75th Anniversary: Recalling a Proud History." *The Campus Echo*, June 14, 1985. https://newspapers.digitalnc.org/lccn/2015236599/1985-06-14/ed-1/seq-7/.

O'Brien, Emma, Stacy M. Warner, and Melanie Sartore-Baldwin. "Eliminating Barriers to Youth Sport in Greenville, North Carolina." *Sport Management Education Journal* 16, no. 1 (April 1, 2022): 86–94. https://doi.org/10.1123/smej.2020-0056.

Obst, Patricia, and Jana Stafurik. "Online We Are All Able Bodied: Online Psychological Sense of Community and Social Support Found through Membership of Disability-Specific Websites Promotes Well-Being for People Living with a Physical Disability." *Journal of Community & Applied Social Psychology* 20, no. 6 (November 2010): 525–31. https://doi.org/10.1002/casp.1067.

O'Connor, Robert. "Feuds and Infighting: A Recent History of Player Mutinies at Major Tournaments." Bleacher Report. Accessed September 29, 2024. https://bleacherreport.com/articles/2649386-feuds-and-infighting-a-recent-history-of-player-mutinies-at-major-tournaments.

Oldenburg, Ray. "Our Vanishing Third Places." *Planning Commissioners Journal* 25, no. 4 (1997): 6–10.

Palmer, C. "Key Themes and Research Agendas in the Sport-Alcohol Nexus." *Journal of Sport & Social Issues* 35, no. 2 (May 1, 2011): 168–85. https://doi.org/10.1177/0193723511406131.

Pardede, Saga, and Velibor Bobo Kovač. "Distinguishing the Need to Belong and Sense of Belongingness: The Relation between Need to Belong and Personal Appraisals under Two Different Belongingness–Conditions." *European Journal of Investigation in Health, Psychology and Education* 13, no. 2 (February 1, 2023): 331–44. https://doi.org/10.3390/ejihpe13020025.

Patterson, Megan S., Christina E. Amo, Tyler Prochnow, and Katie M. Heinrich. "Exploring Social Networks Relative to Various Types of Exercise Self-Efficacy within CrossFit Participants." *International Journal of Sport and Exercise Psychology* 20, no. 6 (November 2, 2022): 1691–1710. https://doi.org/10.1080/1612197X.2021.1987961.

Pearsall, Charlotte N. *The Relationship of Adaptive Sport Participation on Sense of Community and Community Integration.* East Carolina University, 2019.

Peeler, Tim. "One Brick Back: LeRoy Walker: A Man of Olympic Proportions." *One Brick Back* (blog), January 3, 2020. http://timpeeler.blogspot.com/2020/01/leroy-walker-man-of-olympic-proportions.html.

Peiper, Heidi. "Reimagining the Third Place: How Starbucks Is Evolving Its Store Experience." Starbucks Stories, September 13, 2022. https://stories.starbucks.com/stories/2022/reimagining-the-third-place-how-starbucks-is-evolving-its-store-experience/.

Petitpas, Albert J, Allen Cornelius, and Judy Van Raalte. "Youth Development through Sport: It's All about Relationships." In *Positive Youth Development through Sport*, 75–84. Routledge, 2007.

Phillips, Katherine W., Katie A. Liljenquist, and Margaret A. Neale. "Is the Pain Worth the Gain? The Advantages and Liabilities of Agreeing With Socially Distinct Newcomers." *Personality and Social Psychology Bulletin* 35, no. 3 (March 2009): 336–50. https://doi.org/10.1177/0146167208328062.

Phillips, Pamm, and Sheranne Fairley. "Umpiring: A Serious Leisure Choice." *Journal of Leisure Research* 46, no. 2 (April 2014): 184–202. https://doi.org/10.1080/00222216.2014.11950319.

Pickett, Andrew C., Andrew Goldsmith, Zack Damon, and Matthew Walker. "The Influence of Sense of Community on the Perceived Value of Physical Activity: A Cross-Context Analysis." *Leisure Sciences* 38, no. 3 (May 26, 2016): 199–214. https://doi.org/10.1080/01490400.2015.1090360.

Pickleball for Incarcerated Communities. "Resources." Pickleball for Incarcerated Communities. Accessed September 26, 2024. https://www.picleague.org/about-us.

PickleCon | Working with Vets, 2024. https://www.youtube.com/watch?v=OqhgvdWXSjg.

Pilgreen, Daniel G. "Sense of Community in the Campus Recreation Setting: Fostering Community as a Strategy for Student Retention," 2018.

Pillar, Kyle. "Family Affair: McGees Share Memories, Impact of College Football in New Book." *The Richmond Observer* (blog), October 25, 2020. https://richmondobserver.com/local-sports/family-affair-mcgees-share-memories-of-college-football-in-new-book.html.

Platt, John R. "Strong Inference." *Science* 146, no. 3642 (1964): 347–53.

Pollock, Hilary. "Exploring Recreation and Sense of Community in the Canadian Military," 2019.

Porter, Eleanor Hodgman. *Pollyanna*. LC Page, 1913.

President Bush Throws the First Pitch of Game 3 of the 2001 World Series, 2014. https://www.youtube.com/watch?v=lAEXKwQ1f9M.

Prince, Sedona. "Sedona Prince on TikTok." TikTok, March 18, 2021. https://www.tiktok.com/@sedonerrr/video/6941180880127888646.

Putnam, Robert D. *Bowling Alone: The Collapse and Revival of American Community*. 1. touchstone ed. New York, NY: Simon & Schuster, 2001.

Räikkönen, Timo, and Juha Hedman. "Unlocking the Power of Sports: An Exploration of the Nexus between Shared Place, Community Competence, and Sense of Community." *International Journal of Sport Policy and Politics* 0, no. 0 (August 24, 2024): 1–19. https://doi.org/10.1080/19406940.2024.2396836.

Redding, Dave, and Tim Whitmire. *Freed to Lead: F3 and the Unshackling of the Modern-Day Warrior*, 2014.

Richman, Peter. "40 Other Times Sports Have Been Temporarily Interrupted." *Stacker*, June 4, 2020. https://stacker.com/sports/40-other-times-sports-have-been-temporarily-interrupted.

Ridinger, Lynn, Kyungun R. Kim, Stacy Warner, and Jacob K. Tingle. "Development of the Referee Retention Scale." *Journal of Sport Management*, June 28, 2017, 1–36. https://doi.org/10.1123/jsm.2017-0065.

Robertson-Smith, Gemma, and Carl Markwick. *Employee Engagement: A Review of Current Thinking*. Institute for Employment Studies Brighton, 2009.

Rochman, Bonnie. "No Office? No Problem. Meet Me at Starbucks." Starbucks Stories Asia, January 5, 2018. https://stories.starbucks.com/asia/stories/2018/no-office-no-problem-meet-me-at-starbucks/.

Rohan. "When Did Esports Start? When Did Esports Become Popular? The History of Esports." ESPORTS GG, December 30, 2022. https://esports.gg/guides/esports/the-history-of-esports/.

Rowe, K., D. Shilbury, L. Ferkins, and E. Hinckson. "Sport Development and Physical Activity Promotion: An Integrated Model to Enhance Collaboration and Understanding." *Sport Management Review* 16 (2013): 364–77.

Running Insight Staff. "Best Running Stores 2021 | Running Insight." Top 50 Best Running Store by Running Insight, December 28, 2021. https://www.runninginsight.com/best-running-stores-2021.

Rutten, Esther A., Geert Jan J. M. Stams, Gert J. J. Biesta, Carlo Schuengel, Evelien Dirks, and Jan B. Hoeksma. "The Contribution of Organized Youth Sport to Antisocial and Prosocial Behavior in Adolescent Athletes." *Journal of Youth and Adolescence* 36, no. 3 (March 22, 2007): 255–64. https://doi.org/10.1007/s10964-006-9085-y.

Ryan, Shane. "East Carolina University Fans Are Pirates to The Core." Our State, August 31, 2016. https://www.ourstate.com/east-carolina-university-fans-are-pirates-to-the-core/.

Sanz, Carmen. "Why Pickleball Is Becoming the Favorite Sport for All Ages." CarmenSanzPickleball, March 3, 2024. https://www.carmensanzpickleball.com/post/why-pickleball-is-sport-for-all-ages.

Sarason, S. B. *The Psychological Sense of Community: Prospects for a Community Psychology, Jossey-Bass, San Francisco*. CA, 1974.

Sartore-Baldwin, Melanie, and Stacy Warner. "Perceptions of Justice within Intercollegiate Athletics among Current and Former Athletes." *Journal of Issues in Intercollegiate Athletics* 5 (2012): 269–82.

Schultz, Howard, and Joanne L. Gordon. *From the Ground up: A Journey to Reimagine the Promise of America*. First edition. New York: Random House, 2019.

Scott, H. R., A. Pitman, P. Kozhuharova, and B. Lloyd-Evans. "A Systematic Review of Studies Describing the Influence of Informal Social Support on Psychological Wellbeing in People Bereaved by Sudden or Violent Causes of Death." *BMC Psychiatry* 20, no. 1 (December 2020): 265. https://doi.org/10.1186/s12888-020-02639-4.

Seligman, Martin. "Flourish: Positive Psychology and Positive Interventions." *The Tanner Lectures on Human Values* 31, no. 4 (2010): 1–56.

Sharratt, Mark, and Abel Usoro. "Understanding Knowledge-Sharing in Online Communities of Practice." *Electronic Journal on Knowledge Management* 1, no. 2 (2003): 187–96.

Sobers-Outlaw, Gill. "LeRoy T. Walker (1918–2012)," April 16, 2014. https://www.blackpast.org/african-american-history/walker-leroy-t-1918-2012/.

Sparvero, Emily, Laurence Chalip, and B. Christine Green. "The United States." In *Comparative Elite Sport Development*, 2nd ed. Routledge, 2024.

Sparvero, Emily S., and Stacy Warner. "NFL Play 60: Managing the Intersection of Professional Sport and Obesity." *Sport Management Review*, July 2018. https://doi.org/10.1016/j.smr.2018.06.005.

Sparvero, Emily S., Stacy Warner, and Jacob K. Tingle. "RunTex: A Community Landmark Run out of Business." *Sport Management Review* 19, no. 3 (July 1, 2016): 343–51. https://doi.org/10.1016/j.smr.2015.10.003.

Sport & Fitness Industry Association. "2023 SFIA Topline Participation Report Now Availabile." Sports and Fitness Industry Association. Accessed August 19, 2024. https://sfia.org/resources/sfias-topline-report-shows-physical-activity-rates-increased-for-a-fifth-consecutive-year/.

Staff. "The Rise of Collegiate Esports: Universities Embracing Gaming." College Football Poll, August 16, 2024. https://www.collegefootballpoll.com/news/the-rise-of-collegiate-esports-universities-embracing-gaming/.

Starbuck, Peter. "Peter F. Drucker." In *The Oxford Handbook of Management Theorists*, edited by Morgen Witzel and Malcolm Warner, 271–96. Oxford University Press, 2013. https://doi.org/10.1093/oxfordhb/9780199585762.013.0014.

Storey, Daniel. "When Football Came Home (on a Cathay Pacific Flight)." Football365, May 27, 2016. https://www.football365.com/news/when-football-came-home-on-a-cathay-pacific-flight.

Stump, Scott. "EXCLUSIVE: Meet the 3 Female Coaches on the Baltimore Ravens' Staff This Season." Accessed September 2, 2024. https://www.today.com/news/sports/female-nfl-coaches-ravens-rcna167732.

Swyers, H. *Wrigley Regulars: Finding Community in the Bleachers?, University of Illinois Press: Champaign.* IL, 2010.

Swyers, Holly. "Community America: Who Owns Wrigley Field?" *The International Journal of the History of Sport* 22, no. 6 (November 2005): 1086–1105. https://doi.org/10.1080/09523360500286783.

Syers, Kevin. "ECU Named First-Gen Forward Institution for Its Commitment to the Advancement, Success of First-Generation Students." News Services, April 6, 2021. https://news.ecu.edu/2021/04/06/ecu-named-first-gen-forward-institution-for-its-commitment-to-the-advancement-success-of-first-generation-students/.

Taylor, Chris. "On-the-Spot Incentives." Accessed September 2, 2024. https://www.shrm.org/topics-tools/news/hr-magazine/spot-incentives.

The Cigna Group. "The Loneliness Epidemic Persists: A Post-Pandemic Look at the State of Loneliness among U.S. Adults." The Cigna Group Newsroom. Accessed September 14, 2024. https://newsroom.thecignagroup.com/loneliness-epidemic-persists-post-pandemic-look.

The City of Greenville, NC. "Citizen Handbook," 2022. https://www.greenvillenc.gov/home/showpublisheddocument/23306/637933188957600000.

———. "Greenville's 250th Interactive Timeline." Greenville's 250th, October 5, 2023. https://250.greenvillenc.gov/interactive-timeline/.

The University of North Carolina System. "Enrollment Increases across the UNC System – UNC System," September 12, 2024. https://www.northcarolina.edu/news/enrollment-increases-across-the-unc-system/.

Tingle, Jacob K., Brittany L. Jacobs, Matthew Katz, and Stacy Warner. "The Strength of Community: The Role of Social Support Networks in Sport Officials' Retention." *Journal of Sport Management*, 2023, 1–11. https://doi.org/10.1123/jsm.2022-0361.

Tingle, Jacob K., Stacy Warner, and Melanie L. Sartore-Baldwin. "The Experience of Former Women Officials and the Impact on the Sporting Community." *Sex Roles* 71, no. 1–2 (July 2014): 7–20. https://doi.org/10.1007/s11199-014-0366-8.

Torres, Raquel. "San Antonio Sports Names Jenny Carnes as New President and CEO." San Antonio Report, June 14, 2022. http://sanantonioreport.org/san-antonio-sports-jenny-carnes-ceo/.

Tulshyan, Ruchika. *Inclusion on Purpose: An Intersectional Approach to Creating a Culture of Belonging at Work*. MIT Press, 2022.

Twenge, Jean M., Jonathan Haidt, Andrew B. Blake, Cooper McAllister, Hannah Lemon, and Astrid Le Roy. "Worldwide Increases in Adolescent Loneliness." *Journal of Adolescence* 93, no. 1 (December 2021): 257–69. https://doi.org/10.1016/j.adolescence.2021.06.006.

U.S. Department of Education. "A Policy Interpretation: Title IX and Intercollegiate Athletics | U.S. Department of Education." Accessed October 5, 2024. http://www.ed.gov/about/offices/list/ocr/docs/t9interp.html.

U.S. Public Health Service. "Our Epidemic of Loneliness and Isolation: The U.S. Surgeon General's Advisory on the Healing Effects of Social Connection and Community." Washington, D.C., 2023. https://www.hhs.gov/sites/default/files/surgeon-general-social-connection-advisory.pdf.

———. "Under Pressure: The U.S. Surgeon General's Advisory on the Mental Health & Well-Belling of Parents." Washington, D.C., 2023. https://www.hhs.gov/surgeongeneral/priorities/parents/index.html.

USATF. "USA Track & Field | Dr. LeRoy Walker." Accessed October 7, 2024. https://usatf.org/athlete-bios/dr-leroy-walker.

USOPC. "United States Olympic & Paralympic Financial Summary," 2022. https://www.usopc.org/2022-impact-report/financial-summary.

Van de Ven, Andrew H. "Nothing Is Quite so Practical as a Good Theory." *Academy of Management Review* 14, no. 4 (1989): 486–89.

Vey, Jennifer S., and Hanna Love. "Transformative Placemaking: A Framework to Create Connected, Vibrant, and Inclusive Communities." Brookings. Accessed August 31, 2024. https://www.brookings.edu/articles/transformative-placemaking-a-framework-to-create-connected-vibrant-and-inclusive-communities/.

Wade, Luke. "Luke Wade, The Community Creator, LinkedIn." Accessed October 4, 2024. https://www.linkedin.com/in/thecommunitycreator/.

Warner, S. "Sport and Community." In *Sociology of Sport and Physical Activity*, edited by G. B. Cunningham and J. N. Singer, 2nd ed., 237–54. College Station, TX: Center for Sport Management Research and Education, 2012.

———. "Sport and Sense of Community Theory." In *Routledge Handbook of Theory in Sport Management*, edited by George B Cunningham, J. Fink, and A. Doherty, 189–98. New York, NY: Routledge, 2016.

Warner, S, and Vanessa Bright. "Building Community and Culture for Sport Officials." In *Managing and Developing Sports Officials: Officiating Excellence*. 2024, n.d.

Warner, S., Laurence Chalip, and Jules Woolf. "Fan Development Strategy: The Austin Wranglers' Game Plan." *Sport Management Review* 11, no. 3 (November 2008): 309–30. https://doi.org/10.1016/S1441-3523(08)70114-1.

Warner, S., and Marlene A Dixon. "Understanding Sense of Community from the Athlete's Perspective." *Journal of Sport Management* 25, no. 3 (2011): 257–71.

Warner, S, and Tiesha Martin. "COVID-19 and Sport: What Are We Really Missing?" *Sport & Entertainment Review* 6, no. 2 (July 2020). https://serjournal.com/2020/07/03/white-paper-covid-19-and-sport-what-are-we-really-missing/.

Warner, S., Jacob K. Tingle, and Pamm Kellett. "Officiating Attrition: The Experiences of Former Referees via a Sport Development Lens," 2013. http://digitalcommons.trinity.edu/busadmin_faculty/3/.

Warner, Stacy. "Sport and Sense of Community." In *Sport and Sense of Community*. Routledge Resources Online - Sports Studies Edited by Vassil Girginov and Yuhei Inoue. Routledge, 2024. https://doi.org/10.4324/9780367766924-RESS160-1.

Warner, Stacy, Marlene Dixon, and Stephen Leierer. "Using Youth Sport to Enhance Parents' Sense of Community." *Journal of Applied Sport Management* 7, no. 1 (2015): 45–63.

Warner, Stacy, Shannon Kerwin, Matthew Walker, and others. "Examining Sense of Community in Sport: Developing the Multidimensional 'SCS'Scale." *Journal of Sport Management* 27, no. 5 (2013): 349–62.

Warner, Stacy, E Sparvero, S Shapiro, and A Anderson. "Yielding Healthy Community with Sport." *Journal of Sport for Development* 5, no. 8 (2017): 41–52.

Watterson, John S. "Political Football: Theodore Roosevelt, Woodrow Wilson and the Gridiron Reform Movement." *Presidential Studies Quarterly* 25, no. 3 (1995): 555–64.

Webb, Tom, David J. Hancock, Pamm Phillips, and Jacob K Tingle, eds. *Managing and Developing Sports Officials: Officiating Excellence*. 1st ed. Routledge, Taylor & Francis Group, 2025. https://www.routledge.com/Managing-and-Developing-Sports-Officials-Officiating-Excellence/Webb-Hancock-Phillips-Tingle/p/book/9781032442020.

Weed, Mike. "The Pub as a Virtual Football Fandom Venue: An Alternative to 'Being There'?" *Soccer & Society* 8, no. 2–3 (April 2007): 399–414. https://doi.org/10.1080/14660970701224665.

Weingartz, Ashley N., and Stacy Warner. "Big League Social Media: Cultivating Community Online." *Case Studies in Sport Management* 8, no. 1 (January 1, 2019): 44–50. https://doi.org/10.1123/cssm.2018-0011.

Weissbourd, Richard, Milena Batanova, Virginia Lovison, and Eric Torres. "How the Pandemic Has Deepened an Epidemic of Loneliness and What We Can Do About It." Making Caring Common Project. Harvard University, February 2021. https://mcc.gse.harvard.edu/reports/loneliness-in-america.

Wembley Stadium: A Century of Sport, Music and Magical Moments, 2023. https://www.bbc.com/news/av/uk-england-london-65414823.

Wenger, Etienne. "Communities of Practice: A Brief Introduction," 2011.

Whittier College. "Whittier College Athletics' Mission Statement." Accessed June 18, 2024. https://wcpoets.com/sports/2023/7/20/mission-statement.aspx.

Wicker, Allan W. "Undermanning, Performances, and Students' Subjective Experiences in Behavior Settings of Large and Small High Schools." *Journal of Personality and Social Psychology* 10, no. 3 (1968): 255.

Witz, Billy. "Her Video Spurred Changes in Women's Basketball. Did They Go Far Enough?" *The New York Times*, March 15, 2022, sec. Sports. https://www.nytimes.com/2022/03/15/sports/ncaabasketball/womens-march-madness-sedona-prince.html.

Wood, Sarah. "Mental Health on College Campuses: Challenges and Solutions." *US News & World Report*, July 6, 2024. //www.usnews.com/news/education-news/articles/mental-health-on-college-campuses-challenges-and-solutions.

Wood, Zacharias. "Administrator Perceptions of Intramural Coed Flag Football Modifications: A Qualitative Analysis." Master of Science, Louisiana State University and Agricultural and Mechanical College, 2014. https://doi.org/10.31390/gradschool_theses.611.

Woodward, Ronnie. "IN THE JUNGLE." News Services, June 9, 2022. https://news.ecu.edu/2022/06/09/in-the-jungle/.

———. "Professionally Purple Closet Available to Students." HHP News and Events, November 21, 2023. https://hhp.ecu.edu/hhp-news/2023/11/21/professionallypurple/.

Wu, Qiong, and Kathryn Cormican. "Shared Leadership and Team Effectiveness: An Investigation of Whether and When in Engineering Design Teams." *Frontiers in Psychology* 11 (January 18, 2021): 569198. https://doi.org/10.3389/fpsyg.2020.569198.

Yates, Jon. *Fractured: Why Our Societies Are Coming Apart and How We Put Them Back Together Again.* Manchester: HarperNorth, 2021.

Yuen, Felice, and Amanda J. Johnson. "Leisure Spaces, Community, and Third Places." *Leisure Sciences* 39, no. 3 (May 4, 2017): 295–303. https://doi.org/10.1080/01490400.2016.1165638.

Zhang, Chen, Jennifer D. Nahrgang, Susan (Sue) Ashford, and D. Scott DeRue. "Why Capable People Are Reluctant to Lead." *Harvard Business Review*, December 17, 2020. https://hbr.org/2020/12/why-capable-people-are-reluctant-to-lead.

Zhang, J.J., D.W. Smith, D.G. Pease, and E.A. Jambor. "Negative Influences of Market Competitors on the Attendance of Professional Sport Games: The Case of a Minor League Hockey Team." *Sport Marketing Quarterly* 6, no. 3 (1997): 31–40.

NOTES

Preface

1. S. Warner, "Sport and Sense of Community Theory," in *Routledge Handbook of Theory in Sport Management*, ed. George B Cunningham, J. Fink, and A. Doherty (New York, NY: Routledge, 2016), 189–98.

Chapter One. Ghost Runner

1. Saga Pardede and Velibor Bobo Kovač, "Distinguishing the Need to Belong and Sense of Belongingness: The Relation between Need to Belong and Personal Appraisals under Two Different Belongingness–Conditions," *European Journal of Investigation in Health, Psychology and Education* 13, no. 2 (February 1, 2023): 331–44, https://doi.org/10.3390/ejihpe13020025; Edward L Deci and Richard M Ryan, "The" What" and" Why" of Goal Pursuits: Human Needs and the Self-Determination of Behavior," *Psychological Inquiry* 11, no. 4 (2000): 227–68.

2. S. B. Sarason, *The Psychological Sense of Community: Prospects for a Community Psychology*, Jossey-Bass, San Francisco (CA, 1974).

3. Marlene Dixon, Stacy Warner, and Jennifer Bruening, "More than Just Letting Them Play: Parental Influence on Women's Lifetime Sport Involvement," *Sociology of Sport Journal* 25 (2008): 538–59.

4. U.S. Department of Education, "A Policy Interpretation: Title IX and Intercollegiate Athletics | U.S. Department of Education," accessed October 5, 2024, http://www.ed.gov/about/offices/list/ocr/docs/t9interp.html.

5. Dixon, Warner, and Bruening, "More than Just Letting Them Play."

6. Stacy Warner, Marlene Dixon, and Stephen Leierer, "Using Youth Sport to Enhance Parents' Sense of Community," *Journal of Applied Sport Management* 7, no. 1 (2015): 45–63.

7. Shannon Kerwin et al., "Exploring Sense of Community among Small-Scale Sport Event Volunteers," *European Sport Management Quarterly* 15, no. 1 (January 2015): 77–92, https://doi.org/10.1080/16184742.2014.996581; Jacob K. Tingle et al., "The Strength of Community: The Role of Social Support Networks in Sport Officials' Retention," *Journal of Sport Management*, 2023, 1–11, https://doi.org/10.1123/jsm.2022-0361.

8. Daniel H Bowen and Collin Hitt, "History and Evidence Show School Sports Help Students Win," *Phi Delta Kappan* 97, no. 8 (2016): 8–12.

9. John S. Watterson, "Political Football: Theodore Roosevelt, Woodrow Wilson and the Gridiron Reform Movement," *Presidential Studies Quarterly* 25, no. 3 (1995): 555–64.

10. Donald Chu, *The Character of American Higher Education and Intercollegiate Sport*. (ERIC, 1989).

11. Peter Richman, "40 Other Times Sports Have Been Temporarily Interrupted," *Stacker*, June 4, 2020, https://stacker.com/sports/40-other-times-sports-have-been-temporarily-interrupted.

12. S Warner and Tiesha Martin, "COVID-19 and Sport: What Are We Really Missing?," *Sport & Entertainment Review* 6, no. 2 (July 2020), https://serjournal.com/2020/07/03/white-paper-covid-19-and-sport-what-are-we-really-missing/.

13. *President Bush Throws the First Pitch of Game 3 of the 2001 World Series*, 2014, https://www.youtube.com/watch?v=lAEXKwQ1f9M.

14. "Mission Statement - Duke University," July 30, 2005, https://goduke.com/sports/2005/6/30/mission-statement.aspx.

15. "Whittier College Athletics' Mission Statement," Whittier College, accessed June 18, 2024, https://wcpoets.com/sports/2023/7/20/mission-statement.aspx.

16. "Elon University Campus Recreation Mission Statement," Elon University, accessed June 18, 2024, https://www.elon.edu/u/campus-recreation-wellness/about-us/.

17. Warner, "Sport and Sense of Community Theory."

Chapter Two. Perspective on Sport: Sport is Not a Dirty Word

1. The City of Greenville, NC, "Citizen Handbook," 2022, https://www.greenvillenc.gov/home/showpublisheddocument/23306/637933188957600000.

2. Emma O'Brien, Stacy M. Warner, and Melanie Sartore-Baldwin, "Eliminating Barriers to Youth Sport in Greenville, North Carolina," *Sport Management Education Journal* 16, no. 1 (April 1, 2022): 86–94, https://doi.org/10.1123/smej.2020-0056.

3. Shane Ryan, "East Carolina University Fans Are Pirates to The Core," Our State, August 31, 2016, https://www.ourstate.com/east-carolina-university-fans-are-pirates-to-the-core/; Bethany Bradsher, *Never Take This for Granted* (Whitecaps Media, 2024).

4. Andrea L. Buenaño and Stacy Warner, "Girls With Game: Sport and Community Development Strategies," *Case Studies in Sport Management* 12, no. S1 (January 1, 2023): S18–21, https://doi.org/10.1123/cssm.2022-0027.

5. The City of Greenville, NC, "Greenville's 250th Interactive Timeline," Greenville's 250th, October 5, 2023, https://250.greenvillenc.gov/interactive-timeline/.

6. Jessica Jewell, "Greenville Named Sportiest City in the U.S.," *WNCT* (blog), July 15, 2016, https://www.wnct.com/news/greenville-named-sportiest-city-in-the-u-s/.

7. The University of North Carolina System, "Enrollment Increases across the UNC System – UNC System," September 12, 2024, https://www.northcarolina.edu/news/enrollment-increases-across-the-unc-system/.

8. "East Carolina University – UNC System," accessed July 1, 2024, https://www.northcarolina.edu/institution/east-carolina-university/.

9. Kevin Syers, "ECU Named First-Gen Forward Institution for Its Commitment to the Advancement, Success of First-Generation Students," News Services, April 6, 2021, https://news.ecu.edu/2021/04/06/ecu-named-first-gen-forward-institution-for-its-commitment-to-the-advancement-success-of-first-generation-students/.

10. Jay Coakley, *Sports in Society: Issues and Controversies*, 10th ed (New York: McGraw-Hill, 2008); Duygu Harmandar Demirel and Ibrahim Yildiran, "The Philosophy of Physical Education and Sport from Ancient Times to the Enlightenment.," *European Journal of Educational Research* 2, no. 4 (2013): 191–202.

11. Brennan K. Berg, S. Warner, and Bhibha M. Das, "What about Sport? A Public Health Perspective on Leisure-Time Physical Activity," *Sport Management Review* 18, no. 1 (February 2015): 20–31, https://doi.org/10.1016/j.smr.2014.09.005; L. C. Chalip, "Toward a Distinctive Sport Management Discipline," *Journal of Sport Management* 20 (2006): 1–21; Karla A. Henderson, "A Paradox of Sport Management and Physical Activity Interventions," *Sport Management Review* 12, no. 2 (May 2009): 57–65, https://doi.org/10.1016/j.smr.2008.12.004; K. Rowe et al., "Sport Development and Physical Activity Promotion: An Integrated Model to Enhance Collaboration and Understanding," *Sport Management Review* 16 (2013): 364–77.

12. Tiesha Martin, Stacy Warner, and Bhibha Das, "Senior Games: Service-Learning with Older Adults in a Sport Setting," *Sport Management Education Journal* 10, no. 1 (April 1, 2016): 43–53, https://doi.org/10.1123/SMEJ.2015-0004.

13. Jay Coakley, *Sports in Society: Issues and Controversies*, 13th ed. (New York: McGraw-Hill Education, 2021); Chris Imbrogno, Brianna L Newland, and Stacy Warner, "The Role of Community in Athlete Transgressive Behavior," *Journal of Issues in Intercollegiate Athletics* 14 (2021): 285–303; Esther A. Rutten et al., "The Contribution of Organized Youth Sport to Antisocial and Prosocial Behavior in Adolescent Athletes," *Journal of Youth and Adolescence* 36, no. 3 (March 22, 2007): 255–64, https://doi.org/10.1007/s10964-006-9085-y.

14. Travis E. Dorsch, Alan L. Smith, and Meghan H. McDonough, "Early Socialization of Parents through Organized Youth Sport.," *Sport, Exercise, and Performance Psychology* 4, no. 1 (2015): 3–18, https://doi.org/10.1037/spy0000021; Travis E. Dorsch et al., "Toward an Integrated Understanding of the Youth Sport System,"

Research Quarterly for Exercise and Sport, September 22, 2020, 1–15, https://doi.org/10.1080/02701367.2020.1810847; Warner, Dixon, and Leierer, "Using Youth Sport to Enhance Parents' Sense of Community"; Albert J Petitpas, Allen Cornelius, and Judy Van Raalte, "Youth Development through Sport: It's All about Relationships," in *Positive Youth Development through Sport* (Routledge, 2007), 75–84.

15. Emily Sparvero, Laurence Chalip, and B. Christine Green, "The United States," in *Comparative Elite Sport Development*, 2nd ed. (Routledge, 2024).

16. Sparvero, Chalip, and Green.

17. USOPC, "United States Olympic & Paralympic Financial Summary," 2022, https://www.usopc.org/2022-impact-report/financial-summary.

18. William Gasparini, "Council of Europe and Sport: Origin and Circulation of a European Sporting Model | Digital Encyclopedia of European History," June 22, 2020, https://ehne.fr/en/encyclopedia/themes/material-civilization/european-sports-circulations/council-europe-and-sport-origin-and-circulation-a-european-sporting-model.

19. Berg, Warner, and Das, "What about Sport?"

20. D. Stanley Eitzen, *Fair and Foul: Beyond the Myths and Paradoxes of Sport* (Lanham, Md: Rowman & Littlefield Publishers, 2006).

21. So Youn Lim et al., "Sport Participation across National Contexts: A Multilevel Investigation of Individual and Systemic Influences on Adult Sport Participation," *European Sport Management Quarterly* 11, no. 3 (2011): 197–224; Emily S. Sparvero and Stacy Warner, "NFL Play 60: Managing the Intersection of Professional Sport and Obesity," *Sport Management Review*, July 2018, https://doi.org/10.1016/j.smr.2018.06.005.

22. Jay Coakley, *Sports in Society: Issues and Controversies* (New York: McGraw-Hill Education, 2015).

23. Michael F. Bergeron, "Improving Health through Youth Sports: Is Participation Enough?," *New Directions for Youth Development* 2007, no. 115 (2007): 27–41, https://doi.org/10.1002/yd.221; Desiree Leek et al., "Physical Activity during Youth Sports Practices," *Archives of Pediatrics & Adolescent Medicine* 165, no. 4 (2011): 294–99.

24. Berg, Warner, and Das, "What about Sport?"

25. Marlene A Dixon, Stacy Warner, and Christine M Habeeb, "Athlete Concerns: What Can Coaches Do?," *Journal of Issues in Intercollegiate Athletics* 15 (2022): 314–28; H. Gustafsson, S. S. Sagar, and A. Stenling, "Fear of Failure, Psychological Stress, and Burnout among Adolescent Athletes Competing in High Level Sport," *Scandinavian Journal of Medicine & Science in Sports* 27, no. 12 (December 2017): 2091–2102, https://doi.org/10.1111/sms.12797; Christine Habeeb, Stacy Warner, and David Walsh, "Managing Mental Health: Athlete Help-Seeking," *Sport Management*

Review 25, no. 5 (October 20, 2022): 871–91, https://doi.org/10.1080/14413523.2021.2018836.

26. S. Warner, Laurence Chalip, and Jules Woolf, "Fan Development Strategy: The Austin Wranglers' Game Plan," *Sport Management Review* 11, no. 3 (November 2008): 309–30, https://doi.org/10.1016/S1441-3523(08)70114-1; J.J. Zhang et al., "Negative Influences of Market Competitors on the Attendance of Professional Sport Games: The Case of a Minor League Hockey Team.," *Sport Marketing Quarterly* 6, no. 3 (1997): 31–40.

27. Kelly Huang and Marlene A Dixon, "Examining the Financial Impact of Alcohol Sales on Football Game Days: A Case Study of a Major Football Program," *Journal of Sport Management* 27, no. 3 (2013): 207–16; Dan J. Neal and Kim Fromme, "Hook 'em Horns and Heavy Drinking: Alcohol Use and Collegiate Sports," *Addictive Behaviors* 32, no. 11 (November 2007): 2681–93, https://doi.org/10.1016/j.addbeh.2007.06.020; C. Palmer, "Key Themes and Research Agendas in the Sport-Alcohol Nexus," *Journal of Sport & Social Issues* 35, no. 2 (May 1, 2011): 168–85, https://doi.org/10.1177/0193723511406131.

28. Yuhei Inoue, Brennan K. Berg, and Packianathan Chelladurai, "Spectator Sport and Population Health: A Scoping Study," *Journal of Sport Management* 29, no. 6 (November 1, 2015): 705–25, https://doi.org/10.1123/JSM.2014-0283.

29. Chalip, "Toward a Distinctive Sport Management Discipline."

Chapter Three. So What? Why Sport Managers Need to Understand How to Build Community

1. Abraham Harold Maslow, "A Theory of Human Motivation.," *Psychological Review* 50, no. 4 (1943): 370–96.

2. U.S. Public Health Service, "Our Epidemic of Loneliness and Isolation: The U.S. Surgeon General's Advisory on the Healing Effects of Social Connection and Community" (Washington, D.C., 2023), https://www.hhs.gov/sites/default/files/surgeon-general-social-connection-advisory.pdf.

3. Warner, "Sport and Sense of Community Theory"; Amy Chan Hyung Kim, James Du, and Jeffrey James, "A Social Epidemiological Perspective on Local Tennis League Participation: A Multigroup Moderated-Mediation Structural Analysis Using PLS-SEM," *International Journal of Sports Marketing and Sponsorship* 23, no. 2 (April 5, 2022): 437–61, https://doi.org/10.1108/IJSMS-02-2021-0046; Berg, Warner, and Das, "What about Sport?"; Warner, Dixon, and Leierer, "Using Youth Sport to Enhance Parents' Sense of Community"; Stacy Warner, "Sport and Sense of Community," in *Sport and Sense of Community,* Routledge Resources Online - Sports

Studies Edited by Vassil Girginov and Yuhei Inoue (Routledge, 2024), https://doi.org/10.4324/9780367766924-RESS160-1.

4. Warner and Martin, "COVID-19 and Sport: What Are We Really Missing?"

5. Robert D. Putnam, *Bowling Alone: The Collapse and Revival of American Community*, 1. touchstone ed (New York, NY: Simon & Schuster, 2001).

6. Jon Yates, *Fractured: Why Our Societies Are Coming Apart and How We Put Them Back Together Again* (Manchester: HarperNorth, 2021).

7. Miller McPherson, Lynn Smith-Lovin, and James M Cook, "Birds of a Feather: Homophily in Social Networks," *Annual Review of Sociology* 27, no. 1 (August 2001): 415–44, https://doi.org/10.1146/annurev.soc.27.1.415.

8. Maxine Najle and Robert P. Jones, "American Democracy in Crisis: The Fate of Pluralism in a Divided Nation | PRRI," February 19, 2019, https://www.prri.org/research/american-democracy-in-crisis-the-fate-of-pluralism-in-a-divided-nation/.

9. Ruchika Tulshyan, *Inclusion on Purpose: An Intersectional Approach to Creating a Culture of Belonging at Work* (MIT Press, 2022); Jared Nai et al., "People in More Racially Diverse Neighborhoods Are More Prosocial.," *Journal of Personality and Social Psychology* 114, no. 4 (April 2018): 497–515, https://doi.org/10.1037/pspa0000103.

10. Jennifer S. Vey and Hanna Love, "Transformative Placemaking: A Framework to Create Connected, Vibrant, and Inclusive Communities," Brookings, accessed August 31, 2024, https://www.brookings.edu/articles/transformative-placemaking-a-framework-to-create-connected-vibrant-and-inclusive-communities/.

11. Karabi Bezboruah, "Building and Strengthening Communities: What Works? What Doesn't?," in *Building Community and Family Resilience*, ed. Mike Stout and Amanda W. Harrist, Emerging Issues in Family and Individual Resilience (Cham: Springer International Publishing, 2021), 1–17, https://doi.org/10.1007/978-3-030-49799-6_1.

12. Jasmine Linabary, "Working in Diverse Teams," *Small Group Communication*, 2021.

13. Katherine W. Phillips, Katie A. Liljenquist, and Margaret A. Neale, "Is the Pain Worth the Gain? The Advantages and Liabilities of Agreeing With Socially Distinct Newcomers," *Personality and Social Psychology Bulletin* 35, no. 3 (March 2009): 336–50, https://doi.org/10.1177/0146167208328062.

14. Kazi Zainab Khanam, Gautam Srivastava, and Vijay Mago, "The Homophily Principle in Social Network Analysis: A Survey," *Multimedia Tools and Applications* 82, no. 6 (March 2023): 8811–54, https://doi.org/10.1007/s11042-021-11857-1.

15. Warner and Martin, "COVID-19 and Sport: What Are We Really Missing?"

16. Yates, *Fractured*.

17. *Wembley Stadium: A Century of Sport, Music and Magical Moments*, 2023, https://www.bbc.com/news/av/uk-england-london-65414823.

18. Daniel Storey, "When Football Came Home (on a Cathay Pacific Flight)," Football365, May 27, 2016, https://www.football365.com/news/when-football-came-home-on-a-cathay-pacific-flight.

19. Robert O'Connor, "Feuds and Infighting: A Recent History of Player Mutinies at Major Tournaments," Bleacher Report, accessed September 29, 2024, https://bleacherreport.com/articles/2649386-feuds-and-infighting-a-recent-history-of-player-mutinies-at-major-tournaments; Yates, *Fractured*.

20. American Psychological Association, "Stress in America 2023: A Nation Recovering from Collective Trauma," 2023, https://www.apa.org/news/press/releases/stress/2023/collective-trauma-recovery.

21. U.S. Public Health Service, "Our Epidemic of Loneliness and Isolation: The U.S. Surgeon General's Advisory on the Healing Effects of Social Connection and Community."

22. U.S. Public Health Service, "Under Pressure: The U.S. Surgeon General's Advisory on the Mental Health & Well-Belling of Parents" (Washington, D.C., 2023), https://www.hhs.gov/surgeongeneral/priorities/parents/index.html.

23. The Cigna Group, "The Loneliness Epidemic Persists: A Post-Pandemic Look at the State of Loneliness among U.S. Adults," The Cigna Group Newsroom, accessed September 14, 2024, https://newsroom.thecignagroup.com/loneliness-epidemic-persists-post-pandemic-look.

24. Vivek H. Murthy, "Opinion | Surgeon General: Parents Are at Their Wits' End. We Can Do Better.," *The New York Times*, August 28, 2024, sec. Opinion, https://www.nytimes.com/2024/08/28/opinion/surgeon-general-stress-parents.html.

25. Michael Merschel, "How Grief Rewires the Brain and Can Affect Health - and What to Do about It," www.heart.org, March 10, 2021, https://www.heart.org/en/news/2021/03/10/how-grief-rewires-the-brain-and-can-affect-health-and-what-to-do-about-it.

26. Joanne Cacciatore et al., "What Is Good Grief Support? Exploring the Actors and Actions in Social Support after Traumatic Grief," ed. Manuel Fernández-Alcántara, *PLOS ONE* 16, no. 5 (May 27, 2021): e0252324, https://doi.org/10.1371/journal.pone.0252324; Samar M Aoun et al., "What Sources of Bereavement Support Are Perceived Helpful by Bereaved People and Why? Empirical Evidence for the Compassionate Communities Approach," *Palliative Medicine* 32, no. 8 (September 2018): 1378–88, https://doi.org/10.1177/0269216318774995; H. R. Scott et al., "A Systematic Review of Studies Describing the Influence of Informal Social Support on Psychological Wellbeing in People Bereaved by Sudden or Violent Causes of Death," *BMC Psychiatry* 20, no. 1 (December 2020): 265, https://doi.org/10.1186/s12888-020-02639-4.

27. Aoun et al., "What Sources of Bereavement Support Are Perceived Helpful by Bereaved People and Why?"

28. Andrew McClung, "Pickleball for Pearsall Carrying on Life and Legacy of Greenville Pickleball Player," June 28, 2024, https://wcti12.com/news/local/pickleball-for-pearsall-carrying-on-life-and-legacy-of-greenville-pickleball-player.

29. Sarah J Clark et al., "C.S. Mott Children's Hospital National Poll on Children's Health," n.d.

30. Jean M. Twenge et al., "Worldwide Increases in Adolescent Loneliness," *Journal of Adolescence* 93, no. 1 (December 2021): 257–69, https://doi.org/10.1016/j.adolescence.2021.06.006.

31. Lisa Fields, "Why Loneliness Affects Young People More Often Than Older Adults," Cedars-Sinai, accessed September 18, 2024, https://www.cedars-sinai.org/blog/why-loneliness-affects-young-people.html.

32. Richard Weissbourd et al., "How the Pandemic Has Deepened an Epidemic of Loneliness and What We Can Do About It," Making Caring Common Project (Harvard University, February 2021), https://mcc.gse.harvard.edu/reports/loneliness-in-america.

33. Preeti Malani, "Trends in Loneliness Among Older Adults from 2018-2023 | National Poll on Healthy Aging" (University of Michigan, March 13, 2023), https://www.healthyagingpoll.org/reports-more/report/trends-loneliness-among-older-adults-2018-2023.

34. Alison R. Huang et al., "Social Isolation and 9-Year Dementia Risk in Community-Dwelling Medicare Beneficiaries in the United States," *Journal of the American Geriatrics Society* 71, no. 3 (March 2023): 765–73, https://doi.org/10.1111/jgs.18140.

35. Viji Diane Kannan and Peter J. Veazie, "US Trends in Social Isolation, Social Engagement, and Companionship – Nationally and by Age, Sex, Race/Ethnicity, Family Income, and Work Hours, 2003-2020," *SSM - Population Health* 21 (March 2023): 101331, https://doi.org/10.1016/j.ssmph.2022.101331.

Chapter Four. Common Interest: A Shared Mission, Goal or Purpose

1. *2009 Special Olympics World Winter Games Scarf Project*, 2014, https://www.youtube.com/watch?v=ZT5TNtuMtRQ.

2. Lynette Mueller, "Special Olympics Joins With Red Heart Yarns To Inspire Handmade Unity," February 23, 2011, https://omegareporting.com/special-olympics/.

3. Pamm Kellett and David Shilbury, "Umpire Participation: Is Abuse Really the Issue?," *Sport Management Review* 10, no. 3 (September 1, 2007): 209–29, https://doi.org/10.1016/S1441-3523(07)70012-8.

4. Coakley, *Sports in Society: Issues and Controversies*, 2021.

5. Kellett and Shilbury, "Umpire Participation."

6. Kellett and Shilbury.

7. Karissa Niehoff, "With Loss of 50,000 Officials, NFHS Organizes Consortium to Find Solutions," accessed August 14, 2024, https://www.nfhs.org/articles/with-loss-of-50-000-officials-nfhs-organizes-consortium-to-find-solutions.

8. Audrey Lee, "The State of Referee and Umpire Shortage in Youth Sports," Athletic Business, August 20, 2024, https://www.athleticbusiness.com/operations/personnel/article/15682076/the-state-of-referee-and-umpire-shortage-in-youth-sports.

9. Lynn Ridinger et al., "Development of the Referee Retention Scale," *Journal of Sport Management*, June 28, 2017, 1–36, https://doi.org/10.1123/jsm.2017-0065; Jacob K. Tingle, Stacy Warner, and Melanie L. Sartore-Baldwin, "The Experience of Former Women Officials and the Impact on the Sporting Community," *Sex Roles* 71, no. 1–2 (July 2014): 7–20, https://doi.org/10.1007/s11199-014-0366-8; Tingle et al., "The Strength of Community"; S. Warner, Jacob K. Tingle, and Pamm Kellett, "Officiating Attrition: The Experiences of Former Referees via a Sport Development Lens," 2013, http://digitalcommons.trinity.edu/busadmin_faculty/3/; S Warner and Vanessa Bright, "Building Community and Culture for Sport Officials," in *Managing and Developing Sports Officials: Officiating Excellence* (2024, n.d.).

10. Vanessa Bright, Stacy Warner, and Claire Zvosec, "Refereeing as a Postathletic Career Option," *Journal of Sport Management* 36, no. 6 (November 1, 2022): 548–58, https://doi.org/10.1123/jsm.2021-0268; Pamm Phillips and Sheranne Fairley, "Umpiring: A Serious Leisure Choice," *Journal of Leisure Research* 46, no. 2 (April 2014): 184–202, https://doi.org/10.1080/00222216.2014.11950319.

11. Tingle et al., "The Strength of Community"; Minjung Kim et al., "Strengthening Referees' Psychological Well-Being through Engagement and Authenticity," *Sport Management Review* 25, no. 2 (March 15, 2022): 254–74, https://doi.org/10.1080/14413523.2021.1930952.

12. Phillips and Fairley, "Umpiring."

13. Tingle, Warner, and Sartore-Baldwin, "The Experience of Former Women Officials and the Impact on the Sporting Community."

14. Tom Webb et al., eds., *Managing and Developing Sports Officials: Officiating Excellence*, 1st ed. (Routledge, Taylor & Francis Group, 2025), https://www.routledge.com/Managing-and-Developing-Sports-Officials-Officiating-Excellence/Webb-Hancock-Phillips-Tingle/p/book/9781032442020.

15. Sport & Fitness Industry Association, "2023 SFIA Topline Participation Report Now Availabile," Sports and Fitness Industry Association, accessed August 19, 2024, https://sfia.org/resources/sfias-topline-report-shows-physical-activity-rates-increased-for-a-fifth-consecutive-year/.

16. Carmen Sanz, "Why Pickleball Is Becoming the Favorite Sport for All Ages," CarmenSanzPickleball, March 3, 2024, https://www.carmensanzpickleball.com/post/why-pickleball-is-sport-for-all-ages.

17. David Artavia, "Pickleball Is America's Fastest-Growing Sport. Why Is It so Addictive — and Divisive?," Yahoo Life, August 31, 2023, https://www.yahoo.com/lifestyle/pickleball-sport-addictive-divisive-tennis-171700283.html.

18. Sarah Wood, "Mental Health on College Campuses: Challenges and Solutions," US News & World Report, July 6, 2024, //www.usnews.com/news/education-news/articles/mental-health-on-college-campuses-challenges-and-solutions.

19. Mary Ellen Flannery, "The Mental Health Crisis Among Faculty and College Staff | NEA," March 7, 2024, https://www.nea.org/nea-today/all-news-articles/mental-health-crisis-among-faculty-and-college-staff.

20. Colleen Flaherty, "Faculty: 'Gatekeepers' of Student Mental Health?," Inside Higher Ed, accessed August 21, 2024, https://www.insidehighered.com/news/2021/04/08/faculty-gatekeepers-student-mental-health; Meera Komarraju, Sergey Musulkin, and Gargi Bhattacharya, "Role of Student–Faculty Interactions in Developing College Students' Academic Self-Concept, Motivation, and Achievement," *Journal of College Student Development* 51, no. 3 (2010): 332–42, https://doi.org/10.1353/csd.0.0137; George D Kuh, "High-Impact Educational Practices: What They Are, Who Has Access to Them, and Why They Matter," *Peer Review* 14, no. 3 (2012): 29–30.

Chapter Five. Administrative Consideration: People-Focused

1. Terri Byers and Trevor Slack, "Strategic Decision-Making in Small Businesses Within The Leisure Industry," *Journal of Leisure Research* 33, no. 2 (June 2001): 121–36, https://doi.org/10.1080/00222216.2001.11949934.

2. Emily S. Sparvero, Stacy Warner, and Jacob K. Tingle, "RunTex: A Community Landmark Run out of Business," *Sport Management Review* 19, no. 3 (July 1, 2016): 343–51, https://doi.org/10.1016/j.smr.2015.10.003.

3. "Chamber Recognizes 2022 Small Business Leader of the Year," Greenville-Pitt County Chamber of Commerce, May 23, 2023, https://www.greenvillenc.org/news/single-news-page/?no_cache=1&tx_news_pi1%5Bnews%5D=320&tx_news_pi1%5Bcontroller%5D=News&tx_news_pi1%5Baction%5D=detail&cHash=d18acb74d922f5a1c4e953dad038145c.

4. Running Insight Staff, "Best Running Stores 2021 | Running Insight," Top 50 Best Running Store by Running Insight, December 28, 2021, https://www.runninginsight.com/best-running-stores-2021.

5. Kevin Ellis and Natalie Bradin, "Trailblazers 2024: The Seventh Annual Roster of under-40 N.C. Leaders Making Dynamic Local Impacts," *Business North Carolina*, October 1, 2024, https://businessnc.com/trailblazers-2024-the-sixth-annual-roster-of-under-40-n-c-leaders-making-dynamic-local-impacts/.

6. Gary Moss, "Gallo Built a Legacy as a 'Friend to All,'" *University Gazette*, January 12, 2015, sec. Athletics, https://www.unc.edu/posts/2015/01/12/gallo-built-a-legacy-as-a-friend-to-all/.

7. Katie M Heinrich et al., "Mapping Coaches' Views of Participation in CrossFit to the Integrated Theory of Health Behavior Change and Sense of Community," *Family & Community Health* 40, no. 1 (2017): 24; Megan S. Patterson et al., "Exploring Social Networks Relative to Various Types of Exercise Self-Efficacy within CrossFit Participants," *International Journal of Sport and Exercise Psychology* 20, no. 6 (November 2, 2022): 1691–1710, https://doi.org/10.1080/1612197X.2021.1987961; Andrew C. Pickett et al., "The Influence of Sense of Community on the Perceived Value of Physical Activity: A Cross-Context Analysis," *Leisure Sciences* 38, no. 3 (May 26, 2016): 199–214, https://doi.org/10.1080/01490400.2015.1090360.

8. Mariah Rose Moore, "You Belong in the CrossFit Community," CrossFit, February 6, 2023, https://www.crossfit.com/essentials/magic-of-the-crossfit-community.

9. Caroline Mueller, "CrossFit History: Timeline & How It Started," Sports Foundation, January 13, 2024, https://sportsfoundation.org/crossfit-history/.

10. Jannik Linder, "CrossFit Growth Statistics: Market Data Report 2024," July 17, 2024, https://gitnux.org/CrossFit-growth-statistics/.

11. Eddy Martinez, "'Give Them Hope': A Pickleball Program inside a CT Prison Helps Incarcerated People Find Self-Worth," Connecticut Public, August 23, 2024, https://www.ctpublic.org/news/2024-08-23/pickleball-prison-ct-inmates-sports-rehabilitation.

12. Pickleball for Incarcerated Communities, "Resources," Pickleball for Incarcerated Communities, accessed September 26, 2024, https://www.picleague.org/about-us.

13. Martinez, "'Give Them Hope.'"

14. Joe Grobeck, "Iowa Pink Locker Room: How Hayden Fry Gave His Team an Edge," Fan Buzz, accessed September 4, 2024, https://fanbuzz.com/college-football/big-ten/iowa-pink-locker-rooms/; Kembrew McLeod, "The Case against Kinnick's Pink Locker Room," The Des Moines Register, accessed September 4, 2024, https://www.desmoinesregister.com/story/opinion/columnists/2014/05/05/argument-against-kinnick-stadiums-pink-locker-room/8718293/.

15. Hayden Fry and George Wine, *Hayden Fry: A High Porch Picnic* (Champaign, IL: Sports Pub, 1999).

16. Dave Huber, "Color the Opposing Team's Locker Pink and … Risk a Lawsuit?," The College Fix, August 30, 2014, https://www.thecollegefix.com/color-the-opposing-teams-locker-pink-and-risk-a-lawsuit/; McLeod, "The Case against Kinnick's Pink Locker Room."

17. Cork Gaines, "A Shockingly Small Amount Of Money From Pink NFL Merchandise Sales Goes To Breast Cancer Research," Business Insider, accessed September 4, 2024, https://www.businessinsider.com/small-amount-of-money-from-pink-nfl-merchandise-goes-to-breast-cancer-research-2013-10.

18. Beth Cianfrone and S. Warner, "Developing Sport Communities via Social Media: A Conceptual Framework," *International Journal of Sport Management* 19 (2018): 44–56; Kathy Babiak and Richard Wolfe, "Determinants of Corporate Social Responsibility in Professional Sport: Internal and External Factors," *Journal of Sport Management* 23, no. 6 (November 2009): 717–42, https://doi.org/10.1123/jsm.23.6.717; Kathy Babiak et al., "An Investigation into Professional Athlete Philanthropy: Why Charity Is Part of the Game," *Journal of Sport Management* 26, no. 2 (2012): 159–76.

19. Lisa Kihl, Kathy Babiak, and Scott Tainsky, "Evaluating the Implementation of a Professional Sport Team's Corporate Community Involvement Initiative," *Journal of Sport Management* 28, no. 3 (May 2014): 324–37, https://doi.org/10.1123/jsm.2012-0258.

20. Sasha Altschuler, "The Power of Social Responsibility in Sports – Sports Philanthropy Network," accessed September 3, 2024, https://sportsphilanthropynetwork.org/the-power-of-social-responsibility-in-sports/.

21. Dana-Farber Cancer Institute, "Boston Red Sox," accessed September 3, 2024, http://www.jimmyfund.org/about-us/boston-red-sox/.

22. NBA Cares, "About Us," NBA Cares, accessed September 3, 2024, https://cares.nba.com/about-us/.

23. Martin Seligman, "Flourish: Positive Psychology and Positive Interventions," *The Tanner Lectures on Human Values* 31, no. 4 (2010): 1–56.

24. Alice Canavesi and Eliana Minelli, "Servant Leadership and Employee Engagement: A Qualitative Study," *Employee Responsibilities and Rights Journal* 34, no. 4 (December 2022): 413–35, https://doi.org/10.1007/s10672-021-09389-9.

25. Jim Harter, "In New Workplace, U.S. Employee Engagement Stagnates," Gallup.com, January 23, 2024, https://www.gallup.com/workplace/608675/new-workplace-employee-engagement-stagnates.aspx.

26. Dixon, Warner, and Habeeb, "Athlete Concerns: What Can Coaches Do?"

Chapter Six. Creating Leadership Opportunities

1. Dave Redding and Tim Whitmire, *Freed to Lead: F3 and the Unshackling of the Modern-Day Warrior*, 2014.

2. "F3 Nation," 2024, f3nation.com.

3. Jay B Carson, Paul E Tesluk, and Jennifer A Marrone, "Shared Leadership in Teams: An Investigation of Antecedent Conditions and Performance," *Academy of Management Journal* 50, no. 5 (2007): 1217–34; Qiong Wu and Kathryn Cormican, "Shared Leadership and Team Effectiveness: An Investigation of Whether and When in Engineering Design Teams," *Frontiers in Psychology* 11 (January 18, 2021): 569198, https://doi.org/10.3389/fpsyg.2020.569198; Charlotte M. Edelmann, Filip Boen, and Katrien Fransen, "The Power of Empowerment: Predictors and Benefits of Shared Leadership in Organizations," *Frontiers in Psychology* 11 (November 19, 2020): 582894, https://doi.org/10.3389/fpsyg.2020.582894.

4. "About FiA," FiA Nation, accessed September 1, 2024, https://fianation.com/about-fia/.

5. "Home," CoopStrong, October 9, 2024, https://www.coopstrong.org.

6. Bailey Cooper, "Sustainable Success: Motives and Small-Scale Charity Sport Events," 2019, https://thescholarship.ecu.edu/server/api/core/bitstreams/13e5be20-0770-4541-85e8-d25bbfe0329f/content.

7. Cooper.

8. V Kumar and Anita Pansari, "Measuring the Benefits of Employee Engagement," MITSloan Management Review, accessed September 2, 2024, https://sloanreview.mit.edu/article/measuring-the-benefits-of-employee-engagement/?switch_view=PDF; Gemma Robertson-Smith and Carl Markwick, *Employee Engagement: A Review of Current Thinking* (Institute for Employment Studies Brighton, 2009).

9. Cianfrone and Warner, "Developing Sport Communities via Social Media: A Conceptual Framework."

10. Kathryn L Heinze, Sara Soderstrom, and Jennifer Zdroik, "Toward Strategic and Authentic Corporate Social Responsibility in Professional Sport: A Case Study of the Detroit Lions," *Journal of Sport Management* 28, no. 6 (2014): 672–86; Matthew Katz and Bob Heere, "Leaders and Followers: An Exploration of the Notion of Scale-Free Networks within a New Brand Community," *Journal of Sport Management* 27, no. 4 (2013): 271–87; Mark Sharratt and Abel Usoro, "Understanding Knowledge-Sharing in Online Communities of Practice," *Electronic Journal on Knowledge Management* 1, no. 2 (2003): 187–96.

11. Michael McGinnis, "Wrexham Red Dragons | How to Build and Grow the Fanbase," Wrexham Red Dragons Building Community, accessed September 2, 2024, https://www.wrexhamreddragons.com/building-community.

12. Egon G Guba, "Reviewed Work(s): Big School, Small School by Roger G. Barker and Paul V. Gump," *The School Review* 74, no. 2 (1966): 241–46.

13. Allan W. Wicker, "Undermanning, Performances, and Students' Subjective Experiences in Behavior Settings of Large and Small High Schools.," *Journal of Personality and Social Psychology* 10, no. 3 (1968): 255.

14. Robert J. Dekoch and Phillip G. Clampitt, *Leading with Care in a Tough World: Beyond Servant Leadership* (Garden City, New York: Rodin Books, 2022).

15. Chen Zhang et al., "Why Capable People Are Reluctant to Lead," *Harvard Business Review*, December 17, 2020, https://hbr.org/2020/12/why-capable-people-are-reluctant-to-lead.

Chapter Seven. Social Spaces: A Place Where Everyone Knows Your Name

1. S. Warner, "Sport and Community," in *Sociology of Sport and Physical Activity*, ed. G. B. Cunningham and J. N. Singer, 2nd ed. (College Station, TX: Center for Sport Management Research and Education, 2012), 237–54.

2. Holly Swyers, "Community America: Who Owns Wrigley Field?," *The International Journal of the History of Sport* 22, no. 6 (November 2005): 1086–1105, https://doi.org/10.1080/09523360500286783; H. Swyers, *Wrigley Regulars: Finding Community in the Bleachers?*, University of Illinois Press: Champaign (IL, 2010).

3. Tingle et al., "The Strength of Community"; Warner and Bright, "Building Community and Culture for Sport Officials."

4. Betway Insiders, "Most Popular Colleges for Tailgate Parties," Betway Insider, August 29, 2024, https://blog.betway.com/nfl/most-popular-colleges-for-tailgate-parties/.

5. Harry Gerard Bissinger, *Friday Night Lights: A Town, a Team and a Dream* (London: Yellow Jersey Pr, 2005).

6. Betway Insiders, "Most Popular Colleges for Tailgate Parties."

7. Tim Delaney, "The Social Aspects of Sports Tailgating," *The New York Sociologist* 3 (2008): 1–10.

8. Beth Carter, "Tailgate Parties Are a 'Powerful Impulse' and a Microcosm of Society," *Wired*, accessed September 6, 2024, https://www.wired.com/2012/09/anthropology-of-tailgating/.

9. Christopher Klein, "Tailgating: How the Pre-Game Tradition Can Be Traced to Ancient Times," HISTORY, June 1, 2023, https://www.history.com/news/tailgating-history-football-game-traditions-rituals.

10. Kris Boyle et al., "Virtual Tailgating: A Q-Methodology Analysis of Why Sports Fans Visit Online Sports Forums," *Journal of Sports Media* 14, no. 1 (2019): 137–54.

11. Michael Lananna, "East Carolina's Jungle Rocks The Greenville Regional," *College Baseball, MLB Draft, Prospects - Baseball America* (blog), June 4, 2018, https://www.baseballamerica.com/stories/east-carolinas-jungle-rocks-the-greenville-regional/.

12. Bradsher, *Never Take This for Granted*.
13. Ronnie Woodward, "IN THE JUNGLE," News Services, June 9, 2022, https://news.ecu.edu/2022/06/09/in-the-jungle/.
14. *PickleCon | Working with Vets*, 2024, https://www.youtube.com/watch?v=OqhgvdWXSjg.
15. *PickleCon | Working with Vets*.
16. Felice Yuen and Amanda J. Johnson, "Leisure Spaces, Community, and Third Places," *Leisure Sciences* 39, no. 3 (May 4, 2017): 295–303, https://doi.org/10.1080/01490400.2016.1165638.
17. Ray Oldenburg, "Our Vanishing Third Places," *Planning Commissioners Journal* 25, no. 4 (1997): 6–10.
18. Heidi Peiper, "Reimagining the Third Place: How Starbucks Is Evolving Its Store Experience," Starbucks Stories, September 13, 2022, https://stories.starbucks.com/stories/2022/reimagining-the-third-place-how-starbucks-is-evolving-its-store-experience/.
19. Asia Mieleszko, "From Hang Out To Hurry: Why Starbucks Wants To Redefine 'Third Place,'" August 2, 2024, https://www.strongtowns.org/journal/2024/8/2/from-hang-out-to-hurry-why-starbucks-wants-to-redefine-third-place.
20. Nathaniel Meyersohn, "A Major Shift at Starbucks Is Changing Its Personality | CNN Business," CNN, July 19, 2024, https://www.cnn.com/2024/07/19/business/starbucks-mobile-orders-third-place/index.html.
21. Meyersohn.
22. L. A. Times Associated Press Archives, "Starbucks' Drive-Through Service Attracts the Regulars," Los Angeles Times, December 26, 2005, https://www.latimes.com/archives/la-xpm-2005-dec-26-fi-starbucks26-story.html.
23. Meyersohn, "A Major Shift at Starbucks Is Changing Its Personality | CNN Business."
24. Bonnie Rochman, "No Office? No Problem. Meet Me at Starbucks," Starbucks Stories Asia, January 5, 2018, https://stories.starbucks.com/asia/stories/2018/no-office-no-problem-meet-me-at-starbucks/.
25. Howard Schultz and Joanne L. Gordon, *From the Ground up: A Journey to Reimagine the Promise of America*, First edition (New York: Random House, 2019).
26. Patricia Obst and Jana Stafurik, "Online We Are All Able Bodied: Online Psychological Sense of Community and Social Support Found through Membership of Disability-Specific Websites Promotes Well-Being for People Living with a Physical Disability," *Journal of Community & Applied Social Psychology* 20, no. 6 (November 2010): 525–31, https://doi.org/10.1002/casp.1067.
27. Cianfrone and Warner, "Developing Sport Communities via Social Media: A Conceptual Framework."

28. S. Fairley and B. Tyler, "Bringing Baseball to the Big Screen: Building Sense of Community Outside of the Ballpark," *Journal of Sport Management* 26 (2012): 258–70; Mike Weed, "The Pub as a Virtual Football Fandom Venue: An Alternative to 'Being There'?," *Soccer & Society* 8, no. 2–3 (April 2007): 399–414, https://doi.org/10.1080/14660970701224665; Laurence Chalip, "Towards Social Leverage of Sport Events," *Journal of Sport & Tourism* 11, no. 2 (May 2006): 109–27, https://doi.org/10.1080/14775080601155126.

29. Oldenburg, "Our Vanishing Third Places."

30. Gashaw Abeza et al., "Social Media Scholarship in Sport Management Research: A Critical Review," *Journal of Sport Management*, 2015, https://doi.org/10.1123/jsm.2014-0296; Cianfrone and Warner, "Developing Sport Communities via Social Media: A Conceptual Framework"; Ashley N. Weingartz and Stacy Warner, "Big League Social Media: Cultivating Community Online," *Case Studies in Sport Management* 8, no. 1 (January 1, 2019): 44–50, https://doi.org/10.1123/cssm.2018-0011.

31. Boyle et al., "Virtual Tailgating: A Q-Methodology Analysis of Why Sports Fans Visit Online Sports Forums."

Chapter Eight. Equity in Administrative Decisions: The Importance of Clarity and Transparency

1. Brené Brown, *Dare to Lead: Brave Work, Tough Conversations, Whole Hearts* (New York: Random House, 2018).

2. Michael Marot, "Longtime NCAA Exec Donohoe Hands in Resignation," Lubbock Avalanche-Journal, October 26, 2011, https://www.lubbockonline.com/story/sports/2011/10/27/longtime-ncaa-exec-donohoe-hands-resignation/15202766007/.

3. Sedona Prince, "Sedona Prince on TikTok," TikTok, March 18, 2021, https://www.tiktok.com/@sedonerrr/video/6941180880127888646.

4. Billy Witz, "Her Video Spurred Changes in Women's Basketball. Did They Go Far Enough?," *The New York Times*, March 15, 2022, sec. Sports, https://www.nytimes.com/2022/03/15/sports/ncaabasketball/womens-march-madness-sedona-prince.html.

5. Kaplan, Hecker, & Fink, LLP, "KHF Gender Equity Review Phase I Report," August 2, 2021, https://kaplanhecker.app.box.com/s/6fpd51gxk9ki78f8vbhqcqh0b00950xq.

6. Raquel Torres, "San Antonio Sports Names Jenny Carnes as New President and CEO," San Antonio Report, June 14, 2022, http://sanantonioreport.org/san-antonio-sports-jenny-carnes-ceo/.

7. Chris Taylor, "On-the-Spot Incentives," accessed September 2, 2024, https://www.shrm.org/topics-tools/news/hr-magazine/spot-incentives.

8. Ronnie Woodward, "Professionally Purple Closet Available to Students," HHP News and Events, November 21, 2023, https://hhp.ecu.edu/hhp-news/2023/11/21/professionallypurple/.

9. National Football League, "The Rooney Rule | NFL Football Operations," accessed July 1, 2024, https://operations.nfl.com/inside-football-ops/inclusion/the-rooney-rule/.

10. *Evolution of the Black Quarterback - Season 1, Episode 1, Prime Video*, vol. 1, The Beginning (Amazon Studios, 2024), https://www.amazon.com/Evolution-Black-Quarterback-Season-1/dp/B0D7S7XTKX.

11. Nick Igbokwe, "What Is the Rooney Rule? How Effective Has It Been since Its NFL Inception?," accessed September 2, 2024, https://www.sportskeeda.com/nfl/news-what-rooney-rule-how-effective-since-nfl-inception.

12. Charlotte Edmonds, "What Is the NFL's Rooney Rule?," *NBC Sports Philadelphia* (blog), January 19, 2024, https://www.nbcsportsphiladelphia.com/nfl/nfl-rooney-rule-explained/559718/.

13. National Football League, "The Rooney Rule | NFL Football Operations."

14. Scott Stump, "EXCLUSIVE: Meet the 3 Female Coaches on the Baltimore Ravens' Staff This Season," accessed September 2, 2024, https://www.today.com/news/sports/female-nfl-coaches-ravens-rcna167732.

15. Zacharias Wood, "Administrator Perceptions of Intramural Coed Flag Football Modifications: A Qualitative Analysis" (Master of Science, Louisiana State University and Agricultural and Mechanical College, 2014), https://doi.org/10.31390/gradschool_theses.611.

16. Luke Wade, "Luke Wade, The Community Creator, LinkedIn," accessed October 4, 2024, https://www.linkedin.com/in/thecommunitycreator/.

17. KC Crew, "Leagues - Kansas League Sports Event | KC Crew," KC Crew Sports and Events, October 4, 2024, https://kccrew.com/leagues/.

18. *PickleCon | Working with Vets*.

19. KC Crew, "Inclusion," KC Crew Sports and Events, accessed October 5, 2024, https://kccrew.com/leagues/inclusion/.

20. KC Crew.

21. J Stacy Adams, "Inequity in Social Exchange," in *Advances in Experimental Social Psychology*, vol. 2 (Elsevier, 1965), 267–99.

22. S. Warner and Marlene A Dixon, "Understanding Sense of Community from the Athlete's Perspective," *Journal of Sport Management* 25, no. 3 (2011): 257–71.

23. Mary A. Hums and Packianathan Chelladurai, "Distributive Justice in Intercollegiate Athletics: The Views of NCAA Coaches and Administrators," *Journal of Sport Management* 8, no. 3 (September 1994): 200–217, https://doi.org/10.1123

/jsm.8.3.200; Melanie Sartore-Baldwin and Stacy Warner, "Perceptions of Justice within Intercollegiate Athletics among Current and Former Athletes," *Journal of Issues in Intercollegiate Athletics* 5 (2012): 269–82; Daniel F Mahony et al., "Organizational Justice in Sport Organizations: Perceptions of College Athletes and Other College Students," *Journal of Sport Management* 20, no. 2 (2006): 159–88.

24. Marlene A Dixon and Stacy Warner, "Employee Satisfaction in Sport: Development of a Multi-Dimensional Model in Coaching," *Journal of Sport Management* 24, no. 2 (2010): 139–68; Hums and Chelladurai, "Distributive Justice in Intercollegiate Athletics"; Jason A. Colquitt et al., "Justice at the Millennium: A Meta-Analytic Review of 25 Years of Organizational Justice Research.," *Journal of Applied Psychology* 86, no. 3 (2001): 425–45, https://doi.org/10.1037/0021-9010.86.3.425.

Chapter Nine. Now What? Measuring a Sense of Community in Sport

1. Eleanor Hodgman Porter, *Pollyanna* (LC Page, 1913).
2. Chalip, "Toward a Distinctive Sport Management Discipline."
3. Samuel B. Bacharach, "Organizational Theories: Some Criteria for Evaluation," *The Academy of Management Review* 14, no. 4 (October 1989): 496, https://doi.org/10.2307/258555; John R Platt, "Strong Inference," *Science* 146, no. 3642 (1964): 347–53.
4. Andrew H Van de Ven, "Nothing Is Quite so Practical as a Good Theory," *Academy of Management Review* 14, no. 4 (1989): 486–89.
5. Chalip, "Toward a Distinctive Sport Management Discipline"; J. Fink, "Theory Development in Sport Management: My Experiences and Other Considerations," *Sport Management Review* 1 (2013): 17–21; George B. Cunningham, J. Fink, and A. Doherty, eds., *Routledge Handbook of Theory in Sport Management* (Milton Park, Abingdon, Oxon ; New York, NY: Routledge, 2015).
6. Peter Starbuck, "Peter F. Drucker," in *The Oxford Handbook of Management Theorists*, ed. Morgen Witzel and Malcolm Warner (Oxford University Press, 2013), 271–96, https://doi.org/10.1093/oxfordhb/9780199585762.013.0014.
7. Timo Räikkönen and Juha Hedman, "Unlocking the Power of Sports: An Exploration of the Nexus between Shared Place, Community Competence, and Sense of Community," *International Journal of Sport Policy and Politics* 0, no. 0 (August 24, 2024): 1–19, https://doi.org/10.1080/19406940.2024.2396836.
8. Warner, "Sport and Sense of Community Theory."
9. Stacy Warner et al., "Examining Sense of Community in Sport: Developing the Multidimensional 'SCS'Scale," *Journal of Sport Management* 27, no. 5 (2013): 349–62.

10. Shannon Kerwin et al., "Exploring Sense of Community among Small-Scale Sport Event Volunteers," *European Sport Management Quarterly* 15, no. 1 (January 2015): 77–92, https://doi.org/10.1080/16184742.2014.996581.

11. Runyuan Jia, Juan Antonio Sánchez-Sáez, and Francisco Segado Segado, "The Impact of the China Open 500 Event on Sense of Community: Comparisons of Volunteers' Pre- and Post-Event Perceptions," *Sustainability* 15, no. 8 (April 12, 2023): 6547, https://doi.org/10.3390/su15086547.

12. Charlotte N Pearsall, *The Relationship of Adaptive Sport Participation on Sense of Community and Community Integration* (East Carolina University, 2019).

13. Hilary Pollock, "Exploring Recreation and Sense of Community in the Canadian Military," 2019.

14. Erin Leah Morris, "The Impact of Structural Systems on Perceptions of Legitimacy and the Experiences of Female Hockey Players," 2016.

15. Stephen Arkell, "Examining The Impact of Campus Intramural Sports Participation on Students' Sense of Community Using A Pre-Test Post-Test Design," 2020; Stacy Warner et al., "Yielding Healthy Community with Sport," *Journal of Sport for Development* 5, no. 8 (2017): 41–52; Daniel G. Pilgreen, "Sense of Community in the Campus Recreation Setting: Fostering Community as a Strategy for Student Retention," 2018.

16. Kim, Du, and James, "A Social Epidemiological Perspective on Local Tennis League Participation."

17. Rohan, "When Did Esports Start? When Did Esports Become Popular? The History of Esports," ESPORTS GG, December 30, 2022, https://esports.gg/guides/esports/the-history-of-esports/.

18. Sean Burns, "Expanding Esports in Higher Ed: Benefits and Guidance for New Esports Programs," EDUCAUSE, accessed September 11, 2024, https://www.educause.edu/ecar/research-publications/2021/expanding-esports-in-higher-ed-benefits-and-guidance-for-new-esports-programs/introduction-and-key-findings.

19. Staff, "The Rise of Collegiate Esports: Universities Embracing Gaming," College Football Poll, August 16, 2024, https://www.collegefootballpoll.com/news/the-rise-of-collegiate-esports-universities-embracing-gaming/.

20. Chris Hayhurst, "Collegiate Esports Programs Provide Academic Pathways," Ed Tech Magazine, Technology Solutions That Drive Education, August 26, 2022, https://edtechmagazine.com/higher/article/2022/08/collegiate-esports-programs-provide-academic-pathways.

21. James Lowrey, *Protecting the New Student Athlete: Exploring the Mental Health Outcomes of College Esports Athletes and the Supportive Factors of Collegiate Esports Organizations* (Notre Dame of Maryland University, 2023).

22. Lowrey.

Chapter Ten. What's Next? A Call to Action and Community of Practice

1. ECU College of Health & Human Performance, "HHP Alumnus Pledges $333,000 to Establish First Endowed Distinguished Professorship," *HHP Visions: College of Health & Human Performance Alumni and Friends Newsletter*, November 4, 2010, Fall 2010 edition, https://issuu.com/chhp/docs/hhp_newsletter_fall_2010.

2. Dan Kenney, "A Friend of a Friend-Jimmy Grimsley and Charles Jenkins -January 29," *Coach4aday* (blog), January 29, 2015, https://coach4aday.wordpress.com/2015/01/29/a-friend-of-a-friend-jimmy-grimsley-and-charles-jenkins-january-29/.

3. Associated Press, "Wearing a Different Hat When Saturday Comes," New York Times (Online) (New York, United States: New York Times Company, October 18, 2008), https://www.proquest.com/docview/2221144289/abstract/A9474A856F1446A2PQ/1.

4. Kyle Pillar, "Family Affair: McGees Share Memories, Impact of College Football in New Book," *The Richmond Observer* (blog), October 25, 2020, https://richmondobserver.com/local-sports/family-affair-mcgees-share-memories-of-college-football-in-new-book.html.

5. Charles Gaddy, *An Olympic Journey: The Saga of an American Hero: LeRoy T. Walker* (Griffin Publishing Group, 1998).

6. Gill Sobers-Outlaw, "LeRoy T. Walker (1918–2012)," April 16, 2014, https://www.blackpast.org/african-american-history/walker-leroy-t-1918-2012/.

7. Tim Peeler, "One Brick Back: LeRoy Walker: A Man of Olympic Proportions," *One Brick Back* (blog), January 3, 2020, http://timpeeler.blogspot.com/2020/01/leroy-walker-man-of-olympic-proportions.html.

8. Peeler.

9. USATF, "USA Track & Field | Dr. LeRoy Walker," accessed October 7, 2024, https://usatf.org/athlete-bios/dr-leroy-walker.

10. Peeler, "One Brick Back."

11. Gaddy, *An Olympic Journey: The Saga of an American Hero: LeRoy T. Walker*.

12. Gaddy.

13. North Carolina Central University Student Newspaper, "The 75th Anniversary: Recalling a Proud History," *The Campus Echo*, June 14, 1985, https://newspapers.digitalnc.org/lccn/2015236599/1985-06-14/ed-1/seq-7/.

14. Tom Lewis, "Legendary Coach Dr. LeRoy Walker Passes Away at 93," USTFCCCA, April 23, 2012, https://www.ustfccca.org/2012/04/featured/legendary-coach-dr-leroy-walker-passes-away-at-93.

15. "LeRoy T. Walker, Educator, and Athletic Coach Born," African American Registry, accessed October 7, 2024, https://aaregistry.org/story/leroy-t-walker-born/.

16. Lewis, "Legendary Coach Dr. LeRoy Walker Passes Away at 93."
17. ECU News Services, "IOC Selects ECU's Walker Center," News Services, December 15, 1998, https://news.ecu.edu/1998/12/15/ioc-selects-ecus-walker-center/.
18. Etienne Wenger, "Communities of Practice: A Brief Introduction," 2011.

BETTER TOGETHER

ECU SPORT & COMMUNITY DEVELOPMENT LAB

www.ingramcontent.com/pod-product-compliance
Lightning Source LLC
Chambersburg PA
CBHW060952230426
43665CB00015B/2172